CHARLES GRANDISON FINNEY

AND THE

BIRTH OF MODERN EVANGELISM

# CHARLES GRANDISON FINNEY
## AND THE
# BIRTH OF MODERN EVANGELISM

Lewis A. Drummond

**HODDER AND STOUGHTON**
LONDON   SYDNEY   AUCKLAND   TORONTO

**British Library Cataloguing in Publication Data**

Drummond, Lewis A.
  Charles Grandison Finney and the birth of
  modern evangelism.
  1. Finney, Charles Grandison
  2. Evangelists – Biography
  I. Title
  269′ .2′0924      BV3705.F/

  ISBN 0-340-26344-X

This book is dedicated to three preachers of the Gospel, men who have been not only brothers in Christ, but the kind of friends who have been the brothers I never had:

T. D. "Dorrell" Hall, evangelist
Robert J. "Bob" Norman, pastor
Donald H. "Don" Watterson, denominational leader

# FOREWORD

Few men have had such a profound impact on their generation as Charles Grandison Finney. Through his Spirit-filled evangelistic ministry, uncounted thousands came to know Christ in the nineteenth century, resulting in one of the greatest periods of revival in the history of America. In addition, he became one of the most widely-read theologians of his time through his lectures and writings. His concern for education influenced whole generations of students.

But most of all, Charles G. Finney was a deeply-committed Christian. More than anything else he wanted to serve Christ and be used of Him.

I am delighted that Professor Lewis Drummond has written an account of this remarkable man. Although Finney lived and worked over a century ago, the lessons and insights of his life are as applicable today as they were in his own age. This book reveals in a readable and yet scholarly way the life and ministry of one of history's greatest evangelists. It is a story that not only informs us, but challenges us as well to commit ourselves afresh to Jesus Christ and to the task of proclaiming Him to our world.

Billy Graham

Montreal, N. C.
February 22, 1982

# CONTENTS

# Contents

# PREFACE

## The Reasons for the Writing

As a young theological student, I was introduced to an old autobiography: the *Memoirs* of Charles G. Finney. Up to that time, I was moving along on quite traditional lines. As Finney's account of what had erupted in his volcanic ministry flowed as fiery lava before my spiritual eyes, I was captivated, challenged – and *changed*. That the Spirit of God did that kind of work through the life of a man thrilled me. Although I was probably very impressionable in my youthful enthusiasm, that nineteenth-century revivalist became something of my "idol in the ministry". Those early impressions have never really dissipated with time.

When Hodder and Stoughton suggested I do a new biography on the life, service and influence of Charles G. Finney, I accepted the opportunity eagerly. The prospect of putting on paper a fresh glimpse into the life of this fascinating character excited me, but I realised there was already a great deal written about him. A truly new approach would be necessary to make the work relevant and justifiable. After all, the Finney *Memoirs* has stood as a classic for over one hundred years (and still remains in print). That fact put some fear into me. Some will no doubt ask whether Finney has anything of substance to offer today. Is he just a historical witness to a bygone day?

Surely there are answers to these questions. As I dug continually deeper into the life and evangelistic ministry of Charles Finney, my appreciation of the man and his work correspondingly deepened. I have come to believe that in many ways Finney is the "father" of many modern evangelistic philosophies and revivalistic methods. Granted, he did not stand alone as the creator of contemporary evangelism, but he certainly made a most significant contribution. The reader must judge whether this work justifies that claim. I am convinced, however, that Finney, the revivalist, has much to say to the contemporary Church.

Not only did Finney give birth to, or at least popularise modern evangelistic revivalism and make it acceptable, but he also pointed the way to spiritual renewal. That many parts of the present day Body of Christ need a genuine revival is patent. Over thirty years ago, another biographer of the lawyer-evangelist said, "If civilisation survives, there must be another Great Awakening". If that was true three decades ago, it is more true now. Finney is most relevant here. He spent much of his life and ministry in the context of spiritual awakenings, movements historians call the Second Great Evangelical Awakening, the Prayer Revival of 1858, and the like.

In a very real sense, Charles Finney stands as the watershed between men of awakenings like George Whitefield and Jonathan Edwards of the eighteenth century, and mass-evangelists like Dwight Lyman Moody of the nineteenth, thus forming the historical transition between the two approaches. His success in that stance was phenomenal. He is not, however, only a pivotal historical personality, but perhaps can today show us the way to new spiritual heights in evangelism and revival. If that happens, all my efforts to give birth to this new biography will be well repaid.

There are many to whom I must express gratitude in the production of this work. My appreciation is first extended to Mr. Edward England, formerly of Hodder and Stoughton, who proposed the volume, and to Rob Warner who saw it through to its conclusion. I want to thank Billy Graham, America's great contemporary evangelist, for writing the Foreword. He was the logical one to do it, and he graciously consented. Then I wish to express gratitude to Dr. J. Edwin Orr, revival historian and scholar, along with my colleague Dr. Bill Leonard, both of whom read the original manuscript and made many valuable suggestions. Also, I must thank my graduate students, Robert Asa and Harry L. Poe, whose aid was most helpful. To the faithful women in Office Services of the Southern Baptist Theological

Seminary Louisville, Kentucky, who put in long hours of typing, I am most grateful. Then, to my faithful wife I give my love and appreciation. She not only did her regular, superb work of proofreading, she also graciously allowed me many hours in seclusion as I wrote. Without the help of these, this book would never have been possible.

Thus, this biography of Charles Grandison Finney, the man to whom we are in so many ways indebted for our understanding of evangelism and revival, is sent forth with the prayer that in our day we may experience that kind of outpouring of the Holy Spirit that he did in his.

Lewis A. Drummond
Louisville, Kentucky, U.S.A.
1983

# PART I

# CHARLES GRANDISON FINNEY: AN ENCOUNTER WITH CHRIST

# 1

## Introduction: Meet the Man

"He probably led more souls to Jesus than any other man."[1]

"He spearheaded a revival in America which literally altered the course of history."[2]

"The implications of the preaching and example of this towering figure can scarcely be measured."[3]

Such are a small sample of the abundant adulations that extol Charles Grandison Finney. Some have even gone so far as to say, "Students of revival agree that the greatest evangelist since apostolic times was . . . Charles Grandison Finney."[4] Although such tributes of praise to the ministry of one mere man may be somewhat exaggerated, one thing is absolutely certain: here is a personality who impacted his day with profundity and power. He has left indelible footprints on the history of revivalism.

How does one account for such a man and ministry? What lies behind it all? Leon McBeth may well have provided something of the key that unlocks the safe revealing the secret. He said, "Perhaps the greatest leader of the Second Great Awakening was Charles G. Finney, the converted lawyer credited with transforming the style of evangelism in America."[5] That is it! The marvellous ministry of this innovative man can only be calculated in the general context of the last days of America's Second Great Evangelical Awakening and subsequent religious revivals. Finney worked in the setting of significant spiritual awakenings – and made his contribution. McBeth went on to say, "Finney is credited with taming the exuberant camp meeting and tailoring it to fit the local church, thus inventing the local church revival as it is known today."[6] That is no doubt true, for one of Charles' admirers said, "I have heard both Finney and the camp meeting revivalists, and I find no resemblance whatever [except] that Finney used a tent when the church was not big enough." He was an innovator to be sure; yet, only the mighty moving of the Holy Spirit in revival power can explain the entire Finney phenomenon.

What was this Second Great Awakening? It occurred shortly after America's Revolutionary War. At that time the spiritual condition of the new United States of America was deplorable. As astute historian, J. Edwin Orr, has pointed out:

> . . . the Methodists were losing more members than they were gaining. The Baptists said that they had their most wintry season. The Presbyterians in general assembly deplored the nation's ungodliness. In a typical Congregational church, the Rev. Samuel Shepherd of Lennox, Massachusetts in sixteen years had not taken one young person into fellowship. The Lutherans were so languishing that they discussed uniting with the Episcopalians who were even worse off. The Protestant Episcopal Bishop of New York, Bishop Samuel Proovost, quit functioning; he had confirmed no one for so long that he decided he was out of work, so he took up other employment. The Chief Justice of the United States, John Marshall, wrote to the Bishop of Virginia, James Madison, that the Church "was too far gone ever to be redeemed". Voltaire averred, and Tom Paine echoed, "Christianity will be forgotten in thirty years".[7]

Then came the revival.

Historians generally agree that the Second Great Awakening burst into being on the eastern seaboard of early America about 1790. It began in Maine and moved into Maryland, and soon the whole north-east was feeling its impact. It was there it had its greatest influence. But there was more to come. In those days, the East Coast of the young country could contain no more citizens. It was filled to its Appalachian Mountain brim. A spillover was inevitable. As the eighteenth century ended, the dam broke. Streaming through the Cumberland gap in the eastern Kentucky hills, a floodtide of new pioneers flowed to the West. Frontiersmen like Daniel Boone blazed trails, leading the settlers into the new virgin plains. And the revival that had such impact in the East flowed westward with them.

In the turbulent pioneer stream came two mighty revival preachers of the Gospel of Jesus Christ, James McGready and Barton Stone. They had been caught up in the early days of the Second Great Awakening in the Carolinas.

About 1800, God began to do a new thing through the lives of these two men. McGready was termed an "impassioned preacher, diligent pastor, and fervent man of prayer". In the summer of 1800, he called on the settlers of south central Kentucky to lay aside their primitive farm tools and gather for an extended four-day observance of the Lord's Supper. A multitude of people made their way over the rugged trails, first to Red River and then to Gasper River in expectation of blessings. It was time to give attention to religion. God met their faith; the Holy Spirit fell powerfully upon them, especially at Gasper River.

The first few days at Red River saw both repentant tears and exuberant rejoicing. The mixed emotions of the meetings ran high. The Spirit probed even deeper when the Lord's Supper was served. The climax came when John McGee, a Methodist minister, gave the closing exhortation. His own words described the scene: "I . . . exhorted them to let the Lord omnipotent reign in their hearts, and submit to him, and their souls should live . . . I turned again and losing sight of fear of man, I went through the house shouting and exhorting with all possible ecstasy and energy, and the floor was soon covered by the slain."[8]

People had come in unprecedented numbers. Some had travelled scores of miles. The multitudes could not begin to be cared for in the existing buildings of the community, so they brought bed rolls and slept on the ground or in their wagons. The first camp meeting was thus born. It was all quite unplanned, but a tremendously significant new movement and methodology was born. McGready tells us:

> No person seemed to wish to go home – hunger and sleep seemed to affect nobody – eternal was the vast concern. Here awakening and converting work was to be found

in every part of the multitude . . . Sober professors, who had been communicants for many years, now lying prostrate on the ground, crying out in such language as this: "Oh! How I would have despised any person a few days ago, who would have acted as I am now! But I cannot help it!" . . . Persons of every description, white and black, were to be found in every part of the multitude . . . crying out for mercy in the most extreem destress.[9]

Of the many there, none was more caught up in the movement than Barton Stone. He had been faithfully preaching the Gospel at the Cane Ridge Meeting House in Bourbon County, having been invited and urged to serve there by none other than the famous frontiersman, Daniel Boone. Stone was something of a protégé of McGready, and being so blessed at the Logan County revival in May 1801, called for a similar meeting at Cane Ridge. The work began and many were mightily moved. He sent out a call for a second such meeting in August. To the utter astonishment of everyone, over twenty thousand people crowded in for the four-day camp meeting. It was an incredible event, for this was the sparsely populated western frontier of early America.

Among the countless who were converted there was James B. Finley, who later became a well-known Methodist circuit rider. He wrote concerning the event:

> The noise was like the roar of Niagara. The vast sea of human beings seemed to be agitated as if by a storm. I counted seven ministers, all preaching at one time, some on stumps, others in wagons, and one was standing on a tree which had, in falling, lodged against another . . . Some of the people were singing, others praying, some crying for mercy in the most piteous accents, while others were shouting most vociferously . . . My heart beat tumultuously, my knees trembled, my lips quivered, and I felt as though I must fall to the ground. A strange supernatural power seemed to pervade to the entire mass of mind there collected.[10]

The American frontier was set ablaze. The Presbyterians and Methodists immediately caught fire. The flames as a prairie fire soon touched the Baptists in Carroll County Kentucky on the Ohio River. Great personalities emerged from the Awakening: men like the famous Methodist circuit riders. The revivalistic "protracted meeting", which flourishes to this day, had something of its birth in the movement. The camp meeting motif of evangelism spread all over eastern America. Doing battle against gambling, cursing and vice, spirituality and genuine Christianity accompanied the early westward movement. These and many marvellous phenomena characterised the Second Great Awakening as it burst on the American scene. It was God's great hour.

When a genuine spiritual awakening actually erupts, geography and chronology can hardly contain it; no one area or year can hem it in. These movements possess an irresistible ability to cross time and space. The Kentucky revival of 1800, therefore, could do no more than record the events of the Second Great Awakening that took place on that particular frontier at that specific time. The Awakening itself spread far beyond Kentucky and continued for several years into nineteenth-century America. Before it had spent its force, most of the country experienced the power of the revival.

In the second decade of the nineteenth century, the warmth of the Second Awakening began to cool, probably due to the people's preoccupation with the war of 1812. Then about 1820–5, another fresh movement of the Spirit began. It reached its zenith approximately ten years later in 1831. Some historians see it merely as an extension of the Second Awakening, others call it a Third Great Awakening. This was the time in which Charles Finney found Christ and began to preach.

In the heat of significant spiritual stirring, Charles G. Finney, the brilliant young lawyer of western New York State became one of America's leading figures. His own testimony of salvation attests to the power of the revival that was spreading throughout the American scene: "I was powerfully converted on the morning of the 10th of October, 1821. In the evening of the same day, I received overwhelming baptisms (infillings) of the Holy Ghost, that went through me, as it seemed to me, body and soul. I immediately found myself endued with such power from on high that a few words dropped here and there to individuals were the means of their immediate conversion."[11]

What kind of a Christian minister does it take to be a revivalist in the atmosphere of a great awakening? What kind of a man was Charles Grandison Finney?

A Spirit-filled man is the sort of servant of Christ it takes to be a significant revivalist. That Finney was "filled with all the fullness of God" (Eph. 3:19) no one has ever seriously questioned. Probably no preacher has ever ministered with more raw spiritual power than this man. His words were like an artillery barrage, felling multitudes to the floor. His piercing eyes seemed to search out people, boring into their very souls, confronting them with the demands of the Saviour. His plain, pungent, colloquial preaching arrested people in frozen and rapt attention. He was a man "mighty with God".

A "free spirit" is a further prerequisite. Above all, Charles Finney was a free spirit. He gave allegiance to no man, except Jesus Christ. On all occasions he was himself. When you saw Finney, you saw the real Finney, even to the point that at times he seemed reactionary. No system, theological or practical, could contain Finney's fresh, free soul. He challenged the hyper-Calvinistic theology of his day. Refusing to attend Princeton Theological Seminary – as a good nineteenth-century Presbyterian ministerial candidate should never do – he was, for all practical purposes, a self-taught man. Yet he became a professor and president of a theological seminary. Although he would listen to others and seek to learn from them with a simple childlike openness, when he became persuaded he was right on an issue, that free spirit stood unflinchingly and would not be moved. He held his position like the Rock of Gibraltar. He needed to; he was bombarded from every unfriendly ship that sailed by.

Then, effective revivalism demands innovation. What an innovator Finney was! Early in his ministry, he developed what came to be called "new measures". They were the new evangelistic methods he employed in promoting revivals. With these he popularised, developed and legitimatised the entire modern approach to contemporary evangelism. Perhaps it was here he made his most significant and long-lasting contribution.

As could be expected, the "new measures" ignited a flame of fervent resistance from the traditionalists. They accused Finney of being far too mechanical and humanistic, not allowing room for the work of the Holy Spirit in revival. That charge will be fully investigated later.

A good revivalist must also be a thinker – at least he should be. Finney always argued that if revivalism was to have any lasting effect, it must be predicated upon a solid, theological foundation. Genuine revivals transcend the big crowds, countless conversations, and high emotions of the moment. A true spiritual awakening that endures is grounded deeply in well-thought-out biblical truth. Only when revival roots sink deep into the Scriptures and draw their nourishment from God's Word does revival last. Here Finney excelled. His classic *Lectures on Systematic Theology* still remains in print and is studied by students of evangelistic theology around the world.

Further, a revivalist must be human. These giants of spiritual awakenings seem at times bigger than life. But if they themselves think that, they are doomed. The rather stern Finney showed himself a real human being with a sense of humour and unusual balance. For example, one day he visited the home of a fellow professor at Oberlin Theological Seminary, where he taught as a professor of theology. Finney's colleague had a reputation for being a bit slow about everything – even in answering his own doorbell. So Finney rang his bell, turned and left. Surprisingly, however, the tardy professor answered the door immediately, only to see Finney leaving the front gate. Charles turned back on hearing the door open and called out, "Is that you, professor? I thought I would ring the bell, go down town, and be let in when I returned."

On another occasion, a friend relates that someone had said something rather humorous in Finney's presence and the evangelist burst out laughing. The friend complimented Charles on his well-preserved teeth, at which Finney retorted, "I never lost but two in all my life, and they were wisdom teeth, and that some of my theological

friends may say accounts for it.'' Then he laughed loudly
and heartily again. He was human.

Finney had his very serious side, however. He managed
his ministry with absolute earnestness and gravity. His
self-discipline was exemplary.

To put it all together, a revivalist must be a genuine man
of God; one totally open to the Lordship of Jesus Christ in
his life. If ever there were a man wholeheartedly and
genuinely yielded to God's will and purpose, it was Charles
Grandison Finney. He had one consuming passion; to
belong utterly and completely to Jesus Christ. He was a
man of God in the most profound sense of that word. Thus
the revival continued in and through his exemplary life.

Finney was a product of the awakenings as much as he
was an instrument in them. To imply that Finney was the
only effective revivalist of the hour would be historically
incorrect. There were other giants like Barton Stone,
James McGready, Francis Asbury, Asahel Nettleton,
Lyman Beecher, to name but a few. Yet none was more
significant than Charles Finney. With all of his strengths –
and weaknesses, for he had them – he epitomised the
movements. His life from a backwoods preacher in primitive western New York State to the sophisticated pastor of
New York City, finally culminating in the professorship
and presidency of Oberlin College and Theological Seminary, unfolds like a nineteenth-century romance. Now
that we have met the man, let us turn to his romantic life.

# Finney's Aggressive America:
# The Evangelist's Sociological Background

"These are great days – and a great place – to be alive!"
That is how twenty-nine-year-old Charles Grandison Finney would have responded if asked about his native land as
the third decade of the nineteenth century began. The Erie
Canal, built between 1817 and 1825, uniting the Hudson
River to Lake Erie, was just about to be opened. The West
anticipated a sweeping flood of immigration, commerce
and opportunity as the new stretch of water opened its
gates. Settlers pushed toward the Pacific, seeking prosper-
ity. Optimism abounded. The Yankee spirit had been
born – there was a virile young country to conquer.

A man is always to some extent a product of the dynamics of his day, and Charles Finney is no exception. He had
been uprooted in the push west, moving from Warren,
Connecticut, his birthplace, finally settling in Adams.
There he entered the law offices of Judge Benjamin Wright
to study statutory law. He was one of thousands caught up
in the life-moulding move. Because of the Erie Canal and
other such immigration routes, by 1851 half of the population of America lived west of the Appalachian Mountains.
Those decades were days of ferment, expansion and unrest. A new, young country was trying to construct a
national identity.

At the birth of the Finney ministry, several dynamic
factors helped to formulate the emerging national self-
consciousness. The religious factor was certainly central
and primary. The Second Great Awakening, as already
seen, had travelled from New England, through the South
into the West. The First Great Awakening of the 1740s

had a significant impact, and the great George Whitefield from Gloucester, England, was probably its single most prominent figure. Although American personalities like Jonathan Edwards and Gilbert Tennant were significantly used by God, Whitefield was the real catalyst of the Awakening. The Second Great Revival, however, emerged as a Yankee movement through and through. As a result, American Christianity could no longer be labelled as a European import.

Western New York State at the time Finney moved in was accustomed to revivalism. Much of it had proved rather dubious, however. Western New York became known as the "burned over district" as a consequence of certain religious experiments. Dynamic Christianity had stagnated, but a longing for a new spiritual sunrise was growing.

The war of 1812 was also responsible for the shaping of a more vital America. This second war with Britain had an indecisive resolution, resulting in a heightened desire among Americans to establish themselves in the world. That spirit of self-reliance invaded every area of national life. Dependence on Europe was largely laid to rest in the grave of a fading "old country" mentality. This was especially true in religious matters.

A further factor of Finney's century revolved around the gigantic population growth of the explosive New World. In 1810, the census boasted 7,239,881 Americans. By 1850 the number had reached 23,191,876. The potato famine that ravaged Ireland brought immigrants to America in droves to live under the ideals of the American Bill of Rights.

The Irish were not the only immigrants who flooded America's shores in those days. The political, economic and religious oppression, and the general unrest that gripped much of Europe, made the beckoning call of the young republic irresistible to thousands.

At the beginning of this "Century of Progress", the western boundary of America stretched to the Mississippi River. By 1850, the nation extended to the Pacific Ocean. Vast new areas of land were conquered, brought or annexed. The Louisiana Purchase was consummated in 1803 and Florida was brought under the Stars and Stripes in

1819. Texas joined the Union in 1845. By 1850, the border between Canada and the United States of America was finalised.

The national economy took staggering strides. In 1810, the South wrenched from the soil one hundred and seventy-eight thousand bales of cotton. By 1850, that number had multiplied to two millions. During the early days of the colonial period, the North-East was primarily a trade centre. Boston and New York were famous for their docks and banks. King Commerce reigned. Then in Lowell, Massachusetts, an enterprising businessman opened a cotton mill to compete with the British textile industry. Like a chain reaction, mills and factories blossomed all over New England. The Industrial Revolution invaded the States as it had conquered Britain a century earlier. A spirit of materialism was born that has not yet been extinguished.

American expansionism did not change everything, however. The embarrassing "peculiar institution" of the South, slavery, kept rearing its ugly head. Man owned man, and all the strife, misery, exploitation and downright greed that that system generated was like a spectre in the night in southern culture. This would be the pivotal political issue throughout the major part of the century, until it was finally finished by the slaughter of the Civil War.

As a result of the slavery issue, the North and South began to develop along quite distinct ideological and cultural lines. Further, the South had not seen the great influx of continental Europeans and Irish as had the North. These two diverse cultural flows were epitomised in two personalities, Thomas Jefferson and Alexander Hamilton. Jefferson conceived a nation of yeomen farmers with their hands plunged deep into the fertile soil of America's productive farm lands. "The government that governs least, governs best" was his philosophy. Let the individual be individual. The separate states must be allowed to make their own decision. Big central government is taboo. Hamilton, on the other hand, was bent toward industrialisation and urbanisation. He fought long and hard for a strong central government which would exercise control over national life. "States rights" was out. Contemporary conservative southerners would have called him a "liberal damn Yankee".

Strangely enough, it was not until after the war of 1812 that the division between North and South was firmly fixed. Before then, Charleston, South Carolina, and Savannah, Georgia, were as heavily involved in trade as were Boston and New York. The South and North shared many common goals, dramatically demonstrated in the attitude of Vice-President John C. Calhoun of South Carolina. In 1817, he launched a crusade demanding federal expenditures for internal improvements and economic development. Such an approach obviously presupposed a man in favour of industrialisation and commerce. This Calhoun hardly sounded like a right-wing provincial Southerner! But by the end of the first quarter of the dynamic nineteenth century, the picture had reversed itself. Below the Mason-Dixon Line, cotton was fast becoming king. The South grew it, exported it, and soon learned to live on it. So Calhoun began to cry for low tariffs and minimal public expenditures. The large landowners had conquered their politician. As 1825 gave way to the second quarter of the century, the basic diverse economic structures of the south were being firmly planted in sectionalism and self-interest groups.

The North-East scrambled for protection for her industrial goods. High tariffs were mandatory. Daniel Webster, as a young David with a sling of oratory in his hand, burst on to the battle line to champion the cause against the cotton Goliath of the South.

The West posed another problem. The expanding region promoted its progress by the sale of public land at unbelievably cheap rates. If a person could not buy a farm in western New York State dirt cheap, he could trek a bit further west and homestead a farm free, compliments of the federal government. Predictably, the North-East opposed the westward movement, wanting to keep the large, cheap labour force intact.

Yet, go West young men would. With Spain giving up Florida, Mexico the South-West, France selling the Louisiana Purchase, and Britain and America settling their Canadian border disputes, there was land in such abundance that one could own a thousand acres and not have a neighbour for twenty miles. Why be cramped up in a hovel in one of New York City's slums, let alone Dublin or Warsaw, when there was the vast expanse of a beautiful western frontier there for the taking?

In a few years the West was won. The Indians were cruelly conquered and the land began to fill. Prior to the opening of the Erie Canal, New England had enjoyed being the dominant commercial force in American life. Boston boasted of being the pre-eminent American port. But with the new waterway opened and settlers streaming westward, New York City suddenly bounded ahead and seized commercial crown-rights.

Other states reacted. While the Ohio market lay firmly in New York hands, Maryland chartered the Baltimore and Ohio Railroad in 1827. New York countered by establishing the Erie Railroad in 1846 and Pennsylvania got in on the expansion by founding the Pennsylvania Line. The economy was consumed with competition.

Interconnecting canals and railroads began crisscrossing like boot laces in the new territories. Ohio, Finney's final home far to the west, enjoyed an economic boom as the immigrants swept through its virgin forests.

The careful balance that had been maintained up to that moment between free territory and slave-holding lands was now hanging by a thread. There was the constant threat that some new state would join the Union and upset the delicate balance, plunging the nation into conflict.

The first crisis came with Missouri. A battle was avoided by allowing the new state to come into the Union as a slave state, while Maine, which had simultaneously applied for statehood, was admitted as free. Another provision, which came to be known as the "Missouri Compromise", provided that all the new states cut out of the recently acquired Louisiana Purchase north of a line 36° 3′ north would automatically become free states.

The second crisis was over California. The Gold Rush of 1849 brought hordes to the West Coast. Californians wanted to be free. That was understandable; the Mexican war had just recently liberated their land. They had experienced firsthand what "belonging to another" means.

Moreover, the "Wilmot Proviso", hotly debated in Congress, stated:

> That an express and fundamental condition to the acquisition of any territory from the Republic of Mexico by the United States, by virtue of any treaty which may be negotiated between them, and to the use by the Executive of the monies herein appropriated, neither slavery nor involuntary servitude shall ever exist in any part of said territories.[1]

Whatever Mexico gave up to the new Union it was giving up to freedom.

The admission of California brought other compromises. Utah and New Mexico territories were left with no provision. Congress deferred settling their status until they applied for admission to the Union. The southern territories were left to themselves to do about slavery as they would. This guarantee intended to protect the South from abolitionist efforts.

Although the abolitionist movement was growing in popularity, it was still a somewhat unhealthy profession even in the free North. Charles Stewart, an Englishman who had seen the sadism of slavery in Jamaica, was literally whipped out of Plainfield, Connecticut, by local farmers when he agitated for abolition. A school building for free black children in Maine was dragged by oxen to a nearby swamp where it was unceremoniously dunked. In Alton, Illinois, across the river from St. Louis, Missouri, a publisher was actually murdered. He had run an abolitionist press for some time. The harbingers in the wind should have been clear to him. Twice before, his printing machines had been thrown into the Mississippi River. This time the anti-abolitionists freed themselves of his inflammatory press once and for all. In 1835, William Lloyd Garrison, one of the most significant figures in the American abolition movement, was man-handled through a jeering mob on the streets of Boston with a rope around his neck – and all that *above* the Mason-Dixon Line. Abolitionism was not exactly popular! Finney was soon to find that out, for he was a committed abolitionist.

The abolitionists, in their zeal to free the southern

slaves, got on the "political bandwagon". They considered it their duty to keep the slavery issue tied to all political issues that might cross the American scene. The consequence was that many were drawn into supporting the abolitionist cause whether they were fervent about slavery or not. They found themselves standing in the ranks with the abolitionists because of their stance on other political issues.

Abolition had obvious religious overtones. In 1831, a slave revolt erupted in Virginia. A slave by the name of Nat Turner killed his master and the entire family. Although Turner was a fanatic, if not a psychotic, he confessed his crime with these words: "On the 12th of May, 1828, I heard a loud noise in the heavens, and the Spirit instantly appeared to me and said the serpent was loosed . . . and that I should take it on and fight against the serpent . . . on the appearance of the sign, [the eclipse of the sun February, 1831], I should arise and prepare myself, and slay my enemies with their own weapons."[2] Turner's "religious" crusade began. Although few would agree with his methodology, it was indicative of the deep-seated religious emotions that ran rampant through the abolition movement.

Spiritual concerns played a vital role in the nineteenth-century American drama. Revival enthusiasm vied with "old school" tradition and theology. Unitarians battled with the Trinitarians as the Arminians took on the Calvinists. The "new measures" of the evangelists shook every citadel of the religious establishment and Charles Finney played no small part in the sociological and religious ferment.

# 3

## Finney's Family:
## The Evangelist's Heritage

Warren is a tiny New England town hidden away in Western Connecticut that can boast of the birth in 1792 of
Charles Grandison Finney. In that same year were born
Percy B. Shelley, the great poet, Sir John F. W. Herschel,
the astronomer, Lowell Mason, the gifted musician, John
Keble, the British divine and poet, Rossini, the magni-
ficent Italian composer and a host of other notables.

Finney came from good English stock. The family tree
can be plucked of its branches until the roots are reached in
"Mother Finney" who migrated from England sometime
before 1639. Mother Finney gave her husband a daughter
and two sons, Robert and John. The boys married in
America.

To his misfortune, Robert never had a child, so the
entire Finney name must be traced through John. But
where Robert was empty, John had his quiver full. He
married three times and had numerous children. One of his
marriages was to Mary Rogers, the granddaughter of one
of the Pilgrim Fathers. John's maternal grandmother, Sari
Curtis, was of the Curtis family who originally lived in
Nasing, England. So Charles Grandison Finney, like so
many early Americans, had pure Anglo-Saxon blood flowing in his veins. John was his great, great grandfather.

John's ninth child was christened Joshua, a good Bible
name. It was the custom to name children from the Bible in
those days.

Like his father, Joshua loved children and to him and his
wife was born a son, Josiah, on July 26, 1701, at Bristol
where the family eked out a living in the rugged wilderness

of the Colonies. The name of Josiah Finney later appears in the public records of Litchfield County, Connecticut. Josiah had probably transported his family there to seek his fortune. Something of the adventuresome spirit of the westward movement must have been part of the very fibre of the Finney clan.

Josiah and his wife Sarah named their seventh child Sylvester. His birth was on March 15, 1759 – seventeen years before the signing of the Declaration of Independence. Young Sylvester was destined to fight in the Revolutionary War as a zealot for American democracy, before marrying Rebecca Rice.

In 1792 the Sylvester Finney family – by this time boasting six children – were living in Warren, Connecticut. On August 29 of that year, their seventh child, a boy, was born. Sylvester and Rebecca departed from the contemporary custom and did not christen their new son with a biblical name. They call him Charles Grandison after the hero of Samuel Richardson's currently popular novel, *Sir Charles Grandison*. Richardson's novel presented Sir Charles as a "gentleman of high character and fine appearance".[1] Even the New England divine, Jonathan Edwards, who was vehemently opposed to some of the popular literature of his day, was enchanted by *Sir Charles Grandison*. In the naming of their seventh child, Sylvester and Rebecca were almost prophetic.

The choice of the unbiblical name did not mean the family was particularly irreligious. Actually, Sylvester's father, Josiah, was instrumental in the founding of the Congregational Church in their community in 1756. He generously donated a newly-purchased piece of property to the infant congregation and witnessed the actual organisation of the new work in his living-room. Yet, the Finney family into which Charles Grandison was born were far from fervent Christians. After Charles' conversion, he confessed he had never heard a prayer uttered in his home.

When Charles was two, the family joined the westward movement once again. They first settled in the little western New York village of Brotherton in Oneida County, named after the Oneida Indians who had some years before migrated north and settled near Toronto, Canada.

In this county, some thirty years later, the great Western Revivals broke out under Charles' dynamic preaching. The pioneering family soon pushed on to a more settled home in Hanover, now part of present day Kirkland, New York. In Finney's time, Kirkland was a part of Paris, New York.

Western New York State was quite primitive at the end of the eighteenth century, a far cry from the leading state it was soon to become. It stood only fifth in population, superseded by Virginia, Massachusetts, Pennsylvania and North Carolina. Sylvester Finney and his family found themselves in a rugged pioneer setting. Twenty years after the shot at Lexington and Concord that was "heard around the world", there were still only six houses in Utica, New York. Rome, a thriving New York city some years later when Charles held his first revivals there, hardly reflected anything of its Italian namesake: only twenty houses made up the settlement.

Schools were pitifully primitive. None of the amenities of Boston or Charleston could be found. At best, the local schools – the teachers usually college students on vacation – only boasted three textbooks: Webster's *Blueback Speller*, Hodder and Pike's *Arithmetic* and Jebedia More's *Universal Geography*.

In this environment, young Charles grew up and received his early education. It was a Spartan upbringing designed to mould a man out of a boy in short order. This may well explain the tenacity, self-discipline and endurance of the evangelist who never really slowed down until his death at the age of eighty-two. That was a quite remarkable age for those days; he was a *strong* man.

In 1806, young Finney finished his backwoods training and entered Hamilton Oneida Academy at Clinton, New York, named after the illustrious American hero, Alexander Hamilton. This secondary school was situated only a few miles from his father's farm. Here he studied for two years, probably from 1806 to 1808. It proved to be an influential period. Seth Norton, principal and professor at the academy, challenged Finney to give himself to a classical education and music. One never to refuse a challenge, Charles became quite adept in Latin, Greek, Hebrew and learned to play the violin-cello beautifully. The first money he earned was spent to purchase a fine musical instrument.

Charles probably received his first real religious impressions here. Samuel Kirkland, a dedicated missionary to the American Indians, was living in the vicinity, and Charles had apparently made some acquaintance with this devout and influential man of God. Whether Charles ever heard him preach is unknown. In Finney's life at that time, there was no overt moving to God, or even a desire to do so.

Young Charles stood out among his peers. He possessed a splendid physique all through life and excelled in everything to which he put his hand. As a young man, he loved sports, a love he never forsook. Hamilton Oneida Academy offered much to satisfy the sporting desires of a strong, healthy, energetic student. In those days, sports were not nearly as sophisticated as college sports today. Students at the academy took part in running, riding, wrestling and the like – sports that stood them in good stead on the frontier. Finney learned all of these skills. His grandson wrote of him some years later: "when he was twenty, he excelled every man and boy he met, in every species of toil or sport. No man could throw him; no man could knock his hat off; no man could run faster, jump farther, leap higher, or throw a ball with greater force and precision. When his family moved to the shore of Henderson Bay, near Sackett's Harbour, he added to his accomplishments rowing, swimming, and sailing."[2] What the future preacher learned about sailing would, one day out on the Atlantic, prove invaluable – maybe even save his life.

A young man of intellect, as well as an avid sportsman, it was natural Charles should teach school. At the early age of sixteen, until his twentieth year, he taught at Hamilton. In the meantime, in 1808, his parents moved to Henderson on Lake Ontario.

Charles was a popular teacher in Hamilton. The pattern was to teach five months out of the year and then further one's own education in the succeeding months. He was fascinating to his pupils. One of his students said of him: "There was nothing which anyone else knew, that Mr. Finney didn't know, and there was nothing which anyone else could do that Mr. Finney could not do – and do a great deal better. He was the idol of his pupils."[3] Another described him as "a splendid pagan – a young man rejoicing in his strength, proudly conscious of his physical and intellectual superiority to all around him."[4]

That engaging attractiveness never left Finney. Before his conversion in Adams, New York, however, it made him a thorn in the side of the Rev. George Gale, the local minister. Finney captivated all the young people of the community. Being rather irreligious, Charles did little to support Gale's crusade to win Adams' young population. Later in life, of course, his magnetic quality was a tremendous asset in furthering the cause of Christ. Thoughout his career as a minister of the Gospel, he always seemed able to captivate his peers.

When the war of 1812 broke out, Finney's patriotism rose to the surface. He travelled the few miles that separated his home from the Sackett's Harbor Naval Base, intending to enlist in the United States Navy. Rumour had it that the British would soon invade from the north by sea.

At Sackett's Harbor, for the first time in his life, Finney ran into life in the raw – moral raw, that is. At the naval base town, the profanity and crudeness sickened him. One day on the streets of Sackett's Harbor, Charles was accosted by a young prostitute. He was a very innocent young man and did not realise what was actually taking place. When he realised the nature of the proposition, he became so broken-hearted at the woman's moral depravity that he literally broke out weeping. When she saw his genuine, honest concern for her, she wept also. Later in life Charles said, "Oh, if I had only been a Christian at that time! The young woman might have been saved."[5] Although he was a "splendid pagan", the "splendid" should be emphasised. Immorality had no place in his life. He returned home rejecting it all, including the navy. The suspected invasion of the British never developed and the lewdness of naval life never got a foothold in his character.

The autumn of 1812 saw Charles back at his birthplace, Warren, Connecticut, living with an uncle and working on the farm to support himself. His prime purpose in returning to Connecticut was to attend school and further his education. He studied in an institution of higher learning with all of the tenacity and self-discipline he had learned on the frontier. At school he became the editor of a small journal and was known as an orator, wit and poet.

In Warren he encountered, perhaps for the first time, some truly effective preaching. The Rev. Peter Starr, a well-educated man, was pastor in Warren from 1771 to 1822. Starr was a biblical preacher. He would put the four fingers of each hand in his Bible, marking his texts for the sermon, and he would then go finger to finger as he expounded the Scriptures. There is little doubt that Starr's educated preaching was more of a positive religious influence on young Finney than the future evangelist realised at the time, even though Charles said Starr's sermons were "humdrum" stuff. It seems that Finney never gave serious consideration to uniting with the Church. He did join the Warren Masonic lodge, however. His uncle was responsible for that. He convinced Charles it would enhance his social life and contacts. This appealed to the ambitious young man and as a consequence he joined and advanced to the degree of a Master Mason. This commitment he was later to repudiate with some vehemence.

Finney developed a growing desire to enter Yale and take a degree. Charles' teacher in Warren, though a Yale graduate himself, dissuaded his pupil. He convinced Charles that he could do the whole Yale curriculum by himself in two years through private study. Such was the confidence that this teacher expressed in the intellectual ability of his pupil.

About 1814, the man whom God was preparing for destiny left Warren and taught school in New Jersey. After a two-year tenure there, he decided to travel farther south and continue his educational career. However, his mother's health began to deteriorate seriously. At his parents' insistence, he returned to Jefferson County, New York, where they lived at that time. After seeing the condition of his mother, he decided to stay so that he could be close to the family. On the surface, this was something of a setback for the blossoming career of the young teacher. The providence of God was profoundly in the move, however. Finney decided to enter the law offices of Squire Benjamin Wright in Adams, New York, just a few miles' distance from the Finney family home, where he remained for several years. There he met God.

It soon became evident to all that gaining a fine position in law was just what young Charles was destined to accomplish. He had everything in his favour: personality, intellect, connections – all that a flourishing law career demanded. The plan was that after being admitted to the Bar, which he apparently never accomplished, he would practise law for a period and then perhaps enter politics. He could easily become one of the state's political leaders. One thing was certain, everyone in Adams had confidence that Charles would succeed in his chosen career.

The years passed quickly, and Finney became a junior law partner with Judge Wright in the Adams office. At that time Charles was only twenty-nine years old. In the small community, he was the constant centre of attention. He stood six feet two inches tall, weighed one hundred and eighty-five pounds; he was a fine figure of a man. His eyes were a bright blue, and he possessed an unusually penetrating gaze which added a sincerity, if not sternness, to his personality. Dancing, as well as athletics and music, made him the leader of Adams' young set.

Yet, when it came to the Christian faith, the brilliant young man confessed he was "as ignorant of religion as a heathen".[6] Finney may have exaggerated his general lack of understanding of Christianity. He had heard some fine preaching, if only for a limited time. He certainly did not assume a blasé, superior, sceptical attitude concerning vital Christian experience. The opposite was true, for one day while in Adams, he received word that one of his brothers had been converted to Christ. Charles literally wept with gratitude that someone in his family could be saved, having grown up in such a prayerless home. There were few lively churches on the frontier, and even fewer educated ministers who could intelligently present the personal claims of Christ and thus interest the people. The Finneys were not a group of religious rebels, they were simply ignorant of dynamic Christianity. But how that was to change! Charles was soon to be gloriously converted, and the impact of his life would touch family, friends, the entire community and finally the world.

## Finney's Conversion and Call:
## The Evangelist's Spiritual Preparation

Finney's first footprints on his Damascus road journey
were in the sands of his law studies. There was one set of
statutes of which the young lawyer was absolutely ignorant:
the Bible. Authors he read continually quoted it, citing
Moses over and over again. Charles purchased a Bible and
began to study it. Being of an inquiring mind, he found
himself taking a serious interest in the Scriptures.

At the same time, he slowly began to respond to what
was happening in the local Presbyterian church. It had
been a Congregational body, but when a new pastor came,
the church changed affiliation. The "splendid pagan",
strange as it seems, was choir director under the pastor, the
Rev. George W. Gale. It was probably Charles' love of
music more than religion that brought this about, but he
thus found himself in church every Sunday.

Up to Charles' twenty-ninth year, the Church's message
was seemingly of little vital concern, but now the young
lawyer began to pay attention. A problem persisted, however. Even though Pastor Gale was a recent graduate of
Princeton University and delivered quite scholarly sermons, his wooden, unbending theology was illogical to
Charles. His legal, analytical, very practical mind simply
could not put together what Gale was trying to preach.
Charles consequently criticised Gale quite unmercifully.
The pastor would often call at Benjamin Wright's law office
on Monday to get Finney's reaction to his sermon on the
previous day. At times Charles was downright ungracious,
but he was not a radical sceptic. Finney confessed he had an
intellectual belief in the Gospel, a belief he firmly held. But

the problem was that he had no vital *experience* of God, even though he became emotional over the music he led in the church.

Charles' attitude should not be condemned too severely, however. Mass confusion reigned when it came to religion, at least for the uninitiated – and Charles was that. The religious ferment of the nineteenth century made his reaction almost inevitable.

First, the Unitarian controversy raged on unendingly. In 1756, Thomas Emlyn wrote *A Humble Inquiry Into The Scripture Account of Jesus Christ.* This work was the epitome of the Unitarian views concerning the character of Christ. Bellamy, an avid Trinitarian, countered with *A Treatise On The Divinity of Christ.* Thus, the battle was joined.

For some years, there had been a subtle shifting in the theology of New England from the earlier Calvinistic Trinitarian views of the Puritans to the more radical Unitarian position. Like a creeping paralysis, Unitarians filtered in, crippling many congregations. In 1785, King's Chapel, the original Episcopalian Church in Boston, became thoroughly Unitarian. Its pastor, James Freeman, effected that shift. His skilful oratory moved many as he pursued themes such as the divinity of Christ, the depravity of man and the nature of the atonement. Freeman would cry, "There is *one* God." Christ came merely to reveal God's nature. We do not need a divine person on earth, Freeman argued.

The opposing trenches of the battlefield held soldiers like Timothy Dwight, the crusading president of Yale College. Yale had been infiltrated with Deism and "French infidelity" after the American Revolution. Dwight, who ascended to the presidential chair in 1795, took on these heresies. As a result, a remarkable revival burst forth at Yale College in 1800, the same year the frontier awakening gripped Kentucky. Many parts of early America at this time were already basking in the sunshine of the new moving of the Holy Spirit.

Harvard College did not fare as well as Yale; it had fallen on the Unitarian side of the issue. Henry Ware became Professor of Divinity at Harvard in 1805. He was a thorough-going Unitarian. In reaction, at least partially so,

Phillip's Academy at Andover, Massachusetts, became the site of a new theological seminary to provide a place for the education of orthodox ministers.

In 1801, Noah Worchester published *Bible News*, which was solidly Unitarian. Then in 1819, William Ellery Channing, a most influential and popular Boston pastor, preached an ordination sermon that caused no small stir in New England. In his message, he declared that the divinity of Christ was an illogical doctrine. He further rejected the Calvinist view of total depravity. He went so far as to state that the passion of our Lord accomplished no more than a moral or spiritual deliverance through instruction, example and death. The substitutionary aspects of the atonement were laid to rest and buried. Moses Stuart, Professor of Sacred Literature at Andover, answered Channing the same year in his *Letters*. So the battle raged on!

Another fissure in the theological ground opened with the Universalist controversy. Universalism landed on American shores in 1770 with the Rev. John Murray, who had been a follower of James Relly of London. Relly wrote; "Christ's righteousness is upon all his seed; by his simple act . . . many are made righteous."[1] He went on to say that those whom God calls with a knowledge of Jesus Christ go directly to Paradise when they die. Others must wait in a "state of apprehension" until they are enlightened and move from their intermediate state. Thus *all* people are ultimately saved because a *universal* redemption was accomplished by Christ.

John Murray organised the First Universalist Church in Gloucester, Massachusetts, in 1779. A few years later, the Rev. Charles Chauncy, pastor of the First Congregational Church of Boston, preached a sermon on the theme, "Salvation of All Men". By 1785, just one year after Chauncy's sermon, enough Universalist congregations had arisen to call a convention. The gauntlet was thrown down. Samuel Hopkins took it up, holding to the brand of Calvinism as expressed in Jonathan Edwards' classic sermon, "Sinners in the Hands of an Angry God".

Many lesser lights joined the ranks to dispel the darkness of Universalism. Nathan Stag, an ardent Calvinist, fought Joseph Huntington, an avid Universalist. A certain Dr.

Nathaniel Emmons entered the controversy also, propounding a view that Finney would later adopt.

Throughout the nineteenth century, Universalism and Unitarianism were increasingly drawn together. The minister who more than any other achieved this was the Rev. Hosea Ballou. The issues were now fully set out, and even though there was more heat than light generated, it was a controversy of tremendous significance. The consequence was devastating in many areas of the Church in New England.

On top of all of that, another view arose: transcendentalism. This movement was the final contribution in the upheaval of New England theology. Transcendentalism has been called "an intellectual overtone to democracy, a belief in the divinity of nature".[2] The transcendentalist argued that, if Jesus Christ was not divine, then nature must be deified. Deism, another spirit that had made deep inroads into the American theological scene, had put God too far out of reach to be of any personal benefit. That was another reason why nature must become the intimate "god who is with us". The result? Emerson, Thoreau and Whitman sat on the banks of Walden Pond in New England glorifying nature, and many Americans began to listen and be enthralled.

Some of the enthusiastic revivalism that had swept through the area had precipitated some strange aberrations; such as Shakerism and Mormonism. Deviant spin-offs may have been inevitable, but with numerous views developing and becoming entrenched, it is little wonder that western New York at Finney's time was looked upon as the "burned over district".

This, then, is the complex religious milieu from which Charles Finney heard Mr. Gale. The pastor, having just come to his first ministerial charge after his education, was ready to hold forth the orthodox faith at any cost. Being a product of Princeton, there was no question in his own mind of what the orthodox faith was: orthodoxy and Calvinism were synonymous. Gale's sermons were largely an attempt to lead his church to become the predestinarian, trinitarian people that John Calvin would have had them to be. Preaching, as Finney thus heard it, had turned basically into technical polemics. As a consequence, few conversions were taking place. During that period, Charles attended an "inquiry meeting" on salvation. He fell under conviction to the point that he confessed he "trembled so that my very seat shook under me". But, as he further stated, "I never received such instruction as I needed. For if I had, I should have been converted at once."

The religious controversies of the hour that precipitated many of the polemical sermons were not the only impediment to Finney finding faith. The prayer meetings that he attended in the little Presbyterian church were something of a stumbling block. Charles must have felt some need in his heart, for he attended the prayer meetings, but they appeared to accomplish virtually nothing.

He told the praying group on one occasion, "I suppose I need to be prayed for, for I am conscious that I am a sinner; but I do not see that it will do any good for you to pray for me; for you are continually asking, but you do not receive. You have been praying for a revival of religion ever since I have been in Adams, and yet you have it not. You have prayed enough since I have attended these meetings to have prayed the devil out of Adams." Finney was frank, if not gracious.

The Rev. George Gale had given up hope of seeing Finney converted. He told the young people of the church not to pray for the young critic. He said their idol had sinned against so much light that he was incapable of receiving the grace of God. He even despaired of the conversion of the choir that Finney led, so captivating was Charles' influence on them. Yet many faithful believers continued to pray for him including a young lady from Whitestown, Oneida County, by the name of Lydia Root Andrews. She was later to be most important to the unconverted lawyer.

Still, Finney was far more positively impressed by Gale and the ministry of his church than the pastor ever imagined, probably considerably more than Charles himself realised. He later confessed, "At Adams, for the first time, I sat [regularly] for a length of time, under an educated ministry."

In the summer of 1821, Mr. Gale made a trip to visit a

sick sister. He gave his pulpit over to Jedediah Burchard. Although Gale had instructed Burchard to do no more than read sermons from a book and make some exhortation, God's Spirit began to move the congregation and Finney later sensed that a revival was afoot in Adams. One day he heard a man praying in a schoolhouse as he was returning from a legal appointment. He said, "That praying did more to impress my mind with the subject of religion, than all I had heard before."

Charles began to be disturbed about his condition. Circumstances were conspiring to bring about his conversion. He no doubt began to ask himself some serious questions. Did Gale really preach the truth? Were the prayers of the church members truly sincere? Even though the sermons did not make logical sense, and the prayers of the people seemed to go unanswered, was there validity in it all? Above all, there was the Bible itself. The questions deepened: Does a person actually need a personal experience of Jesus Christ more than anything on earth? What must one do to be a genuine Christian?

It was only fair that these questions be honestly faced. After all, Finney had questioned practically everyone else's religious reality, why not question his own? The crisis moment was near. Light was beginning to shine around the sombre clouds of doubt that darkened his sky. When the light fully burst in on Finney, it was a day of astonishing revelation. From his *Memoirs*, written decades later, he recalled with vivid memory his dramatic experience.

Finney penned the account at the age of seventy-five. Thus, he wrote from a sophisticated, theologically mature position. He probably breathed back into the event theological concepts he would not have been able to express in the same words at that time. But like Paul, he no doubt told the story many times. Thus he would recall with vivid clarity all its beautiful details. Furthermore, the fascinating account of his conversion in his *Memoirs* is a tremendous source of insight to the man and his entire approach to the Christian life. So dramatic and personal is the story that we must let Charles tell the thrilling event in his own words. The narrative in the *Memoirs* is somewhat lengthy, but it is classical, so not one word should be missed.

On a sabbath evening in the autumn of 1821, I made up my mind that I would settle the question of my soul's salvation at once, that if it were possible I would make my peace with God. But as I was very busy in the affairs of the office, I knew that without great firmness of purpose, I would never effectually attend to the subject. I therefore, then and there resolved, as far as possible, to avoid all business, and everything that would divert my attention, and to give myself wholly to the work of securing the salvation of my soul. I carried this resolution into execution as sternly and thoroughly as I could. I was, however, obliged to be a good deal in the office. But as the providence of God would have it, I was not much occupied either on Monday or Tuesday; and had opportunity to read my Bible and engage in prayer most of the time.

But I was very proud without knowing it. I had supposed that I had not much regard for the opinion for others, whether they thought this or that in regard to myself; and I had in fact been quite singular in attending prayer meetings, and in the degree of attention that I had paid to religion, while in Adams. In this respect, I had been so singular as to leave the church at times to think that I must be an anxious inquirer. But I found, when I came to face the question, that I was very unwilling to have anyone know that I was seeking the salvation of my soul. When I prayed, I would only whisper my prayer, after having stopped the keyhole to the door, lest someone should discover that I was engaged in prayer. Before that time I had my Bible lying on the table with the law books; and it never had occurred to me to be ashamed of being found reading it, any more that I should be ashamed of being found reading any other of my books.

But after I had addressed myself in earnest to the subject of my own salvation, I kept my Bible, as much as I could, out of sight. If I was reading it when anyone came in, I would throw my lawbooks upon it, to create the impression that I had not had it in my hand. Instead of being outspoken and willing to talk with anyone and everybody on the subject as before, I found myself unwilling to converse with anybody. I did not want to see my minister, because I did not want to let him know how I felt, and I had no confidence that he would understand my case, and give me the direction that I needed. For the same reasons I avoided conversation with the elders of the church, or with any of the Christian people. I was ashamed to let them know how I

felt, on the one hand; and on the other, I was afraid
they would misdirect me. I felt myself shut up to the
Bible.

During Monday and Tuesday my conviction increased;
but still it seemed as if my heart grew harder. I could not
shed a tear; I could not pray. I had no opportunity to pray
above my breath; and frequently I felt, that if I could be
alone where I could use my voice and let myself out, I
should find relief in prayer. I was shy, and avoided, as much
as I could, speaking to anybody on any subject. I en-
deavoured, however, to do this in a way that would excite
no suspicion, in any mind, that I was seeking the salvation
of my soul.

Tuesday night I had become very nervous; and in the
night a strange feeling came over me as if I were about to
die. I knew that if I did I should sink down to hell and I felt
almost like screaming, nevertheless I quieted myself as best
I could until morning.

At an early hour I started for the office. But just before I
arrived at the office, something seemed to confront me with
questions like these: indeed, it seemed as if the inquiry was
within myself as if an inward voice said to me, "What are
you waiting for? Did you not promise to give your heart to
God? And what are you trying to do? Are you endeavouring to work out a righteousness of your own?"

Just at that point the whole question of God's salvation
opened to my mind in a manner most marvellous to me at
that time. I think I saw then, as clearly as I ever had in my
life, the reality and fullness of the atonement of Christ. I
saw that His work was a finished work; that instead of
having, or needing, any righteousness of my own to recom-
mend me to God, I had to submit myself to the righteousness of God through Christ. Gospel salvation seemed to me
to be an author of something to be accepted; and that it was
full and complete; and that all that was necessary on my
part, was to get my own consent to give up my sins, and
accept Christ. Salvation, it seemed to me, instead of being a
thing to be wrought out, by one's own works, was a thing to
be found entirely in the Lord Jesus Christ, who presented
Himself before me as my God and my Saviour.

Without being distinctly aware of it, I had stopped in the
street right where the inward voice seemed to arrest me.
How long I remained in that position I cannot say, but after
this distinct revelation had stood for some little time before
my mind, the question seemed to be put, "Will you accept it

now, today?" I replied, "Yes; I will accept today, or I will die in the attempt."

North of the village inn, and over a hill, lay a grove of woods, in which I was in the almost daily habit of walking, more or less, when it was pleasant weather. It was now October, and the time was past for my frequent walks there. Nevertheless, instead of going to my office, I turned and bent my course towards the woods, feeling that I must be alone, and away from all human eyes and ears, so that I could pour out my prayer to God.

But still my pride must show itself. As I went over the hill, it occurred to me that someone might see me and suppose that I was going away to pray. Yet, probably there was not a person on earth that would have suspected such a thing, had he seen me going. But so great was my pride, and so much was I possessed with the fear of man, that I recollect that I skulked along under the fence till I got so far out of sight that no one from the village could see me. I then penetrated into the woods, I should think, a quarter of a mile, went over to the other side of the hill, and found a place where some large trees had fallen across each other, leaving an open place between. There I saw I could make a kind of closet. I crept into this place and knelt down for prayer. As I turned to go up into the woods, I recollect to have said, "I will give my heart to God, or I will never come down from there." I recollect repeating this as I went up – "I will give my heart to God before I ever come down again."

But when I attempted to pray I found that my heart could not pray. I had supposed that if I could only be where I could speak aloud, without being overheard, I could pray freely. But lo! when I came to try, I was dumb; that is, I had nothing to say to God; or at least I could say but a few words, and those without heart. In attempting to pray I would hear a rustling in the leaves, as I thought, and would stop and look up to see if someone were not coming. This I did several times.

Finally I found myself verging fast to despair. I said to myself, "I cannot pray. My heart is dead to God, and I will not pray." I then reproached myself for having promised to give my heart to God before I left the woods. When I came to try, I found I could not give my heart to God. My inward soul hung back, and there was no going out of my heart to God. I began to feel deeply that it was too late; that it must be that I was given up of God and was passed over.

The thought was pressing me of the rashness of my promise, that I would give my heart to God that day or die in the attempt. It seemed to me as if that were binding upon my soul; and yet I was not going to break my vow. A great sinking and discouragement came over me, and I felt almost too weak to stand upon my knees.

Just at this moment I again thought I heard someone approach me, and I opened my eyes to see whether it were so. But right there the revelation of my pride of heart, and the great difficulty that stood in the way, was distinctly shown to me. An overwhelming sense of my wickedness in being ashamed to have a human being see me on my knees before God took such powerful possession of me that I cried at the top of my voice, and exclaimed that I would not leave the place if all the men on earth and all the devils in hell surrounded me. "What!" I said, "such a degraded sinner as I am, on my knees confessing my sins to the great and holy God; and ashamed to have any human being, and a sinner like myself, find me on my knees endeavouring to make peace with my offended God!" The sin appeared awful, infinite. It broke me down before the Lord.

Just at that point this passage of Scripture seemed to drop into my mind with a flood of light: "Then shall ye go and pray unto Me, and I will hearken to you. Then shall you seek Me and find Me, when ye shall search for Me with all your heart." I instantly seized hold of this with my heart. I had intellectually believed the Bible before; but never had truth been in my mind that faith was a voluntary trust instead of an intellectual state. I was as conscious as I was of my existence, of trusting at that moment in God's veracity. Somehow I knew that that was a passage of Scripture, though I do not think I had ever read it. I knew that it was God's word, and God's voice, as it were, that spoke to me. I cried to Him, "Lord, I take Thee at Thy word. Now thou knowest that I do search for Thee with all my heart, and that I have come here to pray to Thee; and Thou hast promised to hear me."

That seemed to settle the question that I could then, that day, perform my vow. The Spirit seemed to lay stress upon that idea in the text, "When you search for Me with all your heart". The question of when, that is, of the present time, seemed to fall heavily into my heart. I told the Lord that I should take Him at his word; that He could not lie, and that therefore I was sure that He heard my prayer, and that He would be found of me.

He then gave me many other promises, both from the Old and the New Testament, especially some most precious promises respecting our Lord Jesus Christ. I never can, in words, make any human being understand how precious and true those promises appeared to me. I took them one after the other as infallible truth, the assertions of God who could not lie. They did not seem so much to fall into my intellect as into my heart, to be put within the grasp of the voluntary powers of my mind; and I seized hold of them, appropriated them, and fastened upon them with the grasp of a drowning man.

I continued thus to pray, and to receive and appropriate promises for a long time, I know not how long. I prayed till my mind became so full that, before I was aware of it, I was on my feet, tripping up the ascent toward the road. The question of my being converted had not so much as arisen in my thoughts; but as I went up, rushing through the leaves and bushes, I recollect saying with great emphasis, "If I am ever converted, I will preach the Gospel."

I soon reached the road that led to the village, and began to reflect upon what had passed; I found that my mind had become most wonderfully quiet and peaceful. I said to myself, "What is this? I must have grieved the Holy Ghost entirely away. I have lost all my conviction. I have not a particle of concern about my soul; and it must be that the Spirit has left me." "Why!" thought I, "I never was so far from being concerned about my own salvation in my life."

Then I remembered what I had said to God while I was on my knees – that I had said that I would take Him at His word; and indeed I recollected a good many things that I had said, and concluded that it was no wonder that the Spirit had left me; that for such a sinner as I was to take hold of God's word in that way, was presumption if not blasphemy. I concluded that in my excitement I had grieved the Holy Spirit, and perhaps committed the unpardonable sin.

I walked quietly toward the village; and so perfectly quiet was my mind that it seemed as if all nature listened. It was on the 10th of October, and a very pleasant day. I had gone into the woods immediately after early daybreak; and when I returned to the village I found it was dinner time. Yet I had been wholly unconscious of the time that had passed; it appeared to me that I had gone from the village but a short time.

But how was I to account for the quiet in the mind? I tried to recall my convictions, to get back again the load of sin under which I was labouring. But all sense of sin, all consciousness of present sin or guilt, had departed from me. I said to myself, "What is this, that I cannot arouse any sense of guilt in my soul, as great a sinner as I am?" I tried in vain to make myself anxious about my present state. I was so quiet and peaceful that I tried to feel concerned about that, lest it should be a result of my having grieved the Spirit away. But take any view of it I would, I could not be anxious at all about my soul, and about my spiritual state. The repose of my mind was unspeakably great. I never can describe it in words. The thought of God was sweet to my mind, and the most profound spiritual tranquillity had taken full possession of me.[3]

Thus the "splendid pagan" came into the dynamic experience of Jesus Christ. His questioning melted away, and peace, tranquillity and joy filled his life in a quite indescribable manner. Like Paul, the scales had fallen from his eyes and he could see.

More was to come. The Holy Spirit, who indwells the heart of all true believers, deeply desires to fill the life of every Christian with power, wisdom and the conscious presence of Christ. Finney's experience of the Holy Spirit that immediately followed his conversion – on the same day actually – was as traumatic as his salvation encounter with the Saviour.

I went to my dinner, and found I had no appetite to eat. I then went to the office, and found that Squire Wright had gone to dinner. I took down my bass-viol, and, as I was accustomed to do, began to play and sing some pieces of sacred music. But as soon as I began to sing those sacred words, I began to weep. It seemed as if my heart was all liquid; and my feelings were in such a state that I could not hear my own voice in singing without causing my sensibility to overflow. I wondered of this, and tried to suppress my tears, but could not. After trying in vain to suppress my tears, I put up my instrument and stopped singing.

After dinner we were engaged in removing our books and furniture to another office. We were very busy in this, and had but little conversation all the afternoon. My mind, however, remained in that profoundly tranquil state. There was a great sweetness and tenderness in my thoughts and soul. Everything appeared to be going right, and nothing seemed to ruffle or disturb me in the least.

Just before evening the thought took possession of my mind, that as soon as I was left alone in the new office, I would try to pray again – that I was not going to abandon the subject of religion and give it up, at any rate; and therefore, although I no longer had any concern about my soul, still I would continue to pray.

By evening we got the books and furniture adjusted; and I made up, in an open fireplace, a good fire, hoping to spend the evening alone. Just at dark Squire Wright, seeing that everything was adjusted, bade me good-night and went to his home. I had accompanied him to the door; and as I closed the door and turned around, my heart seemed to be liquid within me. All my feelings seemed to rise and flow out; and the utterance of my heart was, "I want to pour my whole soul out to God." The rising of my soul was so great that I rushed into the room back of the front office, to pray. There was no fire, and no light, in the room; nevertheless it appeared to me as if it were perfectly light. As I went in and shut the door after me, it seemed as if I met the Lord Jesus Christ face to face. It did not occur to me then, nor did it for some time afterward, that it was wholly a mental state. On the contrary, it seemed to me that I saw Him as I would see any other man. He said nothing, but looked at me in such a manner as to break me right down at His feet. I have always since regarded this as a most remarkable state of mind; for it seemed to me a reality, that He stood before me, and I fell down at His feet and poured out my soul to Him. I wept aloud like a child, and made such confessions as I could with my choked utterance. It seemed to me that I bathed His feet with my tears; and yet I had no distinct impression that I touched Him, that I recollect.

I must have continued in this state for a good while; but my mind was too much absorbed with the interview to recollect anything that I said. But I know, as soon as my mind became calm enough to break off from the interview, I returned to the front office, and found that the fire that I had made of large wood was nearly burned out. But as I turned and was about to take a seat by the fire, I received a mighty baptism of the Holy Ghost. Without any expectation of it, without ever having the thought in my mind that there was any such thing for me, without my recollection that I had ever heard the thing mentioned by any person in the world, the Holy Spirit descended upon me in a manner that seemed to go through me, body and soul. I could feel the impression, like a wave of electricity, going through and through me. Indeed, it seemed to come in waves and waves of liquid love; for I could not express it in any other way. And yet it did not seem like water but rather the breath of God. I can recollect distinctly that it seemed to fan me, like immense wings; and it seemed to me, as these waves passed over me, that they literally moved my hair like a passing breeze.

No words can express the wonderful love that was shed abroad in my heart. I wept aloud with joy and love; and I do not know but I should say, I literally bellowed out the unutterable gushings of my heart. These waves came over me, and over me, and over me, one after another, until I recollect I cried out, "I shall die if these waves continue to pass over me." I said, "Lord, I cannot bear any more;" yet I had no fear of death.

How long I continued in this state, with this baptism continuing to roll over me and go through me, I do not know. But I know it was late in the evening when a member of my choir – for I was the leader of the choir – came into the office to see me. He was a member of the church. He found me in this state of loud weeping, and said to me, "Mr. Finney, what ails you?" I could make him no answer at that time. Then he said, "Are you in pain?" I gathered myself up as best I could, and replied, "No, but so happy that I cannot live."

He turned and left the office. And in a few minutes returned with one of the elders of the church, whose shop was nearly across the way from our office. This elder was a very serious man; and in my presence had been very watchful, and I had scarcely ever seen him laugh. When he came in, I was very much in the state in which I was when the young man went out to call him. He asked me how I felt, and I began to tell him. Instead of saying anything, he fell into a most spasmodic laughter. It seemed as if it was impossible for him to keep from laughing from the very bottom of his heart.

There was a young man in the neighbourhood who was preparing for college, with whom I had been very intimate. Our minister, as I afterward learned, had repeatedly talked with him on the subject of religion, and warned him against being misled by me. He informed him that I was a very careless young man about religion; and he thought that if he associated much with me his mind would be diverted, and he would not be converted.

After I was converted, and this young man was converted, he told me that he had said to Mr. Gale several times, when he had admonished him about associating so much with me, that my conversations had often affected him more, religiously, than his preaching. I had, indeed, let out my feelings a good deal to this young man.

But just at the time when I was giving an account of my feelings to this elder of the church, and to another member who was with him, this young man came into the office. I was sitting with my back towards the door, and barely observed that he came in. He listened with astonishment to what I was saying, and the first I knew he partly fell upon the floor, and cried out in the greatest agony of mind, "Do pray for me!" The elder of the church and the other member knelt down and began to pray for him; and when they had prayed, I prayed for him myself. Soon after this they all retired and left me alone.

The question then arose in my mind, "Why did Elder B. laugh so? Did he not think that I was under a delusion, or crazy?" This suggestion brought a kind of darkness over my mind; and I began to query with myself whether it was proper for me – such a sinner as I had been – to pray for that young man. A cloud seemed to shut in over me; I had no hold upon anything in which I could rest; and after a little while I retired to bed, not distressed in mind, but still at a lost to know what to make of my present state. Notwithstanding the baptism I had received, this temptation so obscured my view that I went to bed without feeling sure that my peace was made with God.

I soon fell asleep, but almost as soon awoke again on account of the great flow of the love of God that was in my heart. I was so filled with love that I could not sleep. Soon I feel asleep again, and awoke in the same manner. When I awoke, this temptation would return upon me, and the love that seemed to be in my heart would abate; but as soon as I was asleep, it was so warm within me that I would immediately awake. This continued till, late at night, I obtained some sound repose.

When I awoke in the morning the sun had risen, and was pouring a clear light into my room. Words cannot express the impression that this sunlight made upon me. Instantly the baptism that I had received the night before returned

upon me in the same manner. I arose upon my knees in the
bed, and wept aloud with joy, and remained for some time
too much overwhelmed with the baptism of the Spirit to do
anything but pour out my soul to God. It seemed as if this
morning's baptism was accompanied with a gentle reproof,
and the Spirit seemed to say to me, "Will you doubt?"
"Will you doubt?" I cried, "No! I will not doubt; I cannot
doubt." He then cleared the subject up so much to my mind
that it was in fact impossible for me to doubt that the Spirit
of God had taken possession of my soul.[4]

When Finney was finally able to compose himself, he
made his way to the law office. There he told Squire
Benjamin Wright what God had done in his life. The judge
was dumbfounded. He just stared at his young law partner
and remained silent. But God's arrow of conviction sank
deep into his heart.

About that time a client, a deacon in the church, came in.
Finney was to argue a case in court that day for the man. He
said, "Mr. Finney, do you recollect that my case is to be
tried at ten this morning? I suppose you are ready?"
Charles replied, "Deacon, I have a retainer from the Lord
Jesus Christ to plead his cause, and I cannot plead yours."
He looked at Finney with astonishment and said, "What do
you mean?" Finney told him in a few words that he had
enlisted in the cause of Christ, and that only the cause of
Christ must he plead. The deacon dropped his head, and
without making any reply went out. The simple testimony
was the cause of a profound spiritual renewal in the life of
the Christian layman.

As soon as the deacon left the office, Finney sallied forth
to converse with all who would listen. He seemed to sense
that God's hand was mightily upon him. To share the love
of Christ with others became his consuming passion. Since
God had so mightily touched his life, saved him, and given
him the power of the Holy Spirit, he was ready to witness to
the whole needy world. A career in law had no more
appeal.

Share Christ he did. It seemed to Finney that every
person with whom he spoke but a few words was struck
with immediate conviction. It was as if every word he
uttered was driven home to the heart with great spiri-

tual power. People were beginning to be saved all over town.

Adams was astir. Their critical young lawyer, Charles Finney, had been converted. None was more shocked than Pastor George Gale. The pastor had been accustomed to holding prayer meetings in a school building. That night the school filled with people. No regular meeting was scheduled, everyone just came. The folks sat there in frozen attention. No one stood up to lead. Finally, Charles rose to speak. He later confessed that he was "panic-stricken" and exclaimed to himself, "My God, is it I?" It was. God had something to say through the new convert. As he shared his dramatic experience of Christ, the entire congregation was awed at the mighty thing God had done. No one was more impressed and moved than the pastor, George Gale. He stood up, and in humble confession acknowledged that he had doubted Charles' sincerity when he first heard of his conversion. A town sceptic said Finney was trying to pull off a hoax to show how well he could deceive people. The pastor acknowledged the power of God and how utterly wrong he had been.

Charles went after the young people of Adams with zest. He had for some years led them astray; now he must lead them to God. Success surrounded his every effort to witness for Christ, and many of the young people came to salvation.

The story of Finney's experience so impressed several citizens of Adams, that on learning of the details of Charles' conversion, they actually went out into the woods to seek the Lord at the same spot. Even Judge Wright was one of these. A genuine revival was beginning to take hold of the entire Adams community.

A short time later, Charles made his way to Henderson to visit his parents. He met his father at the gate and said that in all the years he lived under his parents' roof, he had never heard his father pray. Smitten with conviction and shame, his father acknowledged Charles was right and urged him to come in and pray with the family. It was not long before the whole household came to Jesus Christ.

In the year following Finney's conversion, sixty-three people were added to the little Adams Presbyterian

Church. Moreover, the revival spirit spread to the surrounding villages and communities.

During those exciting days, if the spiritual fervour of some of the church members cooled, Finney would run to their homes to rekindle the fires. He felt a deep urgency to pray. Early each morning he went to the church for intercessory prayer. Many others joined him.

As history well attests, revival fires flare up and then tend to fade. When attendance at the Adams prayer meetings subsided, Charles would become deeply concerned. It seemed to drive him to even more prayer. One early morning, Mr. Gale alone was found at Charles' side in intercession. Suddenly another touch of the Spirit broke upon Charles, similar in many respects to that which he had experienced on the evening of his conversion. Charles fell prostrate to the ground, overwhelmed with the thought that while all nature was vocal with the praises of God, humanity, the object of heaven's supreme love, remained unmoved and dumb. A light seemed to surround Finney, as he described it, "like the brightness of the sun in every direction". He went on to relate, "I knew something then, by actual experience, of the light which prostrated Paul on his way to Damascus. It was surely a light such as I could not have endured long." He broke out into loud weeping, much to the astonishment of Mr. Gale who had seen no such light. Charles continued to weep until the overwhelming presence of God passed away, then a great calm settled over his mind. He had frequent experiences like this in the years immediately following his conversion – experiences so vivid that he shrank from relating them to others.

God's blessings were surely on Finney, but now he had to face a vital question: Had God truly called him to the Gospel ministry? Did the Holy Spirit want this zealous young convert to devote his whole life to the ministry of the Word? The answer was not difficult to discover. He had little or no desire to practise law after his encounter with Christ. Charles had already confessed that if God ever converted him, he would leave everything and become a minister. Thus he was soon convinced he must preach. As time moved on, he never doubted the call of God to declare the Gospel.

The first year and a half after Charles' conversion is a little obscure – like Paul's three years in Arabia after his conversion. No doubt, God was grooming the young man for a great ministry of preaching. There was, of course, something of a sacrifice to be made. He had studied long and hard for the law profession. One of Charles' former Henderson students said, "When he abandoned the profession and decided to study for the ministry, we all felt that he had made an awful mistake. That if he had continued in the practice, he was destined, in a very short time, to attain the highest position at the Bar and in politics."[5]

But it was the ministry of the Gospel that now captivated Charles, and to that work he gave himself without reservation.

# PART II

# CHARLES GRANDISON FINNEY: AN EVANGELIST FOR CHRIST

# 1

## Finney's Early Evangelism:
## The Evangelist's First Revivals

A call to the ministry is a call to prepare! The principle contained in that often-repeated cliché captivated Finney's imagination. He had studied diligently to be admitted to the legal Bar. Now he had "a retainer from the Lord Jesus Christ". Could he do less as Christ's advocate? He must equip himself to argue His cause. Thus he placed himself under the local Presbyterian presbytery in 1823 to prepare for the Gospel ministry. As could be anticipated, the presbytery urged him to enrol at Princeton Theological Seminary.

Princeton Theological Seminary in New Jersey stood as the impregnable citadel of what was called in the nineteenth century "old school" Calvinistic theology. It had profited much from the influence of the First Great Awakening in America. None other than Jonathan Edwards, revivalist, educator and Calvinist had been at one time president of the institution.

Quite unthinkable to the Rev. George W. Gale was the suggestion that his young protégé should attend any other seminary or embrace any other theology. Yet, that is exactly what the young preacher did. He refused to go to Princeton. Not go to Princeton? The elders wanted to know *why*. Finney told them he could not financially afford the venture. This was true as far as it went. They pressed him, offering to pay all his expenses. He still declined, finally summoning the courage to tell them bluntly that he simply could not put himself under such an influence. He said that the graduates of Princeton were not properly educated for effective Gospel ministry.

How could Finney ever be a successful minister by refusing formal training? That is probably how many on the presbytery reacted. But the future evangelist was far more prepared for a preaching ministry than might have been assumed at first glance. His law career was of excellent use. His adeptness at logic, rhetoric, argumentation, ethics the power of analysis held him in immediate good stead before a congregation.

Furthermore, his fine physical frame gave him a commanding appearance and an exceptional grace of movement. Some have been rather rationalistic about Finney's piercing gaze and influence over his hearers. Fredrick M. Davenport in *Primitive Traits in Religious Revivals*, said Finney's influence had the "quality of a very high hypnotic potential". But surely it was God's Holy Spirit that smote people, not Finney's "hypnotic" human gifts, as important as human gifts are in the hands of God? As a speaker, his resonant voice struck his hearers' ears with a beauty and clarity and rare flexibility. He had a "non-preachy", personal style, and also a fine dramatic flair. Alfred Vance Churchill, a member of Finney's congregation, said, "His language was based on the Bible, Shakespeare and Blackstone." Finney loved Shakespeare all his life, and few contemporaries could read it with the same passion as did the evangelist.

One writer described Finney's power in the pulpit: "the hearer never felt, till the close, that he was listening to a . . . sermon, but rather that he was being personally addressed with such earnestness upon matters that were of great mutual concern."[1] Churchill said of him that his words were "logic on fire", crashing through his listeners "like cannonballs through a basket of eggs".

Above all, there was a rare spirit of grace on the young man. Many of Finney's contemporaries – at least lay contemporaries – may well have agreed with the rather audacious young minister that a theological course at Princeton would probably do him more harm than good.

On June 25, 1823, the presbytery placed Charles under the tutelage of the Rev. George W. Gale and the Rev. George Boardman, pastor of the Presbyterian church in Watertown, New York. These men were tapped as his private tutors in the "verities" of Princeton Calvinism.

Charles was never one to retreat from reality into a superficial piety or rest upon his natural abilities. He possessed a true humility despite his youthful, frontier brashness, and he fully acknowledged his need of training. Thus, Charles gladly and graciously accepted the decision of the presbytery.

Soon he was eagerly engaged in ministerial studies under the leadership of Gale and Boardman. Such a procedure was not unusual in the early nineteenth century. To "read" theology under an able, educated pastor was a common way to prepare for the ministry. But in Charles' case, the arrangement only led to conflict.

Finney still found Gale's Calvinism very difficult to accept. For example, the pastor would preach on repentance, but then never fail to remind his congregation that they could not repent unless God granted it. To his credit, Gale never flinched to demand faith of his hearers. Then, however, he would insist that faith was impossible unless one was elected of God and thus granted faith. That sort of sermonising and reasoning made no sense to Finney.

The "old school" theology of Gale was a puzzle to the young ministerial aspirant on two scores. First, it did not make rational, logical sense. Secondly, he found it impossible to justify this style of Calvinism from a scriptural standpoint. Finney said, "I am sure I was quite willing to believe what I found in the Bible." But he simply could not discover Gale's position in the Bible. So the lawyer set out to refute his tutor; thus, building his theological base on "close and logical reasoning", to use his own words.

Another very important factor forcefully impressed itself upon Finney's theologically-searching mind. He discovered that God honoured his doctrinal views when he preached them by granting far more conversions than were being produced by the preaching of Gale and Broadman. So Finney found the pragmatic test falling in his favour. That may seem somewhat superficial. It may even appear a bit smug on the part of the young preacher. But young, hot-hearted converts are often as concerned for results as for abstract thought.

Finney's greatest problem with Gale's entire approach to the Christian ministry was the pastor's lack of spiritual unction. He felt Gale lacked the profound power of the Holy Spirit in his ministry. To Finney that was of more serious consequence than Gale's systematic theology.

Thus the debates raged between Gale and Finney. The situation degenerated to the point that Finney's learning sessions with Gale were, in his own words, "little else than controversy". They must have been interesting episodes, however. One night, for example, they had a session in the church on the doctrine of the atonement. They were completely absorbed, and unaware that people were coming into the church for a scheduled meeting. The folk were so fascinated with the theological discussion that they insisted the two men continue, replacing the regular worship service.

Finney also ransacked Gale's theological library seeking answers to his questions. There, too, he found nothing but high-Calvinism. This only deepened the conflict between the student and his mentor.

The constant controversy began to exert a depressing effect upon the sensitive Charles. He was almost pressed to the point of giving up his ministerial training altogether. An elder in Gale's church greatly encouraged him at these times. After many a depressing discussion, the elder would meet Charles and pray with him for God's light and help, often until the small hours of the morning. That carried him through the storms.

Despite all the disagreements with Gale and Boardman, there were some positive results from Charles' ministerial education. The young evangelist was becoming a skilful debater. This held him in good stead when he was called upon to defend what he considered "orthodox" Christianity.

In Finney's early days in Adams, a hot argument arose between the universalists and the orthodox. This was precipitated by the arrival of a very skilful Universalist debater. Several citizens of Adams were warming to the comfort of the Universalist's views, and Gale felt the Universalist must be debated and refuted. At that moment, however, Gale became ill. He asked his young pupil, Charles, to engage the "heretic". This Finney did with all the zeal of callow youth. He seemed to relish a good theological fight anyway. He immediately climbed out on a limb, stating that if he could not successfully refute the doctrine of Universalism, he would become a Universalist himself. It is important to realise that the Universalists were quite aggressive in Finney's day. They had an "evangelistic" mentality that made them very eager to propagate their views and win "converts". They were far from passive as they became later.

The Universalist's first arrow came from the quiver of George Gale's own Calvinistic theology. All good Calvinists held that Christ's death was a literal payment for every single sin of those who would be saved. The Universalists reasoned that if Christ died and paid the penalty for every single sin of every person, God could not hold those sins against anyone any more; all sins were already paid for. God could never justly condemn those for whom the debt was already paid once and for all. Hence, all would automatically be saved.

This line of rational reasoning thrust the young preacher into a very difficult position. He felt that he could not refute the Universalist heresy without publicly rejecting Gale's Calvinistic theory of the atoning work of Christ. That would be most embarrassing to Gale, and Charles.

Of course, the hyper-Calvinists had their answer to the quite convincing reasoning of the Universalists. They argued that although Christ paid the penalty for every single sin, it was only paid for the elect. They held that Christ did not die for the sins of the *entire* human race. He only died for the predestined ones. They believed in what is commonly called "a limited atonement". This idea Finney absolutely rejected. Some recent scholars, though a small minority, say John Calvin himself rejected the concept of a limited atonement; they argue that the concept was the product of some of Calvin's successors, such as Theodore Beza and William Perkins. Regardless, Finney firmly believed that Christ died for the sins of *all* humanity. The only way he could refute the Universalist with integrity was to reject Gale's view of the atonement, and that publicly.

Charles' graciously refused to take his stand unless he had his teacher's permission to do so. Gale consented. Charles tells the story of the skirmish in his autobiography.

The young theologian began by contending that Christ's atonement was not a *literal* payment of the sinner's debt in any mathematical, legal sense. Rather, the Lord's death and resurrection merely did what was essential in God's sight to procure the forgiveness of sin and effect salvation. He stated that Christ's passion satisfied what he termed "public justice". He borrowed this phrase from Jonathan Edwards. Of course, he had not read Jonathan Edwards at that time. Thus it is clear that Charles' account of his debate in the *Memoirs* threw the Edwardian phrase back on to the view he began to formulate in his early encounter with the Universalists in Adams. Although he may well have formed his doctrine of the atonement apart from Jonathan Edwards, he could hardly have hit on the same terminology. This view of Christ's atoning work became a central thrust in Finney's later, developed theology. Moreover, by his employment of it, he utterly devastated, at least to his own satisfaction, the Universalist's position. Whether one agrees with Finney's approach to the concept of the atonement or not, it points out the deep divergence that had developed between the pastor and his pupil.

After six months of instruction from Gale and Board-man, on December 30, 1823, the fledgling preacher was up before the presbytery to be examined. In the course of the questioning, Finney was asked if he believed in the *Confession of the Presbyterian Church*. This Confession centred on the well-known *Westminster Confession*. Charles said he did as far as he understood it. In reality, he had never seen it.

He had prepared a sermon of the traditional kind he was expected to deliver before the elders, putting it in writing to demonstrate he could write a sermon; some had seemingly entertained doubts. As Charles began his actual delivery, however, he soon departed from the pages and preached extemporaneously. This pattern of preaching became his style throughout his evangelistic ministry. The examining council took a rather negative view of this. Preaching in those days was somewhat plodding and pedantic; every word spoken was first put on paper and then laboriously read. For a preacher not to read his sermon was almost tantamount to heresy. Charles was successful nonetheless. His performance at the meeting generally pleased the elders. A unanimous vote granted him a licence to preach the Gospel in the Presbyterian churches.

Most men were required to study a full year under the tutelage of their seniors before a licence to preach was granted, yet Finney finished his training in a mere six months. There was another reason besides Charles' brilliance that aided the completion of his course of study in half the normal time: the Adams pulpit was empty. Gale had resigned because of ill health, and it was suggested that Finney take his place. Strangely, the local congregation was not particularly overjoyed at the prospect. One would have thought that the tremendous influence of Charles in effecting so many conversions in Adams would have endeared him to the entire Christian community. But a prophet is not without honour, except in his own country. Our Lord's most difficult time was in Nazareth. A Mr. Hopkins came as the regular pastor to the Adams congregation.

How much George Gale had to do with the negative attitude of certain church members in Adams is uncertain, but he was not happy with his pupil. Gale asked him to preach the Sunday after he had been given his licence. Finney's extemporaneous, personal approach was so different from the tradition of reading a heavy sermon from a manuscript, not to mention the theological deviations, that Gale bluntly said he was ashamed to think he had been Finney's teacher. This rather unkind statement grieved and discouraged the young preacher. In later years, however, Gale turned completely around; he embraced Finney's theology and became a fellow labourer in the revivals.

The next summer, on July 1, 1824, the St. Lawrence presbytery, under which Finney had been placed a year earlier, convened at Evans Mills, a few miles from Adams. The intent of the meeting was to ordain the young licensee to the Presbyterian ministry. Finney was ministering in Evans Mills at that time.

That July 1st night, the ordination meeting was called to order with the Rev. A. W. Platt presiding, and with the Rev. J. Clinton preaching. Hands were laid on Charles, and he became the Rev. Charles Grandison Finney, Presbyterian minister. When the Synod of Albany, New York, met in the First Presbyterian Church of Utica on October 5, 1824, the new minister was there.

The St. Lawrence Presbytery meeting was a monumental moment for Charles. Not only did he receive his official ordination, he also met for the first time the Rev. Daniel Nash, who was later to become a most significant personality in the Finney ministry. Nash had been spiritually cold at one time, when illness overtook him and God performed a deep work in his life. He devoted himself to a ministry of intercessory prayer.

At a later presbytery meeting, Charles was startled when, with no prior notice, they called upon him to preach. He readily obliged, but refused to enter the "high box" pulpit that was typical of church buildings in early America, preferring to address them from the aisle. He took as his text: "Holiness, without which no man shall see the Lord" (Heb. 12:14). The elders, a little stuffy, were somewhat shocked that Charles would lower the dignity of the pulpit by speaking to people in such a colloquial manner, exhorting them with such fervour and vehemence from the aisle. But once again, Charles won the day and the presbytery was pleased.

In the spring prior to Finney's ordination, the young preacher had secured a position with the Utica-based Female Missionary Society of the Western District of the state of New York. He was to serve as a missionary to small congregations in Jefferson County for a three-month period beginning in March 1824. He was delighted. Not only that, this commission was secured for him by none other than the Rev. George Gale. Perhaps Finney's old pastor was a little sorry for the rejection of the Adams congregation. At any rate, that move was to prove most significant in Finney's developing revivalism. It gave him the opportunity to carry on a more itinerant ministry, thus allowing him to preach to different congregations. As a settled pastor, that sort of service would have been quite difficult.

The travelling, itinerant preacher was always a welcome figure in the frontier regions of western New York in those days. Few congregations could support a full-time settled pastor. They had virtually no amenities and little money to pay a preacher. Moreover, these itinerant men of God did much to comfort and help the frontier people in their difficult, primitive life.

Charles seemed well set for the service. Practically everyone in western New York had immigrated from the older settlements farther east, as he had done. In addition, his directness, simplicity and innovative methods were readily received by the western New York frontiersmen. In the pulpit he communicated directly to their needs.

There were still problems to overcome, however.

> I found that region of the country what, in the western phrase, would be called a "burnt district". There had been, a few years previously, a wild excitement passing through that region, which they called a revival of religion, but which turned out to be spurious . . . It was reported as having been a very extravagant excitement; and resulted in a reaction so extreme and profound, as to leave the impression on many minds that religion was a mere delusion . . . Taking what they had seen as a specimen of a revival of religion, they felt justified in opposing anything looking toward the promoting of a revival.[2]

Yet it is right in the heart of the "burnt district" that God visited the land and overcame all obstacles to Charles' ministry.

July 1824 found Finney not only at the presbytery meeting, but also ministering on alternate Sundays between Evans Mills, Jefferson County, and nearby Antwerp. If the presbytery council were not too pleased with Finney's style, Evans Mills, where he was spending most of the weekdays, was very happy with their young missionary. A general revival spirit was developing throughout their small community. The adult population of Evans Mills was only one thousand four hundred and seventy-two, but they were destined to receive bountiful blessings.

There was a small Congregational and Baptist church in little Evans Mills but they did not boast any church building, so the Congregationalists and the Baptists shared an old stone schoolhouse for worship. The congregation was small, just a handful of believers, but they were delighted with their new minister and paid him a stipend of two hundred dollars a year. From the start there was good general interest in the community. Everyone continually complimented Charles on his fine sermons. Yet Finney confessed, "I was very much dissatisfied." He tried to communicate to the citizens that he was not there merely to bring them interesting and enjoyable sermons. Rather, he had come to see their souls saved.

In his rather blunt style, Charles set out to straighten the issue. He entered the pulpit one day, his piercing eyes ablaze, and said:

> Now I must know your minds, and I want that you who have made up your minds to become Christians and will give your pledge to make your peace with God immediately should rise up; but that, on the contrary, those of you who are resolved that you will not become Christians, and wish me so to understand, and wish Christ so to understand, should sit still. You who are now willing to pledge to me and to Christ that you will immediately make your peace with God, please rise up. On the contrary, you that mean that I should understand that you are committed to remain in your present attitude, not to accept Christ – those of you that are of this mind, may sit still.

Shock crossed everyone's face. The people sat in amazement. No preacher had ever put that before them. After looking around for a few moments and seeing the congregation sitting there in stunned silence, the preacher went on: "Then you are committed. You have taken your stand. You have rejected Christ and his Gospel; and ye are witnesses one against the other, and God is witness against you all. This is explicit, and you may remember as long as you live, that you have thus publicly committed yourselves against the Saviour, and said, 'We will not have this man, Christ Jesus, to reign over us.'"

The congregation rose *en masse* in anger. As they made their way out, Finney stopped preaching. As soon as they heard the preacher fall into silence, the people paused and turned around. Charles said, "I am sorry for you; and will preach to you once more, the Lord willing, tomorrow night."

Everyone left. Finney was confounded by his own action. A cloud of depression settled over him; he was sure that his imprudence had ended his ministry in Evans Mills. Everything seemed to be going so well; had his youthful brashness run him aground?

A good Baptist deacon remained behind. He came up to the perplexed young preacher, took him by the hand, smiled and said, "Brother Finney, you have got them. They cannot rest under this, rely upon it . . . I believe you have done the very thing that needed to be done, and that we shall see the results."

The deacon and Finney spent the next day in prayer and fasting, separately in the morning and united in intercession that afternoon. Prayer was becoming of prime importance in Finney's ministry. He saw intercession as the one essential ingredient to bring God's rich blessings. While Finney and the deacon were engaged in prayer, the townspeople were working themselves into an uproar. They threatened to "ride him out on a rail", "tar and feather him", or give him his "walking papers". Others cursed him and generally abused him.

Finney and the deacon prevailed in prayer, however. Late in the afternoon, God gave them "great enlargement and promise of victory", as Charles expressed it. When the time came for the evening meeting, the little place of worship was thronged. Every activity in town had ceased as the people gathered at the stone school building.

Charles had given no prior thought to his sermon. Nevertheless, the Holy Spirit was mightily upon him and the words flowed. As he preached, a deep pervading conviction settled on the entire congregation. Finney said later in recounting the scene, "For more than an hour, and perhaps for an hour and a half, the word of God came through me to them in a manner that I could see was carrying all before it. It was a fire and a hammer breaking the rock; and as the sword that was piercing to the dividing asunder of soul and spirit.''

Finney still assumed the congregation had decided against Christ. He simply dismissed the people, but not before appointing another meeting. As everyone began to withdraw, one woman appeared to be in a faint and was being helped by some friends. The evangelist discerned she was not physically ill; she had been so seized with conviction of sin that she could not even speak. Yet she was a faithful church member and sister of a well-known missionary.

After the meeting, instead of going to his regular lodgings, Charles went home with another family. The next morning, he discovered that many people had been eagerly seeking him throughout the night. Such deep anguish of soul was gripping people that they could not sleep. Not only that, after sixteen hours of speechless stupor, the lady under conviction the night before broke out with a song of salvation. She confessed she had been deceived all the years of her faithful church attendance. For the first time, under Finney's blistering preaching, she saw God's absolute holiness and her sinfulness. That soon became the pattern; what had happened to her became a chain-reaction touching off spiritual explosions all over town. Revival had come.

Opposition to the movement of the Holy Spirit was by no means over, however. There were a number of Deists in the town who seemed determined to thwart the touch of God. The young evangelist met them forthrightly. He preached a direct and convincing sermon against their views. The result: practically every Deist in Evans Mills was converted.

Opposition also came from other sources. One night a man came to the meeting with a loaded gun, intending to kill Finney! In another instance, an old infidel railed and blasphemed against the revival movement in a merciless manner, all over town. But Finney gave no public attention to it at all. One morning, as revival excitement ran high, the blasphemer fell from his chair in what western New Yorkers called a ''fit of apoplexy''. A physician was summoned but to no avail. The last words of the old man were, ''Don't let Finney pray over my corpse.''

Despite every opposition, God's grace prevailed and the revival progressed with an increasing momentum.

Not far from Evans Mills was a German community. The people had no regular minister, so they began attending Finney's meetings. They were soon caught up in the spirit of the revival. At their urging, Finney went out from Evans Mills to preach to them. The Germans turned out to virtually the last person to hear the young evangelist. He preached on what must have been one of his favourite texts: "Holiness, without which no man shall see the Lord". The impact was tremendous. In a few days, the whole community was under conviction of sin and the need of Christ. As a result, in Finney's own words, "The revival among the Germans resulted in the conversion of the whole church, I believe, and of nearly the whole community of Germans. It was one of the most interesting revivals that I have ever witnessed."

At the height of the Jefferson County awakening, Father Nash appeared. He began to pray for the people in Evans Mills. Finney said of this devout man of God, "His gift of prayer was wonderful, and his faith almost miraculous." Nash stayed in the community only a short time, but this was one of the first times Finney and Nash blended their ministry of prayer and preaching in the marvellous fashion that soon developed.

As the revival deepened in the Evans Mills area, Finney grew increasingly sensitive to the "burnt district" syndrome, whether or not he would have used that actual phrase at that time. He was cautious concerning the methods he used to promote the revival and bring about conversions. All he would permit were regular preaching services, prayer meetings, conferences, and gatherings of the concerned that they might be personally counselled in the way of salvation. He also encouraged much private prayer. Although Charles was young and quite inexperienced, God's Spirit was in obvious control.

Charles' caution eliminated any extreme emotional exuberance throughout his days at Evans Mills. He was not an "emotional" preacher himself. His emphasis was on the love of God, especially later, after he read the great revival literature of Jonathan Edwards. What emotions were manifest were in the congregation, not in any excessive emotions of the preacher. Thus meetings were quite orderly, at least for the frontier mentality of the people. He even insisted in the prayer meetings that only one person would be allowed to lead in prayer. Further, to avoid arousing superficial emotions, he would not permit prayer to go on and on without a break. He would calm the rising temperament of the people by giving short talks between each period of prayer. Yet emotions were naturally aroused in the heat of the revival, especially in those under conviction of sin. Finney felt that emotions were involuntary, they would arise whether a person liked it or not. Therefore, he always preached primarily to the intellect. He strongly held that preaching to the emotions was dangerous, because the emotions could overpower the intellect and the will which were in a person's control. Enthusiasm which appeals only to emotions is spurious, he argued. Charles contended that excitement is authentic only as it comes from an encounter with the truth. He thus distinguished between what he called "animal feeling" and "spiritual feeling".

Finney's approach may appear rather legalistic and restrictive today, but this was a time when religious emotions ran high and the evangelist determined not to let matters get out of hand. As a result of this wise approach, no serious "burnt district" problems developed, even though he was accused of such.

During the early days of the dawning revival, the Female Missionary Society still sponsored Finney. According to his contract, he spent alternate Sundays at Antwerp; the adult population being six hundred and sixty. The Antwerp community was what Christian people would have termed in those days "a most wicked place", and generally known in the area as "Hell's Acres". The little town did tolerate a Presbyterian church, but it was very weak and had no regular pastor. A Presbyterian elder who lived some five miles outside Antwerp would hitch up his horse on Sunday and drive over to the church and preach. The road from his home to Antwerp took him through a Universalist community. The Universalists were so antagonistic that they would actually take the wheels off the elder's buggy to prevent him from making his preaching appointment.

Finney flew into the Antwerp fray unafraid. He secured permission to use a school building in Antwerp and announced the services. There is an interesting reason behind the use of the school building instead of the church house. The village hotel keeper had the keys to the church building and was so opposed to Finney's ministry that he refused to open it up for the evangelist. The community abounded with religious rebels, and Finney was quite appalled by the general profanity and lifestyle of the godless village.

On the first Sunday in Antwerp, Finney preached on John 3:16. That was in April 1824. A powerful impression must have been made, for the hotel keeper relinquished the keys and Finney was allowed to hold services in the local church house. Soon people were coming in droves. Finney related, "Appoint a meeting when and where I would, anywhere round about and the people would throng to hear." A spiritual awakening had come to another Jefferson County community.

One of the most fascinating events in the Antwerp revival occurred in another school building service, this one about three miles outside the town. Finney had been invited to speak there by a godly old man. The elder Christian stood in stark contrast to the community which was noted for its irreverence. Charles knew nothing about the place or the gentleman who had invited him, yet he felt he must respond to the plea of the old brother. A Monday evening at 5 p.m. was set for the service.

Since the school was only three miles from town, Charles decided to strike out on foot. He had laboured long on the Lord's day and by the time he had tramped the three miles he was absolutely exhausted. He sat down by the roadside and felt he could scarcely go another step, regretting not taking his horse. But at the appointed hour he trudged up to the schoolhouse, and to his delight found it packed almost beyond capacity. He actually had to stand in an open door himself to lead the services.

The worship began with a hymn. The people were terrible singers. Each one "bawled in his own way", as Charles put it. To the evangelist's musically-trained senses, it was terrible. He finally put both hands over his ears to blot out the discordant bellows. He could still hear them, however. The grating, irritating sound literally drove him to his knees in vocal prayer. God anointed his prayer and soon a deep consciousness of the Holy Spirit's presence settled on the scene.

Finney had taken no thought of his sermon subject, as was common for him. When he rose from his knees, he picked the text, "Up, get you out of this place; for the Lord will destroy this city" (Gen. 19:14). He then proceeded to preach on the story of Lot and the destruction of Sodom. He told in graphic terms of how God's judgment fell upon Sodom and Gomorrah because of their sin and godless-ness. He noticed the people began to look angry – some furious. They seemed so upset he thought they were about to set on him.

He had not been on his feet for more than fifteen minutes, preaching in this manner and applying the truth to the people, when all at once what Charles called "an awful solemnity" settled down on everyone. The people began to fall from their seats and cry for mercy. He described the unbelievable scene by saying, "If I had had a sword in each hand, I could not have cut them off their seats as fast as they fell." In a few minutes, nearly the entire congregation were on their knees, if not completely prostrate.

The preacher could not go on. The people were in such an agony of prayer that loud cries for mercy completely dominated the scene. The old man who had invited Finney to the community sat there in stunned amazement. Finney looked at him and screamed above the din, "Can't you pray?" He instantly fell on the floor and poured out his soul to the Saviour. Finney's own heart was so overflowing with joy that he could hardly contain himself. It was all he could do to refrain from shouting praise to God for His obvious blessings on the meeting.

As soon as the evangelist had controlled his own feel-ings, he moved from person to person whispering in each ear the message of God's grace in Jesus Christ. As he dealt with the people one by one, a wonderful peace settled in their hearts and they began to intercede for others. Finney continued to go from person to person until he had to leave for another preaching appointment in Antwerp. He placed the old man in charge of the meeting and left. So profound was the moving of God's Spirit that the service lasted through the night. As the morning sun broke across the eastern horizon, there were still those who would not go home. But school children would soon be there, so the praying group moved to a neighbouring house. That afternoon, with conviction still running deep, Finney was called for. They could not break up the meeting.

For a second time, Charles made his way to the little community. A significant second service was held. At that afternoon session, the evangelist was told the reason for the hot anger of the people when the service had opened the night before. The community had such a reputation for wickedness that it was commonly called "Sodom". Moreover, the old gentleman who had invited Finney was recognised as the only Christian about, so everyone called him "Lot". The people had, quite naturally, supposed that Finney knew of these facts and had deliberately chosen the subject of his message to humiliate them. But as Finney related, "This was a striking coincidence; but as far as I was concerned, it was altogether accidental." What a moving of God's Spirit! Furthermore, though the awakening came like a sudden avalanche sweeping all in its path, the converts remained steadfast in their commitment. No one could say that it was a mere emotional outburst. For many years after that momentous event, Finney met faithful converts who had come out of the schoolhouse revival. Some had become Christian leaders, ministers and the like. The work was permanent and genuine.

The spirit of revival exemplified in the schoolhouse meetings soon permeated every part of Antwerp as well as some of the neighbouring villages. The Antwerp Universalists rose up in a rage, of course, but Finney took them on in full force, demolishing their views to the satisfaction of most. It is remarkable how the young evangelist could defend the faith and annihilate opposition. An amazing number of conversions were recorded in Antwerp. As the awakening spread and conversions soared, a young man named Denning was procured as pastor. Finney felt that he could now leave Antwerp where he had spent so much time during the past two or three months, and give more effort at Evans Mills.

Charles' time with the Female Missionary Society was rapidly running out. It was actually his second three-month commitment and the question arose whether he should move on. The believers pressed their young minister to remain and after much prayer, Charles concluded he should stay. He gave them his word that he would spend a further year with them as God permitted. Charles worked ardently and tirelessly as a missionary. In one of his reports to the Society, he stated he had preached one hundred and fifty-nine times in a twenty-four-week period.

A whole new chapter opened up for the evangelist in October 1824. He went to Whitestown, also known as Whitesboro, in Oneida County, to claim a bride, the lovely Miss Lydia Root Andrews. Lydia had prayed for Charles' conversion for many years while the young lawyer was still steeped in his spiritual ignorance. He did not realise her concern for him at that time. How she knew of Charles and began praying for him is uncertain. Perhaps the Andrews and the Finney families had some acquaintance in earlier years. Whitestown and Kirkland, where the Finneys lived, are near one another.

Lydia was born in 1804, thirteen years after Charles. Her conversion took place at the age of eleven under the ministry of the Rev. John Frost. She was a spiritually-minded young lady, a perfect match for Charles.

Their love story is a beautiful tale. Charles saw Lydia in the home of Mrs. Sarah Kirkland of Utica, New York. He was there to receive his commission from the Female Missionary Society. Lydia was in Utica at the same time visiting an aunt who was at the commissioning meeting.

Charles could not get the beautiful young lady out of his mind. She even invaded his prayer time. At first this bothered him considerably, thinking it most sinful. He soon came to realise that God is not jealous of those whom He gives to His servants. And that was it: God wanted Lydia and Charles to come together. The young evangelist became convinced of that.

Before long, Charles found himself asking for Lydia's hand in marriage. He looked at her lovingly and said:

"Lydia, you're only twenty, I'm thirty-two. Would you be content to be the wife of a minister?" She joyfully replied, "Oh, Charles, I've loved you secretly ever since I was a small girl. I was one of the band that prayed for your conversion. And I am afraid I prayed as much that you might be mine as that you might be saved." That settled it and they were soon joined as one in Christian marriage.

The two became a "lovable couple", as friends expressed it. They said that Charles provided the serious, she the sunshine. No doubt, it was not too easy to live with such a famous and powerful preacher. On one occasion Lydia said, "Oh my dear, though I know you love me, yet you are terrifying when the power of God comes upon you. You stand there like a mighty angel, shouting the Gospel and wielding the flashing sword of judgment."

The privations that the young Finney family had to endure at times were not easy either. Later, when the couple and their young children left the security and comforts of their happy New York pastorate, it took great resolve and dedication to trek west to the rugged frontier of Oberlin, Ohio, and hack out a life in a primitive new college and seminary.

Oberlin College was not much in those early days. The campus had few buildings to offer. There was a simple log house erected for the president, and the Finneys had to share this for several months until permanent houses could be built. When Charles' eyes first fell on Oberlin's campus, he said the only living thing he saw was a hedgehog, and was so disappointed with the property that he called it a "mud-hole". He thought the location was "unfortunate, ill-considered, hastily decided upon". Perhaps that is why Lydia said, "Why, Charles, the place has nothing. Just a tiny colony in the heart of a big forest. But, Charles, it's just what you want. There is nothing here to upset your ideals of college reform. And I like it here." She truly was a remarkable woman. It was God's will, and that was all that really mattered to the Finneys.

Charles and Lydia were married for twenty-three years, during which time God blessed their union with six children, four of whom survived their father. Charles B. Finney practised law in California for many years and passed away in Ventura, California on April 17, 1876. Another son, Frederick Norton, was a successful businessman in Wisconsin, engaging in the railroad enterprises of the day. The Finneys had several daughters. Helen became the wife of General Jacob Dulson Cox of Cincinnati, Ohio, while Julia married James Monroe of Oberlin. Sarah Finney died at Oberlin on March 9, 1843 at only twenty-one months, while Delia passed away on September 1, 1852 at the age of eight. Finney was strongly attached to his family and he felt deeply the deaths of the children. When Lydia went to be with the Lord, Finney was almost thrown into a traumatic state. Yet God used the event most significantly. His beloved's death brought Finney into an understanding of what it means to yield completely to the will of God. It was on the river of tears that God brought Charles many rich blessings.

It must have been a joyous journey to Whitestown that crisp October 1824 as Finney travelled to claim Lydia. The wedding took place and a short honeymoon followed. The happy preacher left his bride at Whitestown, riding back to Evans Mills to arrange for their move to the little Jefferson County town. He planned to go back in the middle of the next week and bring his new bride to share in the ministry there. Little did either of them know what was in store.

While in Evans Mills, prior to his marriage, Finney had preached in a community called Perch River. The first weekend after the happy wedding ceremony, the Perch River Christians sent a message to Evans Mills pleading for Finney to come and preach to them. They said a revival had been slowly brewing in the area ever since Finney had ministered there some time earlier. Finney never could resist such appeals, so the evangelist arranged a meeting for Tuesday night, seeing no problem as far as Lydia was concerned. He could travel to Oneida County on Wednesday to meet her.

Finney preached on Tuesday evening at Perch River, and God moved mightily upon the people. He simply could not leave. Finney consented to preach on Wednesday and Thursday. It was becoming evident that he would not return to Whitestown that week for his bride. The awakening deepened until it began to spread in the direction of

Brownsville, a village of one thousand nine hundred and ninety-five adults several miles from Perch River. The believers there urged Charles to come to them. Feeling compelled by the Holy Spirit to go, he consented to spend the winter in Brownsville. But what about his new wife? Cold weather was rapidly settling in and winter travel was extremely difficult in the early decades of the nineteenth century. Would Lydia understand? It would mean months of separation, and they had only spent a few brief honeymoon days together. It must have taken some courage to write to Lydia and explain the situation. Lydia, with the gracious and understanding spirit that she always exemplified, seemed content and said she would wait for their reunion until "God seemed to open the door".

The work in Brownsville was not easy. There was little if any true piety anywhere. Even the pastor of the church who had invited Finney seemed rather cold and indifferent to the effort. At times the minister and his wife would be absent from the services, and Finney would discover they had actually gone to a party. With his new bride many miles away and working in such an atmosphere, Charles confessed, "I laboured there that winter with great pain and had many serious obstacles to overcome." There were, nonetheless, some significant conversions, even if the revival did not run as deep as at Antwerp and Evans Mills.

In the spring of 1825, Finney left Brownsville with his horse and buggy to go to his wife. Six months had passed since the marriage. The mail service left much to be desired; few letters had passed between them. But now, at last, he would be with his beloved Lydia. He drove on happily for about fifteen miles, but his horse was smooth-shod and the road was very slippery at that time of the year. So he stopped in the little village of LaRayville, about three miles south of Evans Mills, to have his horse reshod.

As Charles waited for the village blacksmith to do the work, the people of the community heard that the evangelist was in town. They prevailed upon him to preach for them at one o'clock in the afternoon. Finney succumbed, as he always did. There was no church house, so the usual schoolhouse meeting was scheduled. When Charles arrived, the building bulged with eager hearers.

Finney had not preached long before the Holy Spirit fell on the townspeople. They pleaded with Finney not to leave. But he had a bride to claim. As patient as she was, six months was a long time. The believers and the new converts prevailed upon Finney, however, and he consented to spend the night and preach again. The work deepened as Finney arranged more and more meetings. But something must be done about Lydia. So Charles asked a good brother if he would take his horse and buggy and retrieve his wife. This was arranged and at long last the couple was reunited. The movement in LaRayville increased until, as Charles put it, "a powerful revival" took place. After a few weeks, the bulk of the LaRayville citizens were converted. It appears astonishing today to think that practically the entire population of a town could be saved.

In his *Memoirs* Charles does not even hint that Lydia was upset or failed to understand the unusual circumstances. One can only conclude she must have been a deeply devout Christian who put Christ's work first, regardless of personal considerations. As Mrs. Billy Graham said when asked about the frequent absences of her famous evangelist husband, "I would rather live with Billy Graham part-time, than anyone else full-time." That is greatness, too.

While in LaRayville, Finney was invited to preach at nearby Rutland. There God again poured out His Spirit. Finney himself was maturing rapidly during these days, and in Rutland a new evangelistic method developed which had an impact not only in Rutland, but also on succeeding generations. The evangelist's own words record the event:

> The Spirit of the Lord was evidently poured out on the congregation; and at the close of the sermon, I did what I do not know I had ever done before, called upon anyone who would give their hearts to God, to come forward and take a front seat.

The modern evangelistic invitation, so widely used today all over the world, was struggling to be born. Charles Finney was becoming a harbinger of modern revivalistic evangelism. He was developing his so-called evangelistic "new measures", measures that would challenge the old way of doing evangelism in so many areas of the practical ministry (and measures for which he was soon to be called into serious question). Although Charles was still in the youth of his service, the simple, primitive days were obviously fading away and a more mature, sophisticated evangelism was emerging. He was growing into something of a seasoned revivalist.

Few of Finney's contemporaries realised at that stage what great things God had planned for this unusual man, things that were to prove so revolutionary that revivalistic evangelism would never be quite the same again. Many knew something was afoot; a new spirit was beginning to permeate all America. As Finney left Evans Mills and Jefferson County, people were ready and eager for the floodtide of a mighty move by God. They would not be disappointed.

## Finney's Increasing Impact:
## The Evangelist's Developing Ministry

Christian history projects one primary principle: effectiveness in Christian ministry is dependent on one's purpose. *Why* one serves is foundational to God's approval. This, no doubt, is one of the main reasons why Charles Finney enjoyed God's evident blessing: his main motivation in ministry was to perform God's perfect will.

While still in Jefferson County, Charles was deeply impressed that God intended him to minister in the small village of Gouverneur, St. Lawrence County. "God revealed to me, all at once, in a most unexpected manner, the fact that He was going to pour out His spirit at Gouverneur, and that I must go there and preach."

During Charles' last days in LaRayville, before the Gouverneur meeting, Father Nash came. By this time, the evangelist and the prayer warrior had become close friends. Nash had an illness that was used by the Holy Spirit to deepen his commitment to Christ: he contracted an eye ailment that forced confinement in a darkened room for many hours each day. During those long secluded hours he had learned the secret of becoming an intercessor.

Nash's kind of spiritual experience is not always understood. Some criticised his manner of praying. "He prays too loud," the undiscerning complained. Nash did pray vocally, and at times he bordered on being boisterous. Even when he closed himself off in his room or prayed in the woods, he was easily heard. Yet his prayers were powerful and moving.

On one occasion while working with Finney, Father

Nash went out into the forest for a prayer session. In his manner, he prayed with loud cries to God. A bitter opponent of the revival heard him. He could not grasp a single word the man of God was saying, but he knew who it was and what was going on. He was immediately seized with conviction and found no relief until he surrendered his life to Jesus Christ.

"Father Nash, you must go to Gouverneur and see what is there and come back and make your report," Finney urged. Nash journeyed over and in two or three days returned with a good word. Gouverneur is a "land of milk and honey" with much fruit to be harvested, he reported. Nash said that the Holy Spirit was already at work and an air of anticipation was everywhere.

The call to Gouverneur was a call to greater things. The Jefferson County revivals were over and Finney was beginning to expand his evangelistic horizon. Father Nash trekked back to Gouverneur to tell the church that Charles was on the way.

Gouverneur lay some thirty miles distant from LaRayville – a full day's journey in those times, especially in bad weather. As Finney set out, the heavens opened with a deluge of rain. The going was difficult, but perhaps it was a symbol of another kind of outpouring from heaven that Finney was soon to see. The dark clouds that brought the deluge were also prophetic; ominous clouds of resistance were soon to roll across Finney's horizon.

The time for Finney's first meeting had already been set; he was expected to preach the first night he arrived in town. The rain forced him to be late, and at the church the people had given up, not expecting the evangelist to reach there that day. Father Nash was about to dismiss the congregation when Finney burst in. He was introduced and announced a preaching service in an hour or so – he needed a little time for rest and recuperation after the drenching he had just endured. When the set hour arrived, the house was packed. People were on the edge of their seats in expectancy.

The evangelist had spent no time in preparing a formal message yet, as Finney so often said, "The Lord gave me a text," and the Word took immediate and powerful effect.

But as soon as the Spirit of God began to move, opposition made itself felt.

The first wave of resistance came through the person of a noted physician, an avid and committed Universalist. Finney was challenged to debate the issue. But Charles was a more mature man than in his early days in Adams, and no longer relished debate unless exact terms and methods were agreed upon. He had learned how aggressively "evangelistic" Universalists could be. Nevertheless, he felt constrained to enter into dialogue with the Universalistic doctor. His quick lawyer's mind and argumentation soon put him in command of the situation, and the good doctor trudged home devastated. He could not remain still; he paced and paced about the house. His wife, a dedicated Christian, finally asked him, "What is the matter?" He looked at her and retorted, "Nothing." "Doctor, have you seen Mr. Finney this morning?" she asked. This brought the physician to a halt and he literally burst into tears. "Yes," he acknowledged, "and he has turned my weapons on my own head."

In a very short time the doctor was wholly converted. As he was an outspoken leader, his conversion profoundly touched the entire Universalist camp in Gouverneur. One by one they were converted until the revival gripped them all and ended their opposition.

Of all people, the Baptists still opposed Finney. He was a Presbyterian, so baptism by immersion was not emphasised in his meetings. No doubt this upset the Baptists although Finney was not opposed to baptism by immersion for those who wished it. As a matter of fact, he himself baptised by immersion about a dozen people in his Antwerp revival. Finney and Nash recognised that Baptists were thoroughgoing evangelical Christians and that Baptist resistance to the movement could become a serious impediment to the entire work of God. So Finney and his praying partners gave themselves to fervent intercession.

One Sunday, a group of young Baptist men, or at least men under Baptist influence, stalked into Charles' service, obviously intending to stir up resistance to the revival. Tension filled the air and as the service started and the meeting progressed the agitators remained silent. Suddenly Father Nash stood up, struck the pew in front of him with his fist, and with eyes blazing at the young rebels cried out, "Now, mark you, young men! God will break your ranks in less than one week, either by converting some of you, or by sending some of you to hell. He will do this as certainly as the Lord is my God!" The house became still as death. Presumptuous? Finney seemed to think so; he said he regretted Brother Nash had gone so far. But now the gauntlet was thrown down.

Monday came. Nothing happened. On Tuesday, the leader of the young men sought out Finney. He was in obvious, deep distress. As Charles began to speak the words of salvation to the young agitator, the young man began to weep as a child. He soon gave his life to Christ. "What shall I do now, Mr. Finney?" he asked. The evangelist told him to go immediately to all his friends, tell them what had happened, and urge them to receive God's forgiveness. He set out, and before the week was over nearly every young man was wonderfully won to the Lord. Father Nash had spoken in the Spirit after all. But that still did not quench Baptist opposition.

Finney finally decided to face the Baptists man to man. He went first to a deacon who had been most vociferous in his criticism of the work. The evangelist confronted him frankly: "Now you have carried your opposition far enough. You must be satisfied that this is a work of God. I have made no allusion in public to your opposition, and I do not wish to do so, or to appear to know that there is any such thing, but you have gone far enough; and I shall feel it my duty, if you do not stop immediately, to take you in hand, and expose your opposition from the pulpit."

Finney's frankness broke the deacon. He confessed how wrong he had been and promised to oppose the work no more and make full confession of his sin. The deacon departed and fetched the Baptist pastor. Finney had a long conversation with the minister. He, too, confessed his error and sought Finney's forgiveness.

That should have settled it, but the problems kept coming. The next issue emerged when the Baptist pastor opened the doors of his church to receive new members from the ranks of Finney's converts. The pastor had promised not to do that. Charles knew that such an action would create a sectarian spirit. He was right; the Holy Spirit was grieved and conversions dried up for a period of six full weeks. The situation forced Finney – who was never really reticent in tackling a problem head on – to give a series of lectures on the subject of baptism. He urged all in the community, including the Baptists, to attend. He exhibited a very gracious spirit and sense of fairness as he addressed the citizens of Gouverneur. God honoured the move; the strategy was successful. This seemed to pour oil on the troubled waters and the spirit of revival returned.

When the Baptists finally stopped their opposition, resistance from every other quarter likewise dried up. Soon the entire community was being swept along in the moving of God's Spirit. So profound was the outpouring that, as Finney said, "The great majority of them [the Gouverneur community] were converted to Christ."

From Gouverneur, the evangelist moved on to DeKalb, a town about sixteen miles north with an adult population of three hundred and fifty-five. An old feud had festered in the DeKalb community between the Presbyterians and the Methodists. Some years earlier, the Methodists had experienced a great revival, with people literally fainting under searching conviction of sin. The Presbyterians, far more formal in their religious expression, stiffly resisted such a display of emotion. The Methodists considered their experiences genuine. When Finney arrived in DeKalb, everyone thought the old animosities had been buried, but ancient graves can easily be reopened.

At the very beginning of the DeKalb revival, while Finney was preaching one of his first sermons, a man fell from his seat "under the power of God". People gathered around to help. Finney assumed he was Methodist, and feared the old feelings would flare up again and dampen the Holy Spirit's impact. But the revivalist was quite startled when he discovered that the man who had fallen was a leader in the Presbyterian church. Several such cases occurred during the revival, and in each instance it was a Presbyterian who "fell under the power of God". Not a single Methodist was affected in this way. This led to a marvellous healing among the church members of both the Methodist and Presbyterian ranks. A unified spirit emerged that enhanced the entire movement.

And what a movement it was! There was such a manifestation of God's power at times that Finney could not preach. All he did, as he put it, was to "sit still and see the salvation of God". Conversions abounded. The movement seemed so spontaneous, yet in such marvellous order that Charles himself confessed he had never witnessed such an outpouring of God's power.

Father Nash joined Finney in the DeKalb awakening. This was now a quite regular pattern. He interceded fervently, drawing the usual caustic criticisms from the less sensitive of the community. One critic accused him of using the phrase "God Almighty" sixty-three times in one public prayer. But who would actually count the number of times a particular phrase was used in a prayer? Such was the mentality of some, however, even in the context of a mighty outpouring of the Holy Spirit.

The Spirit of prayer was not only on Father Nash, the entire community was caught up in intercession for the revival. This became the most marked feature of the movement in DeKalb. It was not at all uncommon to see Christians gathering in small groups, even on the streets, and before many words had passed, falling on their knees in fervent prayer. The presence of God prevailed throughout the whole town.

Prior to the DeKalb awakening, Charles and his wife Lydia were accustomed to walk from their host's home to the church services. The Finneys were quite poor by modern standards. But while in DeKalb, a wealthy elder of the Presbyterian church in Ogdensburg in northern New York presented them with a new horse and buggy. In this handsome rig they proudly set out for Utica in early October 1825, to attend the Presbyterian synod meeting.

The year 1825 was a notable year for the entire Mohawk Valley of western New York. Governor Clinton officially opened the Erie Canal by emptying a keg of Lake Erie water into New York Harbour. Far more important, 1825 saw a general revival begin to move over much of western New York state. Many evangelists ministered most effectively there that year. Charles Finney was not God's only instrument yet none was of more effect.

The synod of Utica marked a dividing line in Charles' life and ministry. The "new measures" had been found effective and Finney had learned how to handle opposition in a mature Christian fashion. The evangelist's theological concepts were now well formed and he had learned his utter dependence on prayer for the moving of God's Spirit. His ministry had taken on the deeply spiritual tone that characterised his work to the end.

A new phase and a new revival explosion was about to come to the state of New York; Finney was ready to move into that marvellous movement historians call the "Great Western Revivals".

# Finney's Oneida Outpouring: The Evangelist's Great Western Revivals

A significant awakening broke under Charles' preaching in the little community of Western, Oneida County, New York. The movement spread throughout the entire area. The several towns that felt Finney's ministry were not the leading cities of America, but on the crest of this movement the relatively obscure lawyer-preacher was projected forward, gaining widespread public notice as he travelled from community to community. God began to thrust His servant into the limelight of evangelistic popularity.

The Western ministry commenced for Charles and his wife after the synod meeting at Utica. Western was a lovely little New York town on the eastern edge of Oneida Lake. The spot was beautiful, but the religious and moral tone of Western was sadly out of tune when the Finneys arrived. Sabbath breaking, a serious offence in the early nineteenth century, was commonplace.

The couple had journeyed there to visit Charles' old pastor at Adams, the Rev. George W. Gale. Mr. Gale had moved to a farm near Western and was rapidly regaining his vigour. He was increasingly active in the local religious affairs of the community when the Finneys came to visit. Moreover, he had apparently gained far more respect for Charles' ability since the Adams days. Charles and Lydia had no intention of spending much time in Western, but after a few days, Gale persuaded Finney to preach. Almost immediately God's blessings began to flow.

For years before Finney's arrival in Western, the believers had been interceding that God would grant a gracious reviving. But the prayers were lifeless and dry, probably reminiscent to Charles of the Adams days before his conversion. When he first heard them pray, he said he could not honestly call it prayer; it was more like an exhortation or narrative. He was asked to address them, and with something of his frontier frankness, he told them outright that their prayer meeting was a mockery. He sensed they were almost blaming God in their prayers for the present low state of religion in their church and town.

As could be expected, this blunt approach angered some at first. But Finney kept on, "stirred within", until one of the principal elders of the congregation burst into tears and exclaimed, "Brother Finney, it is all true." He fell on his knees and wept aloud. With that the Holy Spirit swept over the entire prayer meeting. Everyone there broke down before the Lord. They all wept and confessed their sins as their hearts melted before the throne of the holy and righteous God.

A wonderful spirit of prevailing prayer blanketed the entire area. Charles himself confessed he had a "mighty hold on God". Many women of the church were greatly exercised in intercession. Finney tells of a husband who was deeply disturbed over his wife's prayer experience, and one day told Charles his distress: "Brother Finney, I think my wife will die. She is so exercised in her mind that she cannot rest day or night, but is given up entirely to prayer. She has been all morning in her room, groaning and struggling in prayer; and I am afraid it will entirely overcome her strength." The evangelist accompanied the man home. They entered the house and walked into the sitting-room. On hearing Finney's voice, the wife came out of her bedroom, and as Charles described it: "Upon her face was a most heavenly glow. Her countenance was lighted up with a hope and a joy that were plainly from heaven." The wife looked at the preacher with her joyous eyes blazing and said, "Brother Finney, the Lord has come! This work will spread all over this region! A cloud of mercy overhangs us all; and we shall see such a work of grace as we have never yet seen." The husband did not know what to say. It was all entirely new to him. But it was not new to the evangelist; Finney, too, had the deep assurance that God would do a tremendous work in the community.

The work spread and deepened. Charles himself moved to a new level of prayer and personal ministry. He tells of the hours he spent visiting those who were anxious concerning their relationship with Christ. Coming home to Gale's house after a strenuous day, he would often find himself, though utterly exhausted, still deeply burdened and driven to prayer. Finney prayed aloud. So as not to disturb the family, he would spread out a buffalo rug in the hayloft of Gale's barn and there pour out his heart in prayer for the revival.

One cold November day, Charles came home exhausted, yet so burdened, he *must* pray. He wrestled with God in the hayloft for some time until he was absolutely assured he had been heard and the victory would be forthcoming. After the peace of assurance flooded over him, he fell into a deep sleep. As time passed, Gale, much concerned, went to seek him out. He found Finney in such a deep sleep that he cried, "Brother Finney, are you dead?" When Finney was finally aroused, he confessed he did not realise he had fallen asleep or how long he had even been there. But, he said, "My mind was calm and my faith unwavering. The work would go on, of that I felt assured."

Gale would often urge his young preacher friend to rest more, warning him that his strength would soon break down. Gale knew about that personally. No man could for long stand the pressure to which Charles submitted himself. Finney always replied that the spirit of prayer was upon him and he could not resist God; he must give the Holy Spirit scope to let out all of his strength in intercession.

Charles was not the only prayer warrior in Western. Many were prevailing before God, and many were the remarkable conversions in the Western revival. One such case was of a well-known personality in the community, known as "the widow Floyd". She was eighty years old and totally blind. Her husband had served as a Revolutionary War officer and had been one of the signers of the Declaration of Independence. He had been a notable sceptic, and died as such. When his widow found Christ at eighty, everyone was astounded.

Perhaps the most outstanding conversion of the revival

was that of none other than the Rev. George W. Gale
himself. Prior to the Finney ministry in Western, Gale had
been a committed Princeton "old school" theologian. This
was seen in Adams. He had pushed his theological Calvinism to a point that even John Calvin himself would probably have found unacceptable and then there was that
disturbing void of God's Spirit in his work. In Gale's earlier
encounters with the newly-converted lawyer, he was certain God could never bless Finney's "new school" ministry.
But he must have had a certain uneasiness about his own
position when he heard of God's work through Finney's
ministry in Evans Mills, Antwerp, LaRayville and other
towns, for he did invite Charles to his home and to the
Western pulpit. Then, when he saw the tremendous results
and profound blessings of God in the Western revival, he
was deeply challenged. He saw that a major overhaul in his
whole understanding of the Christian experience and its
attending theology was demanded. When the revolution
came, it rocked him to the very foundations of his being.
Gale came to the conclusion that he had not only been
swirling around in theological error, he had never even
been genuinely converted. He became convinced that he
had not grasped the essence of the Gospel at all.

After days of inner struggle, Gale confessed to Finney
that God's Holy Spirit had been probing so deeply in to his
heart that he must begin all over again. He came into such a
profound experience of Christ that from that time on he not
only became one of Finney's closest supporters, he also
became an ardent promoter of revivals. A lifelong relationship of service and ministry developed between the two
men. God's providence caused their paths to cross most
significantly in the years that followed. Gale told Charles
that if the new lawyer-preacher had followed the "old
school" approach, as he had presented it to him in Adams,
the great ministry now emerging in the evangelist's life
would no doubt have been ruined. Gale thanked God that
he had now seen the truth of the whole matter.

In the wisdom of God, the Western revivals were not to
be hemmed within the confines of little Western alone. All
of that part of New York was to feel the force of Finney's
revivalistic ministry. The "burnt district" desert was des-

tined to bloom again with the fruits of a genuine spiritual awakening.

One of the spots to which the wind of the Spirit carried the awakening was Rome and its environs. Charles wrote:

> The work went on, spread and prevailed, until it began to exhibit unmistakable indications of the direction in which the Spirit of God was leading from that place. The distance to Rome was nine miles, I believe. About half-way, was a small village, called Elmer's Hill. There was a large schoolhouse where I held a weekly lecture; and it soon became manifest that the work was spreading in the direction of Rome and Utica.

The significant Western revival carried on through the winter of 1825. Before Finney left for Rome, he ministered in the little village of Wright's Settlement. There the Holy Spirit came in power and many found Christ. The pastor of the church related, "The place of worship was thronged by an eager multitude . . . for a week business was generally laid aside."[1] Nearby at Elmer's Hill, the people also experienced a touch from heaven. With these two experiences behind him, the evangelist set his sights on Rome.

The invitation had come from the Rev. Moses Gillett, pastor of the Congregational church in Rome. He had witnessed the significant events going on in Western, arriving just as the awakening was thrust into full orbit. Moved by the blessings of God, Gillett wanted a share in the outpouring. He persuaded Finney to exchange pulpits for a Sunday. Charles did not warm to the idea, but Gillett was so persuasive that finally Finney reluctantly consented. A Sunday was set aside for the pulpit exchange. On Saturday before the set day, Finney travelled to Rome, greatly regretting he had made such a decision. He was fearful that Gillett would not understand how to keep the revival going in Western. He thought Gillett would preach one of his old sermons, and that would do anything but deepen the work. All he was able to do was to trust God in the matter. The evangelist preached three times in Rome that Lord's day. To his satisfaction, the sermons had great effect. A consciousness of sin crept over the entire people as he preached on the text: "The carnal mind is enmity against God" (Rom. 8:7).

On Monday, Gillett came bounding back to Rome. Finney waited for him and related the exciting events. Gillett immediately wanted to call for inquirers. He persuaded Finney to stay and help conduct the inquirers' meeting. Finney went back to Western for the day, but returned that evening for an anxious meeting, scheduled in a deacon's home. When the pastor and evangelist arrived, they found the deacon's large sitting-room jammed to capacity. Gillett was utterly amazed, not only because of the number, but because many of those sitting there were none other than the leading members of his congregation. The pastor started to counsel them, but the feelings began to run so deep that it seemed that at any moment the place would explode with emotion. Finney, never wanting his revivals to be shallow, took over from the pastor: "It will not do to continue the meeting in this shape. I will make some remarks, such as they need, and then dismiss them." Nothing had been done to excite the burning emotions; it was all quite spontaneous under the convicting hand of God.

Such scenes may be difficult to understand today. But as Finney said, "It would probably not be possible for one who had never witnessed such a scene, to realise what the force of the truth sometimes is, under the power of the Holy Ghost." When a true awakening occurs, the Spirit's presence is often so overwhelming that those removed from the events find it quite incredulous.

Charles briefly addressed the inquiry meeting in as gentle and quiet a manner as he could, yet he was plain and honest. After pointing them to Christ as their only hope, he felt he had carried them as far as they could endure for the moment. After his dismissal prayer, Charles told them, "Now please go home without speaking a word to each other. Try to keep silent, and do not break out into any boisterous manifestation or feeling; but go without saying a word, to your rooms." They began to leave, some were sobbing, others sighing.

Finney walked home with one of the men who had attended. They kept silent all the way until they entered the house. Suddenly the man burst into what Finney called "a loud wailing". This, of course, brought the whole family around him. His deep conviction soon spread to all of them. In a moment, the house became a house of prayer. Everyone was saved. Similar scenes occurred all over the town.

At the crack of dawn the next morning, people started coming to Mr. Gillett's home seeking help. After a hasty breakfast, Finney and the pastor went out to aid the seekers. As they walked down the street, people would burst out of the houses as they passed by, begging them to come in and help them find Christ. Finney and Gillett ran from house to house. In every home they entered, all the neighbours would rush in and fill the largest room. As they walked into some homes, they would find people already on their knees or prostrate on the floor in deep distress. Finney recognised the need for another meeting; they could hardly go to every house in the town.

Pastor Gillett agreed and went to the proprietor of the hotel in the centre of town. The dining-room was secured for 1 p.m. in the afternoon. After lunch, the evangelist and pastor made their way to the hotel. People were coming in droves – some actually running. Soon the dining-room was packed. When the meeting opened, the same spirit of crushing concern gripped the group as on the night before. Some of the strongest men were so cut down by Finney's simple remarks that they had to be helped home. The meeting lasted until nearly sunset. In evaluating the day Finney said with considerable reserve: "It resulted in a great number of hopeful conversions, and was the means of greatly extending the work on every side."

That evening Finney preached again in the regular services at the church. Mr. Gillett appointed another inquiry meeting for the next morning. This time the courthouse was secured; it had a much larger room than the hotel. But even that facility proved too small. Although the room was uncomfortably crowded, the pastor and evangelist spent the better part of the day there helping the concerned.

That night another service was held and another meeting of inquiry set. This time the church was the scene for the inquirers, for no other room was large enough to hold everyone. The evening evangelistic services were so powerful that Finney felt he must stay in Rome and preach regularly. For twenty consecutive nights with two services on Sunday he preached the Gospel. A prayer meeting and an inquiry meeting dominated every day. A solemnity and sense of awe pervaded the whole town. In the *Memoirs*, Finney said Rome was in an "extraordinary state of things. Convictions were so deep and universal that we would sometimes go into a house, and find some in a kneeling posture, some prostrate on the carpet, some bathing the temples of their friends with camphor, and rubbing them to keep them from fainting, and as they feared from dying." Apparently, five hundred conversions were reported during those twenty days.

The power of the meetings in a city like Rome was bound to attract attention. The news rapidly spread and ministers converged on the scene from all the neighbouring towns. It was impossible to keep track of all the conversions. The only thing Finney could do was to call upon those who had been converted during the day to come forward at the close of the evening sermon, confess publicly their new faith and receive instructions. The continuing development of this "new measure" gave integrity to the method so widely used today in mass evangelism.

An insight into the sheer, naked power of the meetings is Finney's description of a typical event during the Rome revival:

> At one of the morning prayer meetings, the lower part of the church was full. I arose and was making some remarks to the people, when an unconverted man, a merchant, came into the meeting. He came along until he found a seat in front of me, and near where I stood speaking. He had sat but a few moments, when he fell from his seat as if he had been shot. He writhed and groaned in a terrible manner. I stepped to the pew door and saw that it was altogether an agony of mind.
>
> A sceptical physician sat near him. He stepped out of his slip, and came and examined this man who was thus distressed. He felt his pulse, and examined the case for a few moments. He said nothing, but turned away, and

leaned his head against a post that supported the gallery, and manifested great agitation.

He said afterward that he saw at once that it was distress of mind, and it took his scepticism entirely away. He was soon after hopefully converted. We engaged in prayer for the man who fell in the pew; and before he left the house, I believe, his anguish passed away, and he rejoiced in Christ.[2]

God also performed what the evangelist called "some terrible things in righteousness". Three men stubbornly opposed the revival in Rome. They met on a certain Sunday and spent the entire day drinking and ridiculing the work. Suddenly, one of them fell stone dead. The other two were speechless, convinced that God had judged them for their adamant opposition to the obvious work of the Holy Spirit. This, too, may be rather difficult to comprehend today, because we are historically removed from the heat of such a revival, but it must be understood that God will not allow His work to be sidetracked by the vileness of man, especially when there is such a deep work of the Holy Spirit abroad.

While the awakening was progressing powerfully in Rome, excitement sprang up in all the surrounding area. The prayers of a very devout Christian lady in Utica had the community already astir before Finney arrived. She was spending days and nights in intercession for an outpouring of the Spirit on her town. Others were joining her in extraordinary prayer. Finney, always sensitive to such signs, recognised that God was ready to move on the city. So he went to Utica and started preaching.

The Holy Spirit's influence filled the town and the meetings were crowded every night. Father Nash was also there interceding in prayer for the revival. Especially touched were the two Presbyterian congregations of Utica. The pastors of the two churches, the Rev. Samuel Aiken and the Rev. Samuel Brace, threw themselves wholeheartedly into the work.

During the Utica revival, the evangelist lodged for a time in the leading hotel of the city. Soon the innkeeper and his entire family were converted together with a large number of the guests. Finney related that:

> The stages, as they passed through, stopped at the hotel; and so powerful was the impression in the community, that I heard of several cases of persons that just stopped for a meal, or to spend a night, being powerfully convicted or converted before they left the town. Indeed, both in this place and in Rome, it was a common remark that nobody could be in the town, or pass through it, without being aware of the presence of God; that a divine influence seemed to pervade the place, and the whole atmosphere to be instinct [filled] with a divine presence.[3]

Such happenings were reminiscent of the impact of the first-century church in Jerusalem when "fear came upon every soul" (Acts 2:43).

Utica was also the scene for the well-known story of Finney's visit to the cotton mill. It seems that the owner of the company was not a professing Christian, yet a man of exemplary morals and high standing in the community. Finney's brother-in-law was superintendent of the mill. Finney preached in its locality, Whitesboro, one night and the next morning was given a tour through the factory.

As Charles, his brother-in-law and the factory owner walked through the mill observing the various stages in the production of cotton cloth, they entered a large room where several women were working at the weaving machines. The workers kept eying Finney, knowing who he was and what was going on in the revival effort in the area. Two girls seemed especially taken by his presence, but were laughing light-heartedly. Finney walked slowly towards them. One girl was trying to tie a broken thread on her machine as the evangelist drew closer. His penetrating gape awed her until finally, she was simply overcome. She sank down on her knees and burst into tears. It started a chain reaction. In a matter of moments, practically the entire room was in tears. Conviction spread throughout the whole factory. The owner, himself deeply moved, said to the superintendent, "Stop the mill, and let the people attend to religion; for it is more important that our souls be saved than that this factory run." Everything was shut down and the mass of employees assembled in a large room. Finney preached, and in his own words, "a more powerful meeting I scarcely ever attended". The revival went through the entire group of mill hands until within a few days nearly all were brought to faith in Jesus Christ.

No doubt the outstanding single conversion in Utica – perhaps in the entire Finney ministry – was that of Theodore D. Weld. The intriguing story of Weld's religious experience is a drama in itself, and his succeeding influence in America was most profound. Weld was a student at Hamilton College in Clinton, New York, not a great distance from Utica. The Finney revival attracted so much attention over such a wide area that it generated keen interest at Hamilton College. Many professors and students of the college attended. The movement was the topic of many conversations on the campus. Weld was a leader in the college; his influence over the student body was quite significant. He had a fine Christian heritage: his father was a prominent clergyman in New England, and he had a godly, praying aunt in Utica. Yet, he was an ardent antagonist of much of the Christian faith. On hearing about the Finney revival, he verbally fought against it. Finney was an entire stranger to Weld, yet the young man had nothing good to say about the evangelist. His aunt, on hearing of her nephew's vehement criticisms against the Spirit's work in Utica, grew deeply burdened for his conversion.

At the urgent invitation of his aunt, Theodore Weld came to Utica for a weekend visit. He boasted to his student friends as he left the college that he would show them how to sit through a revival meeting totally unmoved. But he was a bit devious: knowing that Mr. Aiken preached in the morning service and Finney in the afternoon, he planned to go to the early service, thus avoiding the evangelist. His aunt, however, wise to his plans, secretly suggested that Aiken and Finney switch their preaching times. As the time of the service arrived and they entered the family pew, Weld's wise aunt arranged for the young antagonist to sit in the middle. He would have a difficult time getting out if he attempted a hasty exit when he realised Finney would be preaching.

The service began. Mr. Aiken pointed out the young

man to Finney as they entered the pulpit. Charles was aware of Weld's influence on the college campus and of his bitter opposition to the revival. When the evangelist stood to preach he took as his text, "One sinner destroyeth much good" (Eccles. 9:18). Finney said later he had never preached on that theme, or had even heard a sermon on the text. Nevertheless, the Holy Spirit impressed that verse of Scripture on his heart and he preached in his usual extemporaneous yet eloquent style.

Finney's message produced a great effect on the young student. The evangelist confessed, "I suppose that I drew a pretty vivid picture of Weld, and of what his influence was, and what mischief he might do." Weld made several gallant attempts to get out of the pew, but whenever he started a move, his aunt would throw herself forward and engage in silent prayer, preventing him from escaping. She said, "Theodore, if you leave, you will break my heart." So he sat there and endured the entire sermon. The service ended and Weld finally found his freedom from Finney's blistering words.

The next day, Charles visited a store on Genesee Street and whom should he encounter but Theodore Weld! The young man showered Finney with abuse for almost an hour. Finney confessed he had never heard anything like it in his life. Soon the place was crowded with townspeople. Up and down the street businesses closed as a throng gathered in the store to hear Weld's harangue of Finney. The young man was certainly gifted in language. The evangelist patiently let him go on until the critic had vented all his anger. Then Finney said, "Mr. Weld, are you the son of a minister of Christ, and is this the way for you to behave?" That's all Charles said. The evangelist's words stung like an adder. Deeply agitated, Weld said something else cutting and stormed out of the store.

Finney left the crowd and walked to the home of Mr. Aiken. He had only been there a few moments when he heard a knock at the door. He went to answer and there to his amazement stood Weld. The student looked like death and began to pour out the most humble confession and apology. Finney graciously accepted his apology and urged him to give his life to Christ. With that the young man left and made his way to his aunt's home, much subdued. She asked him to lead the family in prayer, but as he knelt down he did anything but pray. The old bitterness arose again, even more vehemently. A blasphemous stream of attacks on the revival fell from his lips that made his aunt shudder. He kept on and on until the oil in the lamp was actually exhausted. The family was dumbfounded. The aunt was genuinely frightened at his blasphemy. When Weld finally finished, she urged him to give his heart to God.

Weld flew out and went to his room for the night. But sleep was impossible. His agitation deepened as the hours dragged on. He paced the floor all night. Just as dawn was breaking, as Weld himself later explained, a great "pressure" came upon him that literally prostrated him. With that "pressure" a voice seemed to say, "Repent, repent now!" Later in the morning, his aunt came to his room to discover why he had not come down. There she found him on the floor, calling himself a thousand fools. His heart was all broken to pieces. He had met Jesus Christ.

That night at the meeting, Weld rose and asked if he could say a few words. He made an eloquent, humble and beautiful confession of Christ; there were no more tirades against the revival. His life had been radically and gloriously transformed. He acknowledged the stumbling block he had been and said now his only wish was that his whole life might count for the cause of Christ.

From the time of his dramatic conversion, Weld proved to be a diligent servant of the Lord Jesus Christ and a profound helper and supporter of Finney. He was destined to become an influential leader in Christian circles, especially in the abolitionist movement. He later entered Lane Seminary in Cincinnati, Ohio, as a student, where he became a leader in the abolition activities of the student body. With his fellow student, William Allen, he led what was known as the "Lane Revolt". He was also one of the organisers and leading figures in the American Anti-slavery Society along with Arthur and Lewis Tappan, notable men we shall meet later. Weld was the one who enlisted James G. Birney, a Kentucky planter, to run as the first abolitionist candidate for president of the United States.

Two important elements in the saga of Charles Finney

surfaced in Utica. First, having moved into Pastor Aiken's home, Finney read the writings of Jonathan Edwards. Those works of the revivalist of the First Great Awakening profoundly influenced Charles and his theology, preaching and revival concepts. Secondly, in Utica the opposition to the so-called "new measures" in evangelism began to spread and deepen, as will be seen more fully in later chapters.

By 1826, Finney's name was becoming popular all over western New York. Dr. Lansing, pastor of the First Presbyterian Church of Auburn, visited Utica and witnessed the power of the awakening. He was thrilled and immediately invited the evangelist to Auburn. Convinced his work was done in Utica, Finney followed what he took to be the Holy Spirit's leading and moved on to Auburn. The fact that Finney never took a new engagement until he felt his work was done where he was at the moment is most significant. This prevented him from being forced to leave an area in the heat of a revival. Thus he could stay one day or one year, as the case warranted.

As the Spirit of God began to move in Auburn, the old spirit of opposition began to exert itself. A theological seminary was situated in Auburn and some of the professors along with several pastors in the area united in opposing the movement. A conspiracy was growing, designed to hedge Finney in and confine his work to central and western New York state. As a single voice, a number of eminent preachers vowed that he would never travel east to disrupt the churches of New England.

Finney had been forewarned of the impending fight. As he inaugurated his ministry in Lansing's Auburn Presbyterian Church, the inner conviction of the Holy Spirit seemed to be preparing him for difficult days ahead.

> I shall never forget what a scene I passed through one day in my room at Dr. Lansing's. The Lord showed me as in a vision what was before me. He drew so near to me, while I was engaged in prayer, that my flesh literally trembled on my bones. I shook from head to foot, under a full sense of the presence of God. At first, and for some time, it seemed more like being on the top of Mount Sinai, amidst its full thunderings, then in the presence of the cross of Christ.
>
> Never in my life, that I recollect, was I so awed and

humbled before God as then. Nevertheless, instead of feeling like fleeing, I seemed drawn nearer and nearer to God – seemed to draw nearer and nearer to that Presence that filled me with such an unutterable awe and trembling. After a season of great humiliation before him, there came a great lifting up. God assured me that He would be with me and uphold me; that no opposition should prevail against me; that I had nothing to do, in regard at all to this matter, but to keep about my work, and wait for the salvation of God.[4]

The passage of Scripture that the Spirit of God constantly kept before Charles, and upon which he relied, was Jeremiah 20:7: "Thou are stronger than I, and hast prevailed."

Finney had preached only a few messages in Auburn when the church broke down in confession. The entire body of believers wanted to make public acknowledgment of their backsliding and spiritual poverty. They drew up a written confession and submitted it to the church. When the unusual document was presented, the congregation as one stood in agreement, many of them weeping. From that point on, the work went forward with great power and many of the lost were converted. Finney went back to Auburn several years later, in 1831, and another powerful revival took hold of the community. He was always welcome there.

Early in the autumn of 1826, Finney accepted an invitation from the Rev. Dr. Nathaniel Beman to labour for a revival of religion in Troy, New York. Charles spent the autumn and winter there as a powerful awakening swept the city. Prayer always formed a central part of Finney's work, but in Troy a most unusual, earnest spirit of prayer developed. A prayer meeting was held each morning at 11 a.m. The praying people would move from house to house for their meetings. These prayer services deepened until they began to be the means of many conversions. At one of the meetings, a bank cashier became so anxious for the conversion of the president of his institution that he could not get up off his knees. The whole group agonised in intercession with him for the bank president's salvation. Needless to say, it was only a short time before their prayers were answered.

One of the students at Francis Willard's Seminary situated in Troy, described Finney in those days as "the equal of Savonarola", the great fifteenth-century revivalist of Florence in Italy. That may be something of an exaggeration, but it is indicative of Troy's gratitude for the Finney ministry.

In the midst of the revival, a young lady travelled to Troy from New Lebanon in Columbia County. She had come to purchase a dress for a ball in her home town. A cousin in Troy, and recent convert of the Finney revival, urged her to attend one of the religious services. She resisted, but finally consented to accompany her cousin to hear Finney preach. God moved mightily that night and she was marvellously converted. The new convert, forgetting all about the dress and the ball, immediately returned to New Lebanon and started to work for a revival there. Soon her father, a deacon in the local church, was moved and revived. The pastor in New Lebanon had an unsaved daughter. She trusted Christ and the two young ladies united in prayer for a revival in their community. In the course of a week or two, a strong conviction developed that Finney should preach there. The young ladies travelled to Troy and urged Charles to come. He did.

Finney began preaching in New Lebanon and God blessed the work almost immediately. Striking conversions were multiplied and what he called a "great and blessed change" came over the entire place. Most of the leading men of the small community were saved.

By the time of the New Lebanon revival, the controversy over the "new measures" was beginning to move to a climax. The so-called "Great Western Revivals" and Finney's methods were a growing topic of conversation. Correspondence between the "Western" brethren who were sympathetic to Finney's revivals and leading "Eastern" brethren such as evangelist Ashel Nettleton and pastor Lyman Beecher who had been opposing them had grown to large proportions. Something had to be done. So a date was set for late July 1927 to hold a convention to consider the whole issue of "measures" in revivals. New Lebanon was set as the venue.

# Finney's Objectors and Opposition:
## The Evangelist's Trials

The Great Western Revivals had scaled the face of the revivalistic mountain; the peak was almost reached. Finney's innovative "new measures" were well developed and being used as the safety lines to enable the evangelist to climb the summit. At the same time, an avalanche of criticism was being loosened to sweep down the mountain and carry the climber away.

In the earlier days, while the young evangelist was labouring in Jefferson and St. Lawrence counties under the auspices of the Female Missionary Society, few negative voices were raised. There were obvious reasons. In the first place, Charles was young and critics can easily excuse the antics of the young, even in the ministry. Furthermore, Finney had achieved little if any notoriety outside the immediate area. Glowing reports of the revivals had appeared in eastern religious periodicals, but Finney's name was not mentioned. Not only that, Jefferson and St. Lawrence counties would raise little opposition; practically everyone was either converted or deeply impressed by the spiritual and social results of Finney's ministry.

Oneida County was another story, however. Revival had burned its way through Gouverneur, Utica and finally Rome and its environs. Although these communities were not large by modern standards, they were growing into New York's greatest cities. Revival there was going to be noticed. The results of these meetings, and the name Charles Grandison Finney, became widespread news for the first time. Even traditional Boston began to hear of the events.

Opposition came first from the unbelieving community. This kind of resistance ranged all the way from simple ridicule to outright violence. Father Nash, writing on the Oneida revivals, May 11, 1826, said: "The work of God moved forward in power, in some places against dreadful opposition. Mr. Finney and I have been hanged in effigy. Sometimes the opposition made a noise in the house of God; sometimes they gathered around the house and stoned it; and discharged guns."[1]

The world itself can never kill a revival, however. The opposition that sidetracks revivals comes from the ranks of the religious. The religious resistance came from three distinct sources: the Unitarians, the "old school" Calvinists and the critics of the "new measures". These latter rebel ranks were, strangely enough, filled by both "old" *and* "new school" proponents. Men of quite divergent theological stances united against Finney and his friends to fight the methodologies utilised in the revival meetings. Paradoxically, many of the "new school" critics were fervent advocates of revivals. Some even used at least one or more of the "new measures" themselves.

Although the rumbling of battle had for some time been heard through Oneida County, it only reached sizeable proportions when Finney was engaged in the Utica revival. One of the catalists was the Rev. William R. Weeks. He was pastor of the Congregational church at Paris Hill in Oneida County, and a "Hopkinsian", that is a follower of the theological system of Samuel Hopkins. As a thinker, Hopkins followed the general pattern of Dr. Nathaniel Emmens, a leading "old school" Calvinistic theologian. Weeks had been unable to impose all his views on the local religious scene in Oneida County, so he broke fellowship and organised a group called the "Oneida Association". After the break, he made several efforts to discredit Finney's "new measures".

In the early days of Weeks' opposition to Finney, he corresponded with men of influence farther east in New England: especially those who were of the revivalistic ilk, no doubt hoping to divide the "new school" camp. He also began a campaign of pamphlets and articles that were circulated widely. His most notorious pamphlet against the "new measures" was published under the title *A Pastoral Letter of the Ministers of the Oneida Association to the Churches Under Their Care on the Subject of Revivals of Religion*. It had a large circulation, probably because it was published in Oneida County where Finney was carrying on his influential revivals.

Weeks used intelligent weapons. First, he did not condemn revivals *per se*. He knew the eastern clergy were generally warm to awakenings. Jonathan Edwards had been a New Englander, and even the "old school" men did not object to Edwards. But, Weeks contended, in those great movements the mature clergy had never permitted any "extravagances" as he accused Finney of fostering. By this devious technique, many men in the East moved over to Weeks' side in the warfare; "old" and "new school" men. This started a general groundswell of distrust towards Finney.

Weeks also aimed specifically to arouse the revivalistic "new school" men of New England. They were really the ones in whose eyes he wanted Finney discredited. The "old school" men had for all practical purposes already written off the evangelist anyway. Exaggeration became the order of the day. The things of which Finney was accused at times were absolutely ridiculous. As a case in point, it was reported that parents were beating their children to force them to become Christians. Accusations of wild emotionalism, weird theology, and bizarre practices confused the situation. Weeks even went so far as to say that Finney tried to undermine the position and respect of the pastors and churches where he held revivals.

One of the most widely disseminated works against Finney's "new measures" along with Weeks' *Pastoral Letter* was called the "Bunker Hill" pamphlet. This tract was a product of the Unitarian opponents. Why did they enter the battle when they were so divorced from the entire revival scene? The answer is simple: they loved to see the orthodox at war with each other. In the "Bunker Hill" pamphlet, they not only raised the "new measures" issue, they even impugned Finney's character and motivations. Below is the title page of the pamphlet. Its innuendoes demonstrate the vindictive spirit of the entire publication.

A
# BUNKER HILL CONTEST
## A.D., 1826.

Between the "Holy Alliance", for the Establishment of
Hierarchy and Ecclesiastical Domination
over the Human Mind

## ON THE ONE SIDE,

And the Asserters of Free Inquiry, Bible Religion,
Christian Freedom and Civil Liberty

## ON THE OTHER

———————

## THE REV. CHARLES FINNEY,

"Home Missionary" and High Priest of the Alliance in
the Interior of New York.
Headquarters: County of Oneida

The work was scurrilous. It spoke of Finney's "anxious"
meetings being held at night in a darkened room with the
atmosphere pervaded by groans and subdued whispers,
surely resulting in false conversions.

The facts of the case were that in the early, more
emotional days of Finney's ministry, the evangelist did not
even use the anxious meeting. He would invite concerned
people to come to the front of the church and after the
service was dismissed, he would counsel them personally
and individually (or in a group if necessary). It was only as
the revivals grew in size that he used the anxious meeting,
and those meetings were quite open and well managed.

The "Bunker Hill' pamphlet was ostensibly written by a
"plain farmer" from Trenton, New Jersey. It was so well
written, however, that no "plain farmer" of the day could
possibly have been responsible. The name Ephraim Perkins has forever become linked with the document, but it
was probably put to press by a certain Henry Ware of
Trenton. The pamphlet raised many questions concerning
Finney personally and the validity of his "new measures".

The most erudite delineation of the actual issues themselves was in the Rev. William Weeks' aforementioned *Pastoral Letter*. He spelled out in precise detail the "evils to be guarded against" in the Finney movement. He listed twenty-nine in all. The great injustice of the *Pastoral Letter* was that Weeks tarred all evangelists with the same brush. That some itinerant evangelists were guilty of wild, bizarre extravagance is a patent fact, but even good pastors who had used some of the "new measures" sensibly and with integrity were judged by innuendo in Weeks' work.

To counter the *Letter*, the Oneida Presbytery issued a tract entitled *A Narrative of the Revival of Religion in the Country of Oneida*. The pamphlet contended that Finney's revivals were conducted with less "excitement and passions" and more "wisdom and discretion" than any could recall in any previous meetings. The most important section came under the heading "Means Which Appear to Have Been Blessed in Promoting Revivals", where thirteen such means of blessing were listed. That section is important for us today because it clearly delineates in objective style what these "new measures" were that caused all the controversy. What were some of the major issues?

First, there was what became commonly known as the "anxious meeting". People "anxious" about their conversion were asked to attend a special meeting for counsel on how to be saved. Finney used this method in his ministry extensively. Its whole purpose centred on helping strugglers find the Saviour. It was never intended to precipitate or force any kind of shallow decision-making, even though Finney was accused of using it to that end. Finney's essential theology prohibited that: he believed people made their *own* decision for or against Christ. His early rejection of Gale's extreme Calvinism makes that self-evident. Finney firmly held that when the Spirit of God convicts an unbeliever of his or her need of salvation, *that person makes a free decision*. All the Christian can do is to point them to God's forgiveness in Christ. The anxious meeting was designed in order that individual care could be given by the Christian to the seeking, anxious decision-maker so that a proper, knowledgeable decision of integrity could be made.

Secondly, Finney's method of house-to-house visitation was considered. Charles' critics could not countenance the practice of visiting concerned people in their homes and personally counselling them on how to receive forgiveness and salvation. This was viewed as far too humanistic.

Thirdly, the use of the "anxious seat" was discussed. To ask people who were anxious about their relationship to Christ to take a special place in the church building was obnoxious, especially to the "old school". This, they argued, undervalued the role of the Holy Spirit. Note that the invitation to the anxious seat was not invariably given at the close of the meeting where a mere emotional reaction might have been evoked. At times, the concerned seekers were asked to come to the stated anxious pew *before* the service began. That would not have been easy for a genuinely convicted seeker, let alone someone caught up in mere shallow, emotional impulse. The origin of the anxious seat, or "mourners' bench" as it was known in some areas, apparently started in the Methodist camp meetings at the turn of the nineteenth century. Finney did not develop it. He never even used it extensively until the great Rochester revival of 1831.

A fourth issue concerned what Weeks would have called "familiarity with God in prayer". Finney did not pray or preach in the usual "language of Zion". Thus, he was constantly criticised as a "vulgar speaker". Charles struggled to be first and foremost a communicator. He believed that to fail to communicate effectively to people proved nothing but the preacher's ineptness in performing the work of Christ. So he spoke the people's language. As he applied this principle in preaching, he also used it in prayer. He wanted people to be enlightened, not to be left in the dark because of stilted language, even as he talked to God. He saw no irreverence in speaking to the Lord in the vernacular; God understood plain talk.

In the fifth place, church membership for new converts became an issue. Finney was accused of throwing open the church doors prematurely and letting new converts into membership too quickly. Yet, upon investigation into the life and ministry of Finney, there is not found one incident where he pressured a pastor into receiving members against the pastor's wishes. He never violated the stated measures the church employed in receiving new members. If a pastor did not go along with Finney's views, all he had to do was say "no". Moreover, there is quite convincing evidence that the converts who did enter the life of the church "stuck" and for the better part made mature church members. Historian R. H. Fowler acknowledged in his *Historical Sketch of Presbyterianism Within the Bounds of the Synod of Central New York* that despite the criticism, converts of the Oneida County revival had generally contributed much to the churches they joined.

The sixth "measure", which perhaps precipitated the greatest emotional controversy, was allowing women to pray in public. Finney did exalt the use of women in revival leadership roles. Women's rights were on the reform agenda in the early nineteenth century, and Finney was certainly a reformer with a wide breadth of concerns. He was an ardent seeker after social justice as well as a fervent revivalist. He blended those two approaches into his ministry in a most significant, balanced fashion, as shall later be seen in detail. It was both Christian and logical to the evangelist to allow any member of the church, male or female, to serve in ways he or she was capable of doing. This shocked the traditionalistic orthodox. The "proof texters" threw their verses at him, to which Finney would reply, "I know some have supposed that the Scriptures plainly prohibit the speaking or praying of women in promiscuous assemblies, but I do not so understand the teachings of the Bible."[2] And that was that.

Some have charged Finney – or credited him, depending on the viewpoint – with giving birth to the whole concept of women's participation in public worship. But women were already speaking publicly in Utica when Finney arrived. He himself acknowledged it was already a local custom. It may have been Theodore Weld who propagated the practice. Weld said, "I was converted to Christ in the city of Utica during a powerful revival of religion under Brother Finney, and the first time I ever spoke in a religious meeting I urged females both to pray and speak if they felt deeply enough to do it, and not to be restrained from it by the fact that they were female."[3]

A seventh and similar method that Finney used was praying for people in public by name. This was just not done by the traditionalists. Feelings on this issue ran especially high among the "old school" theologians. What if the person named in prayer was not one of the elect? That was probably the real crux of the criticism.

The "protracted meeting" itself was an issue to some. For an evangelist to go into a community, stay and preach until a revival broke out was not the way to extend the Kingdom of God, the critics shouted. The reasons for the outcry varied. One argument stated that if the revival meeting were extended, it was usually because there was keen interest. But there was fear that pastors and evangelists might purposely protract a meeting, inferring keen interest, when there really was none. This would put a feather in the evangelist's cap he did not deserve, and furthermore, people could be left exhausted and suffering from nervous strain. Thus they could soon degenerate spiritually and fall into fanaticism or extravagances. That would defame the Gospel.

Now these arguments held some water. Was Finney guilty of these errors? Hardly, for when he saw that his work was done, he left immediately. Moreover, he always said that physical exhaustion was the enemy of revival and saw to it that he did not over-extend the people.

Finney should, nonetheless, be held partly responsible for the situation, since some of those abusing the "measures" were imitating him. Furthermore, Finney at times seemed to imply that if the right methods were employed, God would be duty bound to send a revival. Of course, that philosophy of revival is not true. God is sovereign in all awakenings. If Finney really believed otherwise, he was surely wrong. Several things need to be taken into consideration in this matter.

First, Finney was reacting against a rigid Calvinism in his emphasis on "measures", a Calvinism that emphasised the sovereignty of God to the near-elimination of human responsibilities. People were even seen as passive in receiving the grace of God. Charles could never accept such an approach and hence, he probably overstated his case. He did admit later in life that in his early ministry he placed too much emphasis on human ability to respond to the Gospel and not enough on the grace of God to act in salvation. The more mature Finney struck a much better balance.

Secondly, it is clear Finney *always* emphasised the work of the Holy Spirit in the employment of his evangelistic methods. Moreover, his prime emphasis was on the "measure" of intercessory prayer. He even discouraged singing in prayer meetings, although he used music to good effect in the preaching services.

Thirdly, the wise observer recognises that a significant revival was afoot in Finney's day. God was at work in such a sovereign and unusual manner that almost any method seemed to work. It may be true that Finney did not recognise this fact as clearly as one would have wished. He probably had never seen a "dry season" with which to contrast the work of God going on in his ministry.

Finally, the nature of the "measures" themselves is hardly humanistic. To most contemporary Christians prayer, counselling and personal witnessing are quite spiritual ministries.

Finney still appears to many as having been too mechanical. He did say in effect that as surely as a farmer follows the simple principles of sowing, cultivating and reaping and can hence expect nature to give him a crop, if proper revival "measures" are employed God will invariably grant a revival. To some extent, he must have believed that, but he surely did not mean it in the crass way it may have sounded. His whole philosophy, theology and ministerial approach should make that plain. Yet he probably should have presented his views in a clearer fashion. Later, as happens so easily, many in the Church became either evangelistic technicians on the one hand, or confessional theologians on the other, but Finney himself always combined his evangelistic techniques with a strong, virile theology. This saved him personally from both errors even if later followers fell into the trap.

Other minor matters were raised of much less importance for history, but these were the main "measures" that caused all the stir. The two most important "new school" personalities from the East who took a firm stand against Finney were the Rev. Lyman Beecher and evangelist Asahel Nettleton. Beecher of Boston was a great pastor committed to revivals and Nettleton was a renowned revivalist.

The Rev. Asahel Nettleton was the most significant evangelist of the hour, until Finney's star began to rise. He was nine years older than Charles and was deeply admired by the younger evangelist: "I had the greatest confidence in Mr. Nettleton, though I had never seen him. I felt like sitting at his feet, almost as I would at the feet of an apostle, from what I had heard of his success in promoting revivals. At that time my confidence in him was so great that I think he could have led me, almost or quite, at his discretion."[4]

Nettleton's fame began to develop in the early 1820s, in Saratoga Springs, New York. He was asked to preach in the local church, and as he began to declare the Gospel of Christ a great revival broke out. During Finney's Troy revival, Nettleton was ministering in Albany. Charles rode over to meet with him and to hear him preach, genuinely desiring all the counsel and help he could glean from the more seasoned evangelist. But he was to be disappointed. Although they found themselves in substantial agreement on every point of theology, over the issue of *how* to promote a revival, serious problems surfaced. On those points Nettleton would not even converse with Finney. When Charles told Nettleton he wanted to spend the night in Albany and hear him preach, the older evangelist became uneasy. He finally told Finney that he could not be seen with him in public. So Finney went to the service, accompanied by a layman. Charles was not impressed with the preaching, and finally faced the fact that he would get no help or encouragement from Nettleton.

In a letter to Jay Frost written on February 15, 1827 Nettleton said, "They [Finney and his friends] are driving us back into barbarism under the illusion of a new era." His battle was not against Finney's Christian character. He wrote to Samuel Aiken: "It is no reflection on his [Finney's] talents or piety, that in his zeal to save souls, he should adopt every measure which promises present success, regardless of consequences; nor, after a fair experiment in so noble a cause, to say, I have pushed something beyond what they will bear, that most useful lessons are learned by experience."[5] Writing in that fashion to a very close friend of Finney, it almost seemed that Nettleton sought reconciliation. However, he was adamant that Finney abandon ship completely on his "new measures". But Finney would never surrender his methods. He was the captain of that ship and he would go down with it if Nettleton succeeded in sinking it. Charles was completely convinced that eternal souls hung in the balance, so determined to carry on at any price.

Those were Finney's reasons; why did evangelist Nettleton take his unyielding stand? There are those who say that he was simply professionally jealous of his younger counterpart. There are others who feel that his poor health was the real issue.

The paradox of the whole affair is that Nettleton used "measures" himself. Dr. E. N. Kirk, a well-known clergyman, said of Nettleton, "He was not quite fair, for I am informed that no Revivalist or Evangelist in our day has so abounded in 'new measures', contrivances, and management as he."[6] Nettleton did say he was not opposed to measures as such. But concerning Finney's approach he could say nothing good. He did not oppose Finney's "new measures" simply because they were new, but rather because those measures had "precipitated mischief . . . in bringing the very name of revival into disgrace."[7]

As an orthodox pastor, Lyman Beecher was zealously committed to revivalism because of his war with the Unitarians of New England. He was convinced that the best weapon the orthodox could use was that of a revival. He used some "new measures" too, the inquiry-room method, for example. Beecher was really not opposed to different methodologies for revivals. Then why his complaint against Finney?

First, it must be made clear that Beecher was less violent than Nettleton in his attacks on the "new measures" generally and Finney in particular. He even tried to be something of a peacemaker in the situation. Never did he wish to limit Finney's usefulness. He certainly did not cast any aspersions on Finney's character or piety. Beecher went so far as to say that many churches were in a sad spiritual state and needed strong measures to revive them and no doubt Finney had done many of them much good.

The blame for Beecher's opposition to Finney must be laid primarily at Nettleton's feet. He somehow captured Beecher's ear and convinced him that Finney's brand of revivalism was wrong and extremely dangerous. To compound the problem, Finney refused to answer the charges publicly. Charles was trying to heal the wounds by silence, but as a consequence, most of the information travelling to the East Coast from Oneida County was emanating from sources like Weeks and Nettleton. Thus no counter move developed to better inform Beecher and his friends. Charles considered Lyman Beecher and even Nettleton good men, but misinformed. He said, "These brethren were grossly deceived by misinformation that they received from some source, we were sure. We regarded them as good men, and true; but we know that somebody was giving them most unreliable information."

About that time, a group of Nettleton's cohorts from New England came west to see what was actually happening in Finney's ministry. They returned with a negative, damaging report. As circumstances would have it, Finney released his first published sermon right at that moment. The text was Amos 3:3: "Can two walk together except they be agreed?" The message was originally preached in Utica and repeated again in Troy. The people there heard it with great appreciation, so Finney decided to put it in print. But it came bounding back with a vengeance. Nettleton felt it was directed towards him personally, and reacted sharply. That did anything but help Finney's public relations with Beecher and the eastern men. So there was the problem: Lyman Beecher's main source of information was Asahel Nettleton and his crowd. Beecher's own son and editor of his father's autobiography attested to this: "In short, Mr. Nettleton was clearly master of the position."[8]

As a consequence, the most influential and famous minister of the day took his stand against Finney. Beecher wrote to a friend in a personal letter that Finney was "not to be believed at all . . . make a manful stand against him".[9]

The tragedy was that the issue had been raised at all. A true revival had never swept over the church scene without the employment of "measures". Some of Finney's own friends felt that he should defend himself by stating that the "new measures" had been used through the years. The Rev. John Frost, one of Finney's ardent admirers, encouraged him to defend himself on that basis. But Finney seemed reluctant to follow this advice. Perhaps he realised that when emotions run deeply, reason absents itself. To answer may merely have accentuated the division.

It was at this point that a general meeting was called for to air the differences. Once and for all, the issues needed to be settled. Beecher and Dr. Nathaniel S. Beman, pastor at Troy, set a time and place for the conference and invited men from both factions. July 1827 and the town of New Lebanon, New York were agreed upon. It so happened that Finney was preaching in New Lebanon that summer. New Lebanon was not chosen for that reason: the selection was made because of its convenient location. The town was situated just a few miles west of the Massachusetts state line on the Albany-Pittsfield turnpike. All sides could get there easily. So on Wednesday, July 18, the "Watchmen of the East", as they were known and the men from the West met. The assembly came to be called the "New Lebanon Convention". It must have been quite an exciting event.

By this time, a general mood of compromise was growing in the minds of many. Finney and his friends gladly welcomed the conference so that the actual facts, devoid of the gross exaggerations, could be set forth. Invitations had been issued from the pen of Lyman Beecher and Nathaniel Beman. The prospects for a satisfying solution looked good. The New Lebanon Convention in no sense should be seen as an actual trial for Finney and his "new measures". The purpose and spirit was primarily conciliatory. Further, it was in no sense an official meeting of the Church; therefore, no one had authority to make any binding decisions on anyone. Understanding was the sole goal.

On the appointed day the invited members arrived. They met in the home of Dr. Betz of New Lebanon. The notables from the East were Dr. Lyman Beecher, Asahel Nettleton, Dr. Humphrey (President of Amherst College) and several other well-known clergymen. From the West came Dr. Beman, Mr. Lansing of Auburn, Mr. Aiken of Utica, Gillett of Rome, Gale of Western, and others involved in the Finney ministry. Finney had a sizeable and influential following as did Beecher and Nettleton.

The gavel fell, prayer was offered, and the convention commenced. Although there was some tension in the air, the opening session unanimously passed a conciliatory resolution. A positive spirit was instilled as the sessions got under way, but the more emotional agenda items on the "new measures" issue soon began to surface. Finney and friends had nothing to hide; they fully presented the unvarnished facts. Tension began to rise.

When the true issues began to be plainly presented, it started to look bad for Beecher and Nettleton. It became clear that they had not projected an unbiased, objective assessment of Finney's methods. Nettleton who had been vocal in spreading the stories became so nervous he could not attend the sessions for several days.

Lyman Beecher also found himself in a difficult position. He tried to prohibit Finney and the western men from probing into the source of the criticism: "We have not come here to be catechised, and our spiritual dignity forbids us to answer any such questions."[10] The Boston pastor further argued that the Finneyites could not be heard as witnesses. He said they were the ones to be questioned, therefore they were not admissible as witnesses. They were the objects of censure, so facts should not be received from them.

Beecher's strategy was plain. He and Nettleton had written much of the opposition material. It was obvious why he did not wish to divulge the source of their information. Beecher and Nettleton were on the defensive and knew it. The eastern brothers were disturbed. Dr. Humphrey from the East said the men from the West were the best witnesses they could get. Why not hear them? The men from the East genuinely wanted to know the truth. Finney acknowledged that he found many of these brethren open and brotherly.

In one of the sessions, Nettleton read a lengthy letter that he said was the basis of his attacks on Finney's revivals.

He apparently realised that he had to give some sort of documentation for his accusations; he was under pressure. Finney had already seen a copy of the document. He informed the assembly that not one accusation in it was true. Charles said, "All the brethren are here, with whom I have performed all these labours, and they know whether I am chargeable with any of these things, in any of their congregations. If they know or believe that any of these things are true of me, let them say so here and now."[11]

The western clergymen rose and to the last man made it clear that Finney was guilty of none of the abuses the Nettleton letter outlined. Not even Weeks, who was present throughout the entire proceedings, said a single word in defence of the Nettleton letter. That placed Beecher and Nettleton in a bad light. They had expected Weeks to justify their attacks, since he was probably the author of the document. Yet not a word fell from his lips.

The handwriting was now clearly on the wall. In an effort to save the situation, one of the men from the East, a Mr. Justin Edwards, brought in a long string of resolutions condemning excesses in revivals. He laboriously read each single item. The men from the West said they agreed wholeheartedly with the resolution. But Edwards' subtle strategy was clear: if they voted on the resolution and published it, that would leave the impression that excesses were actually being practised, which they clearly were not. After some debate, the men from the West went along with it nevertheless and voted in favour of the motion.

The New Lebanon Convention had gone on now for several days. The whole matter was fully aired. As the assembly began to draw to a close, most felt that the differences between the eastern and western clergymen were really very few indeed. Actually, the only issue that could not in some sense be resolved was that of women praying in public. That was hardly a major issue, even if it had emotional overtones. In something of that conciliatory spirit, the conference adjourned. No one won; it was not for that purpose. But Finney surely came out justified.

At the end of the convention, Beecher said to the evangelist, "Finney, . . . I know your plan, and you know I do; you mean to come to Connecticut, and carry a streak of fire to Boston. But if you attempt it, as the Lord liveth, I'll meet you at the state line, and call out the artillery men, and fight every inch of the way to Boston, and then I'll fight you there."[12] But that unkind word seemed to be merely the emotional outburst of the moment. Two years later, Kathryn Beecher, Lyman's daughter, told Finney he would be well received in Boston. Charles reminded her of her father's statement at the New Lebanon Convention. He told Kathryn Beecher he would never come to New England unless invited by Dr. Beecher himself. So the Boston pastor invited him – even to his own church! Beecher gave a final touch to the story in his own words: "So we wrote and invited him, and he came and did very well."

Lyman Beecher was a good man even if seriously misled. He was apparently considerably shaken by the New Lebanon Convention, and by Nettleton in particular. He lost confidence in the older evangelist. After the convention, Beecher is reported to have said, "I would not have had Mr. Nettleton come to Boston for a thousand dollars." Travelling back to Boston humbled by the experience, he said, "We crossed the mountains expecting to meet a company of boys, but we found them to be full grown men."[13]

Perhaps Beecher unconsciously put his finger on the real issue. The whole problem may have been no more than the sophistication of the East in conflict with the frontier ruggedness of the West. The radically different cultural backgrounds were bound to result in different ministerial methods. Both sides were made up of true Christians and could thus resolve their differences. So the issue seemed to be basically settled.

Evangelist Asahel Nettleton could not be satisfied, however. George Gale had warned Finney to watch out for Nettleton after the New Lebanon Convention. Gale said the old evangelist would be looking at Charles' revivals "with an eagle's eye". He was right. Nettleton persisted in publishing papers against the "new measures". Lyman Beecher tried to persuade him to forget it, and finally said to the evangelist, "Dr. Taylor and I have made you what you are, and, if you do not behave yourself, we will shoot you down."[14] The evangelistic ministry of Nettleton was brought into disrepute because of his constant wrangling. Nettleton finally broke with Beecher and the Newhaven men, even assisting in the conservative retort against their views.

The New Lebanon Convention was a blessing for Finney. The religious newspapers of the day had given complete coverage to the meeting. Now his name was heralded all over the East. Furthermore, the convention put an end to any serious opposition from the eastern clergymen, save Nettleton. The brethren had seen the clear facts of the case. Before long, Finney was found on the East Coast preaching and ministering with great effect, even in Beecher's own city.

The "new measures" controversy was formally put to rest on May 27, 1828 when the General Assembly in Philadelphia passed the following resolution:

> The subscribers having had opportunity for free conversation on certain subjects pertaining to revivals of religion, concerning which we have differed, are of the opinion that the general interest of religion would not be promoted by any further publication on those subjects, or personal discussion; and we do hereby engage to cease from all publications, correspondence, conversations, and conduct designed and calculated to keep these subjects before the public's mind; and that, so far as our influence may avail, we will exert it to induce our friends on either side to do the same.
> Signed by Lyman Beecher, Erick C. Lansing, S. C. Aiken, A. D. Eddy, C. G. Finney, Sylvester Holmes, Ebzener Cheever, John Frost, Nathaniel S. S. Beman, Noah Cole, E. W. Gilbert, Joel Parker.[15]

Warfare was still to rage in Finney's life; he was too controversial a figure for that not to happen. But the "new measures" issue never generated serious and heated debate again. Near the end of his life, Finney wrote, "Were I to live my life over again, I think, that with the experience of more than forty years in revival labours, I should, under the same circumstances, use substantially the same measures that I did then."[16]

## Finney's Far-reaching Frontiers:
## The Evangelist's Broadening Ministry

Finney often experienced the Macedonian call through
someone who attended his meetings and then cried "come
over and help us". As Charles came out of the New
Lebanon pulpit one Sunday, the convention now closed
and the revival in good progress, Maria, a young lady from
Stephentown, approached the evangelist with concern
written all over her face. Her urgent plea was that Finney
come to her community and preach. Finney was touched,
but told her that as much as he would desire to do so, his
hands were full. Yet, when he sensed her deep burden, he
began to search out the facts about Stephentown.

He soon discovered what kind of community it was; it
stood in desperate need of a spiritual awakening. Under
the previous pastor of the Presbyterian church, the congregation began to deteriorate seriously. It finally lost so
much ground that the pastor left and became an outright
infidel. On top of that, he stayed in town to become a
cynical critic of Christianity. The entire community was in
the grip of spiritual decay. The moral foundations of the
town had virtually crumbled away. Such a situation was
always too much for the evangelist. He consented to preach
to the community on Sunday at 5 p.m.

One of the recent converts at New Lebanon offered to
drive the evangelist over to Stephentown in his buggy.
Finney inquired if he had a steady horse. The young
Christian replied he had. "What made you ask the question?" he inquired. "Because", Charles answered, "if the
Lord wants me to go to Stephentown, the devil will prevent
it if he can; and if you have not a steady horse, he will try to

make him kill me." So the young men set out. Finney was prophetic! Before many miles, the horse suddenly bolted and started to run away, nearly killing the two men. Twice the cantankerous animal tried his tricks. The owner of the horse was dumbfounded; he assured Finney his docile steed had never acted like that before. But then, the devil deals in death.

When the evangelist arrived in Stephentown, the meeting place was crowded. The first service produced nothing of any spiritual significance, however, and Finney, somewhat disappointed, did not appoint a further meeting. But Maria pleaded with him so earnestly that he consented to return the following Sunday. On the next Lord's day the same atmosphere prevailed, yet Finney sensed an increase in the seriousness of the congregation. Charles left, this time taking the initiative and appointing a third service. Perhaps God was at work after all. During the next service the Holy Spirit fell in revival power and a tremendous work was under way.

Finney was soon forced to say farewell to New Lebanon and take up residence in Stephentown. Once in the harness, great blessings abounded. Finney was aided in his labours by the Rev. Zebulon R. Shipherd, the father of John J. Shipherd, one of the founding fathers of Oberlin College. As the work deepened, some of the strongest men in the community fell before the power of God. As the great Welsh revivalist, Christmas Evans, would have expressed it, "hearts were wounded by the arrows of divine love, through the strongest breastplate ever made in hell". Finney gives a graphic account of a man who was "of strong nerve, and of considerable prominence as a farmer in the town. He sat almost immediately before me, near the pulpit. The first that I observed was that he fell, and writhed in agony for a few moments; but afterwards became still, and nearly motionless, but entirely helpless. He remained in this state until the meeting was out, when he was taken home. He was very soon converted, and became an effective worker in bringing his friends to Christ." These sort of events parallel the great Wesley-Whitefield Awakening in Britain nearly one hundred years earlier.

The spirit of prayer was everywhere – as is always the

case when a true revival of religion is in progress. The evangelist stated, "I have seldom laboured in a revival with greater comfort to myself, or with less opposition, than in Stephentown . . . [there was] such power . . . set home by the Holy Spirit, that I soon heard no more complaints."

Now that the "new measures" controversy had been sufficiently eradicated, the Finney ministry progressed and developed in a marvellous fashion. While the revival was still in progress in New Lebanon, the Rev. Mr. Gilbert, pastor of the Presbyterian Church in Wilmington, Delaware, had visited Finney. He was a committed "old school" type, but a good and devout man with a deep desire to help people come to Christ. His joy in seeing sinners saved overrode any theological problems he found with Finney. He earnestly urged the evangelist to leave Oneida County and come east to Delaware. After the Stephentown outpouring, Finney set his sights on that new field.

When Finney commenced his ministry in Wilmington he ran into a new situation. Gilbert had so ingrained "old school" thought into the people that when the evangelist preached, they simply did not understand what he was talking about. Charles immediately saw that their theology would have to be completely overhauled if a revival were to develop. They seemed frightened to make any effort at all to promote effective evangelism lest they blunder into God's domain.

It was evident to Charles that Gilbert would have to be changed as well as his congregation. After two or three weeks of labour and much discussion, Finney felt that the time had come for a resounding "new school" theology sermon. He spoke on the text "Make you a new heart and a new spirit: for why will ye die?" (Ezek. 18:31). The reaction of the pastor and people was mixed: some laughed, some cried, and some were furious. A strange excitement filled the entire house. Gilbert himself was so convicted he could hardly sit still. As soon as Finney finished, Gilbert fled the pulpit. A friend took hold of him and asked, "Mr. Gilbert, what do you think of that?" He replied, "It is worth five hundred dollars." "Then you have never preached the Gospel," the friend replied. "Well," the pastor said, "I am sorry to say I never have." A revolution was in the making.

The pastor's wife had a disturbing feeling that Finney was right. Before the evangelist's message, she had toyed with the idea that God in justice actually owed her salvation. But Charles undermined this foundation. She secluded herself in her room for two whole days and emerged not only transformed in theology, but in life as well. The radiance of Christ beamed from her face. From that point on, the work took off like the dove from Noah's ark. Gilbert became a new minister.

In the meantime, Finney accepted an invitation to preach in the growing metropolitan centre of Philadelphia, Pennsylvania. For a short time, the evangelist alternated between Philadelphia and Wilmington; they were only forty miles apart. But as the work deepened in Philadelphia, Finney felt he must give himself full-time to the Pennsylvania city. He was convinced that Gilbert could carry on the work in Wilmington, so Charles and Lydia moved to Philadelphia.

Charles' work in Philadelphia took strong hold from its inception, even though he was moving into Nettleton's eastern territory. The pastor in Philadelphia, the Rev. James Patterson, was an "old school" Presbyterian. But like Gilbert of Wilmington, he was a godly man and deeply committed to seeing people converted. Finney said that he was "one of the truest and holiest men that I have ever laboured with". Patterson's wife, unlike her husband, held to Finney's "New England" theology. All dogma was laid aside, however, as the work of evangelism began. Moreover, the fact that God honoured the preaching of Finney's "New Divinity" sermons greatly affected Patterson. Never once did he raise a protest at Finney's theological stance. The pastor's wife would say to her husband after a good sermon, "Now you see Mr. Patterson, that Mr. Finney does not agree with you on these points upon which we have so often conversed." The good man of God would simply reply, "Well, the Lord blesses it." That surely pleased Charles' pragmatism!

Finney had a new and unusual experience in Philadelphia – not that every community did not present excit-

ing new things. Philadelphia was considerably larger than
any town he had previously encountered, and there were
several Presbyterian congregations in the city, so Charles
developed a preaching circuit. He would alternate services
among the various churches.

Most of the Philadelphia pastors were "old school" men.
Patterson was fearful that the ministers of the churches, if
they found out Finney's doctrinal position, would reject
him and his ministry. But such was not the case. Finney was
accepted in every Presbyterian church save one, the old
Arch Street Church. Nor did Charles trim his theological
sails to catch more favourable breezes. In fact, he preached
forcefully on his "radical" view of the atonement. He chose
as his text: "There is one God and one mediator between
God and men, the man Christ Jesus" (I Tim. 2:5). It had
such effect that invitations flooded in from far and wide to
preach it. Finney was many things, but he was never
reticent to preach what he believed, to challenge people
with what he saw as truth. He said, "I felt it my duty to
expose all the hiding places of sinners, and to hunt them out
from under those peculiar views of orthodoxy, in which I
found them entrenched."

As the spirit of revival grew, it became evident that
shifting from church to church was not the best methodology. Philadelphia boasted a large German church house
seating some three thousand people. The building was
acquired and Finney settled down in that venue. Night
after night the church was filled to capacity; even the aisles
were filled. Converts of the revival were soon found in
every corner of the city. Finney continued evangelising in
the German church for several months.

An incident occurred in the spring of 1829. When the ice
melted and the Delaware River was high, lumbermen
would come floating down the stream on rafts of timber
they had cut during the long winter months. Philadelphia,
situated on the Delaware River, was the stopping point
where the lumbermen would break up their rafts and sell
the wood for a good profit. Most of these lumbermen came
from the area called "the Lumber Region", an area some
eighty miles in length. In 1829, that region was a pure
wilderness – no schools, churches, or any amenities. Many

of the lumbermen coming to Philadelphia that spring attended the Finney revival and were converted. They made their way back to their wilderness homes to pray earnestly for an outpouring of the Holy Spirit in "the Lumber Region". The new converts began to share their faith with friends. God blessed wonderfully: a great revival broke out. The movement spread to such an extent that in case after case men would be converted who had never even attended any meetings and were "almost as ignorant as heathens", as Finney put it. People would be saved while completely alone in the woods.

One man, for example, was living alone in a little shanty in the wilderness. He began to feel he was a sinner. He became so burdened that he broke down, fell on his knees, confessed his sins, and genuinely repented. In that broken frame of mind, the Spirit of God marvellously revealed the way of salvation to the lumberman; he found Jesus Christ as Saviour. He had never attended a prayer meeting or heard a prayer in his life. After his conversion he felt drawn to tell some of his friends what had happened. He discovered them in their wilderness house, feeling just as he did and actually having a prayer meeting. They all turned to Christ.

The movement continued with few if any ministers. Moreover, there was no fanaticism as, perhaps, one might expect. It was simply a remarkable work of God. Over five thousand people were converted in two years. Finney said of the wilderness revival, "I have regarded that as one of the most remarkable revivals that have occurred in this country."

As Finney's fame was spreading, he was invited to preach at the General Assembly of the Presbytery when it was held in Philadelphia. That was no mean honour, and only five or six years after the first Evans Mills revival. One of Finney's friends, John Frost, warned him not to be taken in by such heady wine: "Brother Finney, I have said before, keep humble; I repeat it. Don't think more highly of yourself than you ought."[1] Charles, because of his blunt personality, did at times appear arrogant, but he was above all a man of God who recognised his utter dependence upon the work of the Holy Spirit and never forgot that the boatman waxes careless when his craft glides gently along on a smooth sea before a pleasant breeze.

Finney stayed in Philadelphia for one and a half years. The historic Pennsylvania city, which saw the birth of the nation, witnessed one of the greatest religious revivals in its days. The length of time, the general acceptance of a big eastern city, the spotlight of attention, all pointed to grander things ahead. Could it be that Philadelphia was God's testing ground for a greater ministry than any at the time realised?

From Philadelphia, Finney travelled to Reading, Pennsylvania in the winter of 1829–30. Reading was a blossoming young city which proudly possessed a population of ten thousand. It nestled in the hills some fifty miles west of Philadelphia. The days of revivals in little villages seemed over for Charles.

The invitation to Reading had come from a Dr. Grier, pastor of a Presbyterian church. Finney soon found that neither pastor nor people possessed any idea of what a revival was, or even that they needed one. A worldly spirit pervaded the people – and Grier said little if anything about it. Finney could not even generate significant prayer meetings for a revival.

With the pastor's consent, Finney preached directly to the church members for three weeks. The most formidable opponents were the local newspapermen, who published continual articles against Finney and the revival. He soon demolished that problem, however, with a thundering sermon. He could be as vociferous as they when necessary.

As conviction began to deepen among the people, Finney called for an inquiry meeting. Dr. Grier did not object, but it was evident he felt few if any would respond. Even Finney was a little doubtful himself. The invitation was given on Sunday. They were to assemble the next night in a lecture room. Monday was a cold, snowy day, hardly conducive to interest in salvation. Yet, as Finney and the pastor entered the lecture hall, they were amazed to see practically the entire congregation of the church. The pastor opened the meeting, then turned to the evangelist: "I know nothing about such a meeting as this; take it into your own hands." Finney took the helm, and after conversing personally with each one there, he addressed the group. Charles brought the meeting to a climax by asking all who would to kneel, pray and receive Christ. Grier said nothing, and after the meeting the two went to their respective homes.

About eleven o'clock that same night, a man ran to Finney's lodging. He burst in announcing that Dr. Grier was dead. "What happened?" Finney inquired. Grier had retired. Suddenly he was taken with what Victorian people called a "fit of apoplexy" and died immediately. As could be expected, the pastor's untimely death shocked and totally disoriented the people. Grier was a highly-educated man with a gentle spirit. Even if Grier did not speak out against sin in his congregation as perhaps he should, Finney still admired him as a Christian minister. When the shock and grief subsided, the revival went on with increasing impact until many in Reading were converted.

Yet the work was not easy in that Pennsylvania town without the help of a pastor and in the midst of opposition. God honoured the effort, however, and a sound work of the Spirit spread over the entire community.

Late in the spring of 1830 Charles travelled to Lancaster, Pennsylvania. There the evangelist found the Presbyterian church without a pastor and the spiritual life of the community low. God was seemingly leading His servant into increasingly difficult fields, perhaps preparing him for the big cities of the East Coast which were soon to host him. He remained in Lancaster a very short time. Nonetheless, in the evangelist's own words, "The work of God was immediately revived, the Spirit of God being poured out almost at once upon the people."

Finney's movements during the next few months of 1830, nine years after his dramatic conversion in Adams, are difficult to trace. The evangelist never kept a daily journal and his *Memoirs* were written decades later. One or two things are clear, however. He visited his father-in-law back in Oneida County, his "home base", where he received a letter from his friend, Mr. Cushman, in Troy, New York. Cushman related that even after the decision of the New Lebanon Convention, the pastor Beman was still under attack for his use of "new measures". Mr. Kirk of Albany was also receiving his share of criticism for the methods. But this was probably no more than a final rearguard action of a retreating army.

While in Oneida County, Finney was invited to Albany, the capital of New York, and asked to preach while the State Legislature was in session. To be invited to address members of the legal profession was high praise and indicative of his growing stature.

At some time during those obscure months, Finney made the big leap: he went to New York City and preached in the Old Laight Church. The pastor, Mr. Cox, apparently did not support Finney's ministry and Beman mildly rebuked Charles for even going: "You have no Lansing, or Aiken, or Frost, or Gillett, or Beman to stand by you and assist you."[2] George Gale felt that any large city was no place to seek a revival, and warned Finney that he might lose his evangelistic zeal in a city like New York.

While in the metropolitan area, Finney visited Poughkeepsie, a few miles north of New York. The Presbytery session that met in that community resolved: "That we in a Session highly approve to the labours of the Rev. Charles G. Finney among us the past week and do now invite him to return and labour among us as God in his Providence shall open the way."[3] Finney later developed a far-reaching ministry in New York. Not only that, but Finney's first son, Charles Beman, was born on March 26, 1830 while the family was in New York City.

In that summer of 1830, a call came from Columbia in Herkimer County, to which the Finneys responded. Columbia had a strong German congregation, and their fine building and large number of members made it look a perfect place for Finney to begin a revival effort. At this time, Finney's revivals were usually held in single churches. As his ministry grew, several churches would co-operate in the revival effort, but that pattern became more significant later. The members of this church, though doctrinally orthodox, were unconverted. The church suffered from what historians call "Protestant scholasticism", the idea that correct theology is all that is required to be a good Christian. Could one plant revival seeds in this kind of "fallow ground"? In his early days, the pastor had studied under a German doctor of divinity who had tenaciously discouraged any form of dynamic religious experience. The pastor himself acknowledged that he had no real religion at all.

The German minister's mother, on the other hand, was a vibrant believer and deeply concerned for her son. When the young pastor received the call to the Columbia church, his mother had a serious talk with him, sharing what Christ truly can mean to a person. The sense of need burdened the young preacher for months, but he had no one with whom he could talk. His wife was unconverted also. Finally, after a severe struggle of soul, he broke through and came to trust Christ as his personal Saviour. The joy of salvation flooded his life. He flew into his work as never before. First, he had to see his wife converted. She was soon saved. Next was the church. The pastor went all over town witnessing to his elders and members.

The newly-converted pastor set a special church business meeting at the apex of all of the excitement. Before the assembly, he shared his experience as well as that of his wife. The few elders and members who did have a real relationship with Jesus Christ also gave their testimony. With that the pastor outrightly dissolved the church and on the spot reconstituted another congregation on the basis of genuine Christian experience. This bold move threw the congregation into a near panic. Not to be able to take the sacraments or have one's children baptised was terrifying to these German people. But the die was cast. After the new church with its whole new approach was organised, the pastor laboured with all his might to secure conversions. At that moment, he heard that Finney was visiting in Oneida County, and urged him to come to minister. Charles complied and the revival began at once. It was a refreshing outpouring.

A little later, a group of converts from the revival travelled west, settled in Illinois, and established the city of Galesburg. The leader of the group and founder of the Illinois town that exists to this day was none other than George W. Gale. Gale took a group of these German people to the new territory, founded the township and established Knox College which has educated thousands through the years.

Shortly after the Columbia meeting, Finney apparently returned to his in-laws. There he was visited by Hansan G. Phelps, a wealthy philanthropist, who asked him to come and preach in New York City once again. Charles consented and revival followed. He stayed in New York for a protracted period preaching the Gospel.

The New York revival resulted in several very important moves. First, it paved the way for the organisation of the so-called "free Presbyterian churches" in the city. These churches were composed largely of the converts of the Finney revival. Secondly, the New York ministry enabled Finney to grow close to the Tappan brothers. This proved very providential in the evangelist's future ministry. Finally, Finney came to understand New York. In return, New York grew to know the evangelist. Before long, the Finneys would move to New York City to engage in a completely new venture: Charles was destined to become a pastor-evangelist in America's largest metropolitan centre.

Charles' career as an itinerant evangelist was rapidly reaching its climax. But there was still the highest mountain peak to scale. It came in the great Rochester, New York, campaign of 1830–1. The invitation to that city came from Josiah Bissell, an elder in the Third Presbyterian Church and the owner of the stage-coach line. He began corresponding with Charles in 1829, laying on Finney's heart the needs of Rochester. The Rev. Joel Parker, pastor of Rochester's Third Church from 1827 until 1830 had also urged Finney to come to the city. Several other invitations from various places came to Finney while he was resting in Oneida County, all putting him in a quandary – he did not know what to do.

The prospects for a revival at Rochester did not appear to be very bright. The Second Presbyterian Church, called the "Brick Church", had a good pastor, but he was about to leave. Parker, pastor of the Third Presbyterian Church, had left and taken up the ministry of one of the new free Presbyterian churches in New York City. To tarnish the prospects further, there was a controversy between an elder in the Third Church and the pastor of the First

Presbyterian Church. Still, the friends at Rochester were most anxious and urgent that Finney come. He prolonged his stay at his father-in-law's home, trying to find God's will. Finally, the family packed and went down to Utica where Charles had many praying friends.

The Finney family arrived in the afternoon, and in the evening a number of the faithful friends and admirers gathered for prayer and consultation. One by one they expressed their feelings to Finney. They were unanimous in their conviction that Rochester was far too uninviting to start a revival. New York City or Philadelphia, from whom Finney had received invitations, seemed much more promising. Finney agreed, drawn especially to New York.

The family went to their lodgings expecting to take the canal boat the next day to New York City. (That was before the railroad opened the West, when much travel was done on canal boat.) Finney could not sleep, however. He kept asking himself, "Why am I not going to Rochester?" Charles began to see that the reasons others felt were detriments were actually what should compel him to go there. He finally came to the conclusion that God wanted him in Rochester. He even felt ashamed that he was avoiding the city because of the difficulties. God gave him the assurance that He would be with him and give him great victories.

Finney was never one to delay when he found God's will. He immediately informed his family and early the next morning the Finneys went west instead of east.

## 6

## Finney's Rochester Revivals:
## The Evangelist's Greatest Meetings

The Finney family disembarked from the canal packet boat
on September 10, 1830. The thriving, sophisticated city of
Rochester, New York, lay before them. It would soon be
conquered for Christ.

The Finneys took up residence in the home of elder
Josiah Bissell. Feeling there was no time to waste, Charles
started preaching immediately in the Third Presbyterian
Church. A cousin of Finney who lived in Rochester had, in
the meantime, arranged for the evangelist to meet Dr.
Penny, pastor of the First Presbyterian Church. Penny
came to hear Finney preach and right from the outset a
kindred spirit welded them in Christian fellowship. The
two men became fast friends and Penny invited the
evangelist to his pulpit. Charles already knew there was a
problem between an elder of the Third Church and the
First Church pastor. Bissell, Finney's host, and Dr. Penny,
Finney's new friend, were the two men.

The conflict centred on the calling of a pastor to the
Second Presbyterian Church of Rochester. Bissell, a
strong-willed man, and Penny, equally adamant, disagreed
over the issue. The ensuing rift between the two men
extended its influence over others. But as soon as the Spirit
of God began to move upon the city, the two men saw their
error, and patched up their differences. As far as records
show, Finney had said nothing to them, yet had surely been
the catalyst in the healing.

The entire city began to feel the impact of Finney's
ministry. People came from every corner. They travelled in
from the surrounding communities of Henrietta, Pittsfield

and Canandaiqua. As well as preaching in Rochester itself, Finney moved out from his central location and preached in Clarkson, Brockport, Ogden and Penfield.

Rochester had always been proud of its large number of lawyers, and many of these men came out solidly for Jesus Christ. They were powerfully influenced by Finney's logical, legal style. Lawyers, businessmen, teachers, ordinary workers, all classes of people came to Christ in numbers Charles had never before experienced in his ministry.

Soon, no building in the entire Rochester area was large enough to hold the crowds. This problem was compounded by an accident that occurred on October 1st, early in the revival. In the middle of the service at the First Presbyterian Church as Dr. Penny was offering prayer, an ear-splitting sound filled the building. The stone walls began spreading out and with a thunderous crash a large timber from the ceiling fell through the plaster and landed in front of the organ. The building was situated near the canal and the wet soil was causing the dangerous settling.

All made for the doors and windows. One elderly woman even jumped out of a rear window and landed in the canal itself. Others leaped out of the gallery. It was pandemonium. Finney sprang to his feet and cried at the top of his voice, "Be quiet! Be quiet!" Dr. Penny ran into the street; the building looked as if it were exploding with people. Finney, not thinking there was any real danger, thought it quite ludicrous and could scarcely stop himself laughing. Fortunately, no one was killed, although some suffered minor injuries.

Finney feared the near-tragedy would detract the people from the revival, but the positive spirit that pervaded the community prevailed and the work went on with increasing momentum. The Brick Church opened its doors immediately after the First Church accident and Charles began alternating between various Presbyterian churches in the city. Inquiry meetings and prayer meetings were held in different churches as well. All the denominations of the city threw themselves into the work: the movement became ecumenical in a most profound sense.

A high school was located in Rochester, directed by the son of a pastor in nearby Brighton. Many of the students began attending the revival services and soon conviction began to invade the whole student body. One day, the director found his class unable to recite their lessons because of their deep consciousness of sin. The director called for one of his associates who was a Christian and told her that his young people were so concerned for their souls that school work was impossible. Despite his scepticism, he suggested that she send for Finney to come and speak to them. Charles came, spoke, and the revival took powerful hold on the students. Nearly every person in the school was saved – including the sceptical director.

Out of the significant Rochester revival, some forty men dedicated their lives to the gospel ministry. Of that forty, many became foreign missionaries. The Rochester revival also witnessed Finney's first regular use of the "anxious seat". In his *Memoirs* he wrote:

> I had never, I believe, except in rare instances, until I went to Rochester, used as a means of promoting revivals, what has since been called "the anxious seat". I had sometimes asked persons in the congregation to stand up; but this I had not frequently done. However, in studying upon the subject, I had often felt the necessity of some measure that would bring sinners to a stand. From my own experience and observation I had found, that with the higher classes especially, the greatest obstacle to be overcome was their fear of being known as anxious inquirers. They were too proud to take any position that would reveal them to others as anxious for their souls.
>
> I had found also that something was needed, to make the impression on them that they were expected at once to give up their heart; something that would call them to act, and act as publicly before the world, as they had in their sins; something that would commit them publicly to the service of Christ. When I had called them simply to stand up in the public congregation, I found that this had a very good effect; and so far as it went, it answered the purpose for which it was intended. But after all, I had felt for some time, that something more was necessary to bring them out from among the mass of the ungodly, to a public renunciation of their sinful ways, and a public committal of themselves to God.

This "new measure" was only regularly employed by

Charles years after the controversies over revival method-ologies, although it was discussed at the New Lebanon Convention. It shows clearly that Finney was constantly changing and seeking new ways.

Extensive newspaper coverage was given to the Rochester events. Contrary to Charles' early days, the upper classes in intellect, education and culture, as well as average citizens, were now impressed by Finney's ministry. This was an important turning point in the work. The *Rochester Observer* gave excellent coverage. One report read:

> We have never known a revival more general among all classes, the youth, and those who are preparing for, and those who have just entered upon, the great theatre of life – the student, the mechanic, the professional man, and the politician – those who were seeking for, and those who are in possession of office and worldly honours, have been arrested by the Spirit of God, and a new song has been put in their mouths.[1]

A writer in the *New York Evangelist* wrote:

> Mr. Finney is preaching to overflowing houses. Multitudes assemble who cannot get within the reach of the preacher's voice. Conversions are daily occurring. The Spirit of God is subduing all orders and ranks of society . . . So large a proportion of men and wealth, talent, and influence have rarely, if ever, been known to be the subjects of the revival in that vicinity.[2]

Henry B. Stanton, a lawyer, journalist, and man of powerful influence, all but eulogised Finney when he wrote:

> In October, 1830, Charles G. Finney, the famous evangelist, came to Rochester to supply the pulpit of the Third Presbyterian Church. I had been absent a few days and on my return was asked to hear him. It was in the afternoon. A tall, grave-looking man, dressed in an unclerical suit of grey, ascended the pulpit . . . I listened. It did not sound like preaching, but like a lawyer arguing a case before a court and jury . . . The discourse was a chain of logic,

brightened by felicity of illustration and enforced by urgent appeals from a voice of great compass and melody. Mr. Finney was there in the fullness of his power . . . His style was particularly attractive to lawyers. He illustrated his points frequently and happily by reference to legal principle. It began with the judges, the lawyers, the physicians, the bankers, and the merchants, and worked its way down to the bottom of society, till nearly everybody had joined one or the other of the churches controlled by the different denominations. I have heard many celebrated pulpit orators in various parts of the world. Taking all in all, I have never heard the superior of Charles G. Finney.[3]

Finney had learned an important lesson about speaking to people when he was a law student. A supreme court judge had advised: "Charlie, you win a legal case by telling it simply; repeated as many times as there are men in the box. Tell it *simply*. And *never read it*! Have it so well in hand that you can look the jury in the eye and see if you are moving them. If you *are not*, you will have to change your tactics so that you will move them."[4]

Charles was colloquial, direct and pungent. In his later days, as a professor of theology and an instructor of young preachers, he would say: "What would be thought of a lawyer who should stand up before a jury and read an essay to them? He would lose his case! I talk to the people as I would have talked to a jury." His illustrations were from real life, not so much from classical literature. They were down to earth and on the level where the people lived out their lives. He broke all the conventions of the preaching style of the day – but he communicated.

Finney was no less a thinker. He wrote in the preface to the *Systematic Theology*: "My brother, sister, friends – reason, study, think . . . you were made to think . . . God designed that religion should require thought; intense thought and should thoroughly develop our powers of thought. The Bible itself is written in the style so condensed as to require much intense study."[5]

A contemporary wrote: "As the preacher . . . he stood at his full height, tall and majestic – stood as if transfixed, gazing and pointing toward the emblazened cloud, as it seemed to roll up before him; his clear, shrill voice rising to its highest pitch, and penetrating every nook and corner of the vast assembly. People held their breath. Every heart stood still. It was almost enough to raise the dead – and there were no sleepers within the sound of his clarion voice."[6] Another admirer said: "Why, it didn't seem like preaching. It seemed as if Mr. Finney had taken me alone, and was conversing with me face to face."[7]

Despite the enthusiasm for Finney's preaching and the overflowing crowds and excitement, dignity was still the order in the Rochester revival. There was no falling in the aisles, or shrieks, or groanings, as was reminiscent of Evans Mills and Gouverneur. The *New York Evangelist* reported that: "From all that can be learned by private letters, and by oral testimony, that almost every town within forty or fifty miles of Rochester is favoured more or less with the special presence of the Lord."[8] Finney himself said, "The great majority of the leading men and women of the city, were converted." Every service was a witness to the power of God.

Unknown to Finney, Mr. Abel Clary was in Rochester. He had been converted during the revival in Adams, New York ten years earlier, as had Charles himself. Clary was licensed to preach, but most of his energy and strength was devoted to prayer. He did very little preaching. Being a quiet man, fading into insignificance as far as the public eye was concerned, he was a man of deep, sacrificial prayer. He was much like Father Nash in prayer, if not in Nash's loud praying style.

One day a friend asked Finney if he knew Clary. Charles said he did. The friend went on, "Well, he is at my house, and has been there for some time, and I don't know what to think of him." Finney remarked he had not seen Clary at any of the meetings. "No," the man replied, "he cannot go to the meetings, he says. He prays nearly all the time, day and night, and in such an agony of mind that I do not know what to make of it. Sometimes he cannot even stand on his knees, but will lie prostrate on the floor, and groan and pray in a manner that quite astonishes me." Finney answered, "I understand it; please keep still. It will all come out right; he will surely prevail."

Father Nash also came to the Rochester campaign to aid Finney in prayer. During those exciting days, Finney also became a fast friend of John J. Shipherd, founder of Oberlin College. He was travelling west with his family and they stopped off in Rochester. Finney tried unsuccessfully to get Shipherd to stay in the city for a short time, and despite Shipherd's urging that Finney go west, he refused to leave such a profound revival. But the paths of these two men were destined to cross in the future.

The father of Augustus Hopkins Strong, the great Baptist theologian, was converted in the Rochester crusade. A. H. Strong himself was converted in a later Finney revival in Rochester. Strong became one of the most influential theologians in evangelical circles and his works still remain in print.

Other notables who joined the host of Finney's admirers as a consequence of the Rochester crusade were Asa Mahan, pastor in Pittsford, Theodore J. Keep and his father John, pastor of the Presbyterian church in Homer, New York, plus a large group of dedicated laymen. All these men were to figure prominently in the Finney ministry as it progressed and developed through the years.

The longer Finney ministered in the city, the more his fame spread. He began to receive calls to preach from every part of the North; Albany, Utica, Syracuse, Potsdam and from as far as the Mississippi. The most insistent request, however, came from New York City. Dr. L. Brown wrote to Charles from the metropolis and said, "Prejudices against you are very much done away here from the revival in Rochester." Joshua Leavitt even expressed the hope that a reconciliation between Nettleton and Finney could now be accomplished. Timothy Dwight at Yale College addressed a letter to Charles relating the events of a great revival at the college and inviting him to come to Yale and preach. That was a great honour.

The Rochester revival, the first of three Finney conducted in that city, began on September 10, 1830, and continued until March 6, 1831. During that period, Finney preached ninety-eight sermons in Rochester alone, not counting many other meetings where he ministered in nearby communities.

All Christian groups benefited from the tremendous campaign. The Baptist church added two hundred and three members during the revival. The Methodists built a new church building seating two thousand – and there were only ten thousand people in the whole of Rochester. Approximately one thousand two hundred converts were added to the Rochester Presbytery with eight hundred joining Rochester churches. In addition, the church members themselves were mightily revived. Many of Finney's messages were directed towards the deepening of believers as well as to reach the unconverted. As one person said of his preaching, "The duties and responsibilities of the Christian life were so portrayed as absolutely to amaze and frighten the cold and backslidden professor."[9]

The *Rochester Democrat* recorded these words: "No real history of Rochester, probably, has ever been written that did not give space to the Finney revival . . . no epic in the city's religious life thus far seems to have quite so deeply impressed the general public."[10] That article was penned in 1926, almost one hundred years after the event itself.

Later, remarking on the Third Great Awakening, the general religious revival sweeping America in which Finney played his part in Rochester, Lyman Beecher said "That was the greatest work of God, and the greatest revival on religion, that the world has even seen in so short a time. One hundred thousand were reported as having connected themselves with churches as the result of that great revival. This is unparalleled in the history of the church, and the progress of religion."[11] Lyman Beecher said that no year during the Christian era had seen an account of so great a revival of religion.

Some of the statistics that came out of that awakening along with the effects of the Second Great Awakening are phenomenal in retrospect. From 1800 to 1830 the Presbyterians increased from 40,000 to 173,329; a four-fold increase. The Baptists during the same three decades increased in like manner from 100,000 to 313,138, a three-fold increase. Others grew similarly. This growth was preceded by serious losses in the American Church. From 1793 to 1795 the Methodists lost eleven thousand six hundred members. But, with the awakening, Church growth mushroomed. The Methodists had a membership of 1,323,361 by 1850. The Baptists, by the middle of the nineteenth century, increased to 815,212, and the Presbyterians to 487,691. At the same time, Bible and tract societies, the Sunday School movement, young peoples' organisations and similar evangelical works grew and multiplied.

The Rochester revival was a microcosm of the general American awakening, and one of God's great hours in Finney's ministry.

With the thrill of that revival surging through their hearts, Charles and Lydia set their faces towards New York City and a new ministry.

# Finney's Travels Terminate:
# The Evangelist's Last Itinerant Days

Charles' roving days were coming to an end. Spring and summer of 1831 saw Finney evangelising in Auburn, Buffalo, Providence and finally Boston. He was physically exhausted, and several physicians expressed the fear that he would never preach again. They were quite certain he had the fatal disease of consumption. Charles was convinced they were absolutely wrong, and determined to carry on.

He set out for Schenectady, New York. Early in the spring of 1831, Dr. Mott, President of Union College, had invited the evangelist to hold student meetings in the college. Travel was very difficult, and after three, trying, tiring days, Charles finally rode into Auburn where he decided to stop and rest.

Before the stage-coach pulled away from the inn the next day, a man appeared with a written appeal to stay and preach. As Charles read the signatures he was quite amazed by the large number of influential, leading men of the city who had signed. Many of the signatures were of those who had fought Finney's first revival effort in Auburn. This touched Charles quite profoundly. He turned away from the stage-coach, went back to his room, and spread the matter out before God. He soon got his answer. The evangelist went to the pastor of the local congregation and said he would stay and preach provided certain conditions be met due to his extreme fatigue. Charles consented to preach twice on Sunday and two nights during the week. This was all he felt physically capable of doing. The rest of the labours must be placed in the hands of others. He further stipulated that he could see no visitors except under extreme circumstances. During the time he was not conducting services, he needed to rest.

The conditions were gladly accepted and the revival was launched. In the evangelist's typical words, "The word took immediate effect." The first Sunday, upon reaching the climax of his sermon, Finney asked those who would renounce their sins and receive Christ to come forward publicly declaring their decision. Giving a public invitation to respond to Christ was by now one of his reasonably regular "new measures". The first among the many who came forward was the very man who had led all the opposition in the previous Auburn revival.

The next Lord's day, Able Clary, one of Finney's prayer warriors, sat in the revival services. The burden of prayer rested heavily upon him. After the service, Charles and Clary went to dinner with Clary's brother, a physician in Auburn. At the dinner table, the physician brother asked Clary to express thanks for the food. As the dear man of God began to pray, he simply broke down. He left the table and went to his room. The spirit of prayer had come mightily upon him; it was obvious that God was about to do a tremendous work.

A powerful revival began to take hold in Auburn. Professor Richards of Auburn Theological Seminary, a man who had supported Nettleton in the New Lebanon Convention, was caught up in the spirit of the meeting and no longer stood in Finney's way.

Finney ministered in the community for six weeks. During that time, approximately five hundred people professed faith in Jesus Christ. Finney said of the revival, "This revival seems to be only a wave of divine power, reaching Auburn from the centre at Rochester, whence such a mighty influence had gone out over the length and breadth of the land." The Rochester movement was still having its impact. Many years later, the historian of the First Presbyterian Church of Auburn gave a graphic account of the tremendous impact of Finney and his work:

> He was then at the prime of life and at the height of his fame. As a preacher . . . he was without a rival. The glance of his full sharp eye and the tones of his commanding voice

were in keeping with the sterner aspects of truth, which he never failed to present with searching discrimination and powerful effect . . . Mr. Finney preached in no other pulpit than this, but the results were by no means limited to this congregation. Many, who ascribe their conversion to his instrumentality, united with other churches in the village and vicinity; and now, after a generation has passed, and with it the prejudice of the time, there can be no question of the service then rendered to the cause of vital religion.[1]

Invitations had been coming to the evangelist from every quarter during the Auburn days. Probably because of this, Finney finally decided not to continue his trip to Union College in Schenectady. He felt strongly moved to accept an invitation to Buffalo. Finney spent approximately one month in that New York community. Although the time there was short, the same revival pattern emerged. A large number were converted, including many influential citizens. Finney's revivals were more and more reaching the so-called upper classes of New Yorkers.

In June, Finney again retreated to his father-in-law's home in Oneida County for rest and recreation and spent most of the summer attempting to regain his strength. In the early autumn of 1831, Charles set his face toward Providence, Rhode Island.

Charles' ministry in Providence was fruitful but continued only a brief three weeks. Finney himself admitted, "My stay was too short to secure so general a work of grace in that place, as occurred afterwards in 1842, when I spent some two months there." While in Providence, Charles cemented a close relationship with Josiah and W. C. Chapan, who were later to figure in Finney's ministry.

In the meantime, the clergymen of Boston were holding conversations as to whether or not Finney should be invited to their city. The New Lebanon Conference was still an issue to some, even four years after the event. As a consequence, a certain Dr. Wisner, pastor of the Old South Church, was dispatched by the brethren to "spy out the land". He visited Finney's services in Providence, and was duly impressed. Finney immediately received an invitation to minister in Massachusetts' greatest city. Wisner's report to the body of Boston's clergy, that bastion of Presbyterian and Congregational orthodoxy and propriety, had tilted the scale in Charles' favour.

Finney began his labours by preaching in various churches on Sundays. Each week night he preached in the Park Street Church where Edward Beecher, Lyman's son, was the pastor. With this arrangement, the work got under way. The believers of Boston were spiritually rather cold. They showed little concern for prayer, no deep burden for the unconverted and little interest in a revival. Finney, when he saw the real situation, changed his tactical approach and began preaching some very probing, penetrating sermons.

To Finney's surprise, however, the congregation began to dwindle away. Each night witnessed fewer and fewer people in attendance. This was a new experience for the evangelist. He had never seen Christians "shrink back", as he put it. The believers kept saying, "What will the Unitarians say, if such things are true of us who are Orthodox? If Mr. Finney preaches to us in this way, the Unitarians will triumph over us, and say, that at least the Orthodox are not better Christians than Unitarians." They resented Finney's frank dealing with them, and were so obsessed with their warfare over Unitarianism that they had little time for their own spiritual development. They just did not have the Christian maturity to take Charles' pointed preaching. So they resisted.

God soon overcame their subtle rebellion, however. Before long the Holy Spirit moved in power on the congregation and the atmosphere was radically changed. The Christians not only started listening to searching sermons, they came to appreciate them.

Lyman Beecher, now generally reconciled to Finney, thrust himself into the work with enthusiasm. He was a genuine man of God and a preacher of outstanding ability. Inquiry meetings were held in the church basement of Lyman Beecher's church. Beecher gave himself to those meetings, yet when it came to dealing with inquirers, he managed less well. Finney was conscious of this, but most gracious. When he had to take the meetings out of Beecher's hands, he did it in such a gentlemanly and gracious manner that Beecher was never embarrassed nor was the impression left that the great pastor was not conducting the meeting with propriety and skill.

Beecher had no serious theological problems with the evangelist at any stage in their ministries. The only doctrinal issue that he raised with Finney centred on the influence of the Holy Spirit in regeneration. The question was: is the influence of the Holy Spirit a "moral" influence or a "physical" impression? Although there was some disagreement over the point, in Finney's own words, "In any of the discussions that we had at that time, nothing grieved the Spirit or produced any unkind feelings among the brethren . . ."

While in Boston, Finney received some interesting correspondence from his brother, George Finney. He warned Charles to stay humble in the light of all of his fame. Father Nash also cautioned him of the danger of losing his spirituality if he used written notes in his preaching. But their fears were groundless. Finney always remained a devout, humble man of God.

A short time after Father Nash gave Finney his word of caution, God called the great intercessor to his reward. Finney felt he had lost a true father in the faith.

At this point, Theodore Weld and several other leading ministers began begging Charles to go to the West. No doubt, it was a spiritual "land of opportunity". Did God want His servant on the western frontier with its ruggedness as well as its challenge? Finney had now been involved in itinerant revival work for almost ten years. He was *seriously* fatigued. Not only that, the Finney family had grown: there were now three children. This made it impossible for Lydia to travel with her husband.

At the same time, the pastors of the free churches in New York City were urging Finney to come there on a more permanent basis. The Tappan brothers, devoted and influential Christian businessmen, were also involved in the invitation. New York City had its own powerful appeal. As one of Finney's friends, a Mr. O. Smith, reminded him, "This city exerts a most powerful influence upon the whole United States: *and upon Europe.* It is the same to this country, that Paris is to France. All the revolutions in that country you know are 'effected in Paris'. What they do there is imitated all over the kingdom."[2]

After much prayer, Finney made his move. It was to New York. He accepted a call from the Second Free Church to work as their pastor-evangelist. The change was timely. As one person described Finney after ten laborious, self-denying years; he was virtually "burnt to a cinder". In the pastoral role, he could regain his strength and also make a vital impression on the most influential city in America.

Finney, of course, would always be an evangelist, even while undertaking pastoral responsibilities. His full-time itinerant days were over, but evangelism must never end. Thus Finney left Boston in April of 1832 to become pastor of the Second Free Presbyterian Church at Chatham Street.

The whole free church movement had its birth in Finney's previous New York ministry of 1829–30. When Finney left New York for his great Rochester meeting, he left a thriving congregation. They called Joel Parker as pastor. That became the first free Presbyterian church in New York, the term "free" denoting the fact that the pews were rent-free. Anyone could come and sit where he or she wished, free. Up to that time, pew rentals were the way most established churches in the East financed many of their activities. For example, the sale of eighty-five pew rentals in Lyman Beecher's Boston church covered two-thirds of the expenses of the building.

There were obvious problems with the pew-rental system. In the first place, the wealthiest members of the congregation got the best seats in the house. Not only that, they tended to dominate the entire financial structure of the church's life. Furthermore, many felt that the practice flew in the face of a "free" gospel of grace. Worse, there were poor people who could hardly even find a place of worship. The feelings ran so strong against this practice in some quarters that a Baptist wrote, "splendidly carpeted aisles, pews to match, cushioned and completed; with brass spittoons, brass nameplates on the doors may be compared to the devil's turnpikes in the aisles, and his coal gates in the labelled pew doors. Let not the pew-seyites call this a rude or harsh comparison . . . God's temple should have inscribed on their portals, 'Open to all, closed to none' . . . Two or three hundred dollars paid for a spot in the church to sit in! Oh! This is money-changing."[3]

The free church movement was obviously a revolt against exploitation and discrimination. The movement caught on and spread rapidly. As free churches multiplied, Finney sent in pastors from central New York State to further the work. As could be expected, some of the "old school" Presbyterians took a negative view of the new approach; all new methods of any sort seemed to upset them. Some even invited Finney to leave the Presbyterian fold if he could not accept their views and methodologies.

By 1840, there were eleven free churches in New York. Lewis and Arthur Tappan, who had grown very close to Finney, were tremendously helpful in the new development. Strangely, however, after 1840 the movement began to decline, largely because it became so identified with the abolitionist movement – at least this is what Lewis Tappan felt.

As the Scriptures state, "we are changed from one degree of glory to another". This was certainly true of Charles' ministry. Though his days as a travelling evangelist had come to a close, there lay before him vast fields of ministry that were white unto harvest in New York. The way he rose to the challenge is indeed a token of the degree of God's glory on the man.

# Finney's Powerful Pastorate:
## The Evangelist's New York Ministry

"Having had no training for the ministry, I did not expect or desire to labour in large towns and cities, or minister to cultivated communities. I intended to go to the new settlements, and preach in schoolhouses and barns and groves, as best I could." So spoke Charles Grandison Finney. Nothing could be further from the realities he faced.

In old Chatham Street in New York City was an empty theatre. Lewis Tappan, along with a group of concerned Christian laymen, leased the site, renovated the building, and shaped it into a structure fit for the worship of God. The Second Free Presbyterian Church was born.

After a short time, "the Spirit of the Lord was immediately poured out upon us and we had an extensive revival that spring and summer." That is how Charles characteristically described his early days as a new pastor of a new church. At the very first service two thousand people arrived – a sizeable congregation for even a large metropolitan area.

The first year of Charles' pastoral ministry was spent in a very turbulent time. About midsummer, just three or four months after the evangelist moved his family to New York, a devastating cholera epidemic broke out. People fled from the area as if escaping from a sweeping prairie fire. The plague was the most severe in the city's history. The section around Chatham Street was especially affected. Finney records that one morning as he looked out of his bedroom window, he saw five hearses pulled up at different houses to collect the dead.

The new pastor, with genuine pastoral concern, stayed

with his people throughout the epidemic. He laboured with the suffering and dying in a sacrificial manner. He gave of himself to the extent that soon his own strength was seriously depleted. After travelling into the country for two or three weeks of rest, he returned to the city for the formal installation service as pastor of the Second Free Presbyterian Church.

The installation service was a happy and blessed time, but right in the middle of it, Charles began to feel very ill. After the benediction, he went home, got in to bed, called a doctor and steeled himself for the diagnosis. Cholera. His next door neighbour came down with the disease the very same day; in the morning the neighbour was dead.

Finney was given drastic treatment. It became clear that Charles would not preach for a long time – and he had just been installed in his first church. But he must convalesce. Help was sought, and during the time of the pastor's recovery, Jacob Heffenstein stepped in to occupy the Chatham Street pulpit. In November 1832, Heffenstein was officially installed as the associate pastor to serve with Finney.

Records are scanty of the long convalescent months. No doubt it was a terribly trying time for Charles. Towards the spring of 1833, almost a year after coming to New York, Finney was finally able to begin preaching again. He immediately invited two fellow preachers to come and serve with him in a series of revival meetings. Finney's revival blood must have heated to fever pitch during the many days of confinement. The two revivalists preached in turn for some two or three weeks. It did not work: in Charles' own words, "very little was accomplished".

Finney learned that New York was different and such a method was "not the way to promote a revival there". Charles thus drew the series of meetings to a rapid close. There is something quite revealing about the affair. First, Finney was honest and objective enough to admit a mistake and not attempt to defend the indefensible. When his plans went awry, he would quickly abandon them. Moreover, as observed before, Charles was constantly looking for "measures" that were effective. His fertile, inquisitive mind and spirit were always on the lookout for different ways of accomplishing the salvation of people. Finally, and perhaps of prime importance, it demonstrated his commitment to the principle of human instrumentality in revivals. God does not scatter revivals in a capricious manner: Christians must do their part, and that with dedication and plain common sense.

With this basic revivalistic philosophy before him, the following Sunday Finney began a programme of nightly preaching. Almost instantaneously a powerful revival commenced. He preached for twenty evenings in succession. His health was still quite precarious, but in those twenty days over five hundred conversions were recorded.

If Finney's friends were wary of his first venture into New York City, they were probably even more concerned now that he was there permanently. His friend, E. N. Clark, felt that Finney would be drawn into abstract theological sophistication. Clark warned him, "I fear that the peculiar circumstances in which you have been placed have led you rather to a discussion . . . of abstract theological subjects than to those soul stirring appeals to the heart and conscience by which you once brought so many sinners to the feet of Jesus."[1]

Finney's friends could have laid aside their fears, for Charles' evangelistic impact on the city was tremendous. The Second Free Presbyterian Church grew in a matter of months to the extent that a "colony", as Finney expressed it, was sent off to form another Free Presbyterian Church. This new congregation constructed a building on the corner of Madison and Catherine Street and it grew swiftly. Further, the mother of Arthur Tappan Pierson, who later became one of America's great missionary leaders, was profoundly influenced by the Finney ministry. Charles also grew in popularity with the young people of the city. As they struggled to gain confidence in their faith, he helped them tremendously with his reasoned sermons.

It may be true that Finney's preaching style changed as he addressed the more sophisticated New Yorkers. He was always adept at getting on to the cultural level of the people to whom he ministered. This was another facet of the flexibility and evangelistic genius of the man.

The work went forward in a fascinating fashion. His

ministry methods were essentially the same. Recognising the basic centrality of a praying, witnessing, committed people, he relied heavily upon lay involvement. And the people in the Chatham Street Church were a working, praying, united people. Moreover, they were well trained in evangelistic skills. Finney saw to that. They could be found constantly "in the highways and hedges" of New York City. Men and women alike would fan out with printed invitations, contact friends and acquaintances, and "compel them to come in". Finney regularly preached to a full house. Even the ladies were fearless. They would go to any neighbourhood and urge people to come to the services. Old New York was beginning to feel the grip of revival.

The theatre building in Chatham Street was itself a positive attraction. To attend worship in a theatre rather than an old, grey stone, cheerless building was novel. The Tappans had renovated it to make it adaptable to evangelism. The front section of the building contained rooms ideally suited for prayer meetings, lectures and conferences. The sanctuary had three galleries, all connecting to smaller rooms. As Finney expressed it, the arrangement was "exceedingly convenient". The church members would scatter themselves throughout the congregation during the evangelistic services. When they observed someone clearly moved by the Holy Spirit, they would approach him after the preaching and engage him in conversation concerning his relationship to Jesus Christ. Many were led to life and salvation in this way.

Lewis Tappan was particularly helpful in this manner of witnessing. For example, a leading executive of the New York branch of the well-known Naylor and Company, cutlery manufacturers of Sheffield, England, attended the services one evening. He had been urged to come by a Christian clerk in his office. As God's providence would have it, he sat opposite Lewis Tappan. As the Gospel was preached by the pastor, the executive became deeply disturbed. He was obviously under conviction. Tappan immediately sensed the situation, and after the service he introduced himself. Of course, every New York businessman knew the Tappan firm very well. Lewis actually took

gentle hold of the button of the businessman's coat and
began to tell him of Jesus. The executive tried to excuse
himself, but Tappan was so kind and gracious he could not
very well get away. Soon the Spirit broke through upon the
man and he was marvellously converted. Afterwards he
said of Lewis Tappan, "He held fast to my button, so that
an ounce weight at my button was the means of saving my
soul."

The Second Free Presbyterian Church was constantly
growing with a host of new converts. Much time and
counsel was given to each individual inquirer. The pastor-
evangelist saw every person as a precious life for whom
Christ died and hence worthy of all the help available to
effect spiritual conversion.

As the church in Chatham Street grew to a certain
number, a new "colony" would be sent off. By the time
Finney left New York some two or three years later, seven
Free Presbyterian Churches had been born from the
mother congregation. Moreover, every new congregation
became soul-seeking bodies of Christ. The churches were
not made up of New York's wealthy. For the better part,
the members were average middle- and low-middle income
New Yorkers. They were a gracious, generous people.
Though their incomes were not high, they supported their
churches well and "great grace was upon them all" (Acts
4:33). As Finney expressed it: "A more harmonious,
prayerful, and efficient people I never knew; than the
members of these free churches."

At the height of Finney's New York ministry, an issue
arose that had a far-reaching effect. A man sought
membership in the Chatham Street Church from an old,
established Presbyterian congregation. His credentials
were sent for from his former church. He was recom-
mended as a member of good standing. It soon came to
light, however, that the man had committed an offence in
his old church that demanded discipline. Something had to
be done. Finney was convinced that the man's previous
church should administer the discipline.

The question was brought before the Third Presbytery of
New York to which Finney belonged. The presbytery
decided that the Chatham Street Church should carry out

the discipline since the offender was now a member there. Finney disagreed, but in the name of co-operation, the man was disciplined.

It was not long before another similar case arose in the Second Church. This time a woman came into the church with the same sort of circumstances. So in accordance with the previous ruling of the presbytery, the Chatham Street Church excommunicated her. She appealed to the presbytery and they did a complete turn-around. They chided Chatham Street for their action on the grounds that she had not committed the offence there.

Finney "expostulated" with them. He wanted to know how his church was to act when the presbytery was so vacillating. A presbyter, Dr. Cox, replied that they would not be governed by their own precedence, or by any other precedence for that matter. He spoke with such heat and vehemence that he carried the entire presbytery with him.

Wedges were being driven deeper between Finney and his Presbyterian connections. First, the theological controversy with the "old school" kept brewing. Then the "new measures" issue boiled over. And now this! Circumstances were conspiring for the Presbyterians to lose the greatest evangelist they had ever produced.

Soon after the discipline debate erupted, a group of Christian laymen, led by the Tappan brothers, struck upon the idea of erecting a large new church building on Broadway. The people wanted two things for their new church. First, they wanted a Congregational church. That they could accomplish with little difficulty: there were many Congregational ministers about. Secondly, however, they wanted Charles Finney as their pastor. That was different, because he was Presbyterian and had been so all of his Christian life and ministry. Would he leave and sever those long ties? In his autobiography, he says nothing of the decision that must have caused him some sorrow. He simply says, "I then took my dismission from the Presbytery, and became pastor of that congregational church."

The Broadway Church was to become Finney's greatest New York platform. But before looking into this phase of the evangelist's ministry, we must go back a year or two. A situation which was tremendously significant surfaced during Charles' convalescence from his serious illness. In 1834, while Finney was still recuperating from cholera, the doctor decided that an ocean voyage to the Mediterranean might be helpful in restoring the evangelist's strength. So, in the winter of 1834, he left on a small brig going east across the stormy Atlantic, leaving his family and friends on the pier.

The Atlantic is always turbulent, and in January it is almost unbearable on a small ship. The little brig bobbed like a cork. Charles' cabin was small and the entire voyage was unbelievably uncomfortable. To add to the misery, the captain of the ship was an alcoholic. On one occasion during a storm, with the captain completely out of action, the command of the ship actually fell to Finney. That was when his experience of sailing on Lake Ontario in his earlier years stood him in good stead. He put his skill to use that well may have saved his life and that of his fellow travellers.

Finney spent some weeks on the island of Malta and in Sicily. Yet, the voyage did little to restore his health. He sailed for home as exhausted as when he had left.

Finney had a deep experience of God on the voyage home. He met God in a new, fresh way. It is so personal he must be allowed to tell the story himself. In the *Memoirs* he wrote:

> On my homeward passage my mind became exceedingly exercised on the question of revivals. I feared that they would decline throughout the country. I feared that the opposition that had been made to them, had grieved the Holy Spirit. My own health, it appeared to me, had nearly or quite broken down; and I knew of no other evangelist that would take the field, and aid pastors in revival work. This view of the subject distressed me so much that one day I found myself unable to rest. My soul was in an utter agony. I spent almost the entire day in prayer in my stateroom, or walking the deck in such agony as to wring my hands and almost to gnaw my tongue, as it were, in view of the state of things. In fact I felt crushed with the burden that was on my soul. There was no one on board to whom I could open my mind, or say a word.
>
> It was the spirit of prayer that was upon me; that which I

had often experienced in kind, but perhaps never before to such a degree, for so long a time. I besought the Lord to go on with his work, and to provide himself with such instrumentalities as were necessary. It was a long summer day, in the early part of July. After a day of unspeakable wrestling and agony in my soul, just at night, the subject cleared up to my mind. The Spirit led me to believe that all would come out right, and that God had yet a work for me to do; that I might be at rest; that the Lord would go forward with his work; and give me strength to take any part in it that he desired. But I had not the least idea what the course of his providence would be.

While Charles was still at sea, the members of the Chatham Street Church, together with a group of abolitionists, held a liberation rally on July 4th, America's Independence Day. The meeting at the church stirred up serious reaction. Anti-abolitionists thought it was an anti-slavery rally. American vehemence vented against the abolitionist was not restricted to the "Old South". The entire issue had grown out of proportion. Rumours started that the new church building on Broadway was going to be a centre of abolitionist sentiment. While the building was still under construction, someone set fire to it. Feelings were so vehement that when the building was ignited, the local fire brigade refused to put it out. The whole interior and roof of the partially completed building were consumed, leaving only the walls standing.

When Finney returned to the city from his voyage, his friend the Rev. Joshua Leavitt met him. Leavitt was the editor of the *New York Evangelist*, which had grown up in the heat of the "new measures" battle with Nettleton. The *Observer*, a popular religious periodical, had taken its stand with Nettleton. The *Observer*'s editors were so biased towards Nettleton that they even refused to publish anything on Finney's side of the case. So some of Finney's friends and supporters, known as the "Holy Band", got together and developed a new revivalistic periodical to redress the balance. It became known as the *New York Evangelist*. Finney himself helped to produce the initial issue. A Mr. Saxton was chosen as the first editor. He had been a close friend and former labourer with Nettleton, until Nettleton levelled his guns on Finney's Western Revivals. Saxton was a capable young man, but his editorship was short-lived. Two or three other editors followed in rapid succession. Finally, the Rev. Joshua Leavitt accepted the editorial chair. He was a most able leader, despite some errors in judgment.

When Finney returned to New York from his rather tiring trip, anti-abolitionist fever was at its peak. Leavitt had entered the fray during Finney's absence. He was a fervent abolitionist and had written with a fiery pen. Finney had cautioned him about this. Keep evangelism first in the *New York Evangelist*, Finney urged, regardless of the importance of social issues. Charles was simply trying to maintain the correct balance between evangelism and social action. When Leavitt met Charles, he burst out emotionally, "Brother Finney, I have ruined the *Evangelist*. I have not been as prudent as you cautioned me to be, and I have gone so far ahead of public intelligence and feeling on the subject [of abolition], that my subscription list is rapidly failing; and we shall not be able to continue its publication beyond the first of January, unless you can do something to bring the paper back to public favour again." Finney told the distraught editor that his health was such that he did not know what he could do.

Leavitt said if Finney would write a series of articles on revivals, he had little doubt that that would immediately restore the paper to public favour. After pondering this for a day or two, Charles suggested he would preach a course of revival lectures to his church, which would then be published in the paper. The editor was delighted: "That is the very thing [to do]." In the next issue of the *New York Evangelist*, Leavitt advertised the forthcoming course of lectures and the subscriptions immediately increased. He told Charles, "I have as many new subscribers every day, as would fill my arms with papers."

Finney delivered one lecture a week on revival throughout the winter of 1834–5. Leavitt would take down the gist of Charles' message in longhand, since he knew no shorthand, and the next day would fill in the sketchy notes as he recalled the sermon. Finney did nothing to edit or develop the articles. They went to press directly from Leavitt's pen.

The verbal lectures usually lasted approximately one and a half hours. The messages as Leavitt recorded them can be read in about one-third of that time. The *New York Evangelist* omitted much, yet these lectures have become timeless in their appeal.

The interest in Finney's revival lectures was tremendous. Every Friday night the building was crowded with eager listeners. Not only did it save the *New York Evangelist*, it was soon published in book form under the title *Lectures on Revivals of Religion*. A revivalistic classic was born. Twelve thousand copies were sold immediately. As fast as the press could produce new editions, they were snatched up. The *Lectures* were translated into French, German and Welsh. England absorbed them by the tens of thousands, and so did the entire English-speaking world.

The most significant impact of the *Lectures* were the revivals that the book spawned. In Merioneth, Wales, revival broke out in 1840. The book was instrumental in causing great numbers of conversions in England and Scotland, and many young men were also called to the ministry. Spiritual awakenings occurred all over America as the volume gripped the hearts of people.

Finney's spiritual victory while at sea was being gloriously achieved, as he remarked:

> This was not of man's wisdom. Let the reader remember that long day of agony and prayer at sea, that God would do something to forward the work of revivals, and enable me, if he desired to do it, to take such a course as to help forward the work. I felt certain then that my prayers would be answered; and I have regarded all that I have since been able to accomplish, as in a very important sense, an answer to the prayers of that day. The spirit of prayer came upon me as a sovereign grace, bestowed upon me without the least merit, and in spite of all my sinfulness. He pressed my soul in prayer, until I was enabled to prevail; and through the infinite riches of grace in Christ Jesus, I have been many years witnessing the wonderful results of that day of wrestling with God. In answer to that day's agony, he has continued to give me the spirit of prayer.

Even though the fire had gutted the partially complete

Broadway building, construction carried on. The building was of Finney's own design. The architect, a certain Mr. Archi Tack, objected to the pastor's plan, because he feared the final product would not be artistically attractive and his reputation as a church architect would be injured. In his forthright and forceful manner, Finney told the architect that if he would not build it as planned, he would get someone who would. The building was soon finished according to Finney's plan. In Charles' evaluation, "It was a most commodious and comfortable place to speak in."

Before Finney entered the new Broadway Tabernacle, several young men approached him asking if he would tutor them as students in theology. Finney graciously refused, feeling that there was too much work to be done in his church. Nonetheless, a seed was sown in the heart of the evangelist.

The students persisted, and applications mounted for a series of theological lectures. Finney finally decided to deliver a series of messages on the basic theological concepts of the Christian faith and students could come as they desired. A room had been drawn into the design of the new Broadway Tabernacle for the purpose of lecturing.

In the meantime, out West a rebellion at Lane Seminary in Cincinnati, Ohio, had erupted. The student body were fervent abolitionists and the trustees of the seminary attempted to curb their actions. The students rebelled and the Lane Seminary revolt took place after Lyman Beecher went to serve as president of the institution. Beecher not only served the seminary in Ohio, he also ministered as pastor of the Second Presbyterian Church of Cincinnati.

Beecher said, "I have thought seriously of going over to Cincinnati to spend the remnant of my days . . . and in consecrating all my children to God in that region, who are willing to go. If we gain the West, all is saved; if we lose, all is lost."[2]

Lyman Beecher was back in the East in 1833 when the trustee executive committee took the action that sparked the Lane rebellion. When he returned to the seminary campus, he issued a statement with other members of the faculty affirming that the trustees were right in their decision. No doubt Beecher agreed with the trustees' action, believing this would defuse the issue, but the students left the seminary in large numbers. The rebellion left the ranks of the seminary seriously depleted. Many outsiders were very happy, however, as they were glad to be rid of the abolitional "radicals". An editorial in the *Cincinnati Journal* stated:

> Parents and guardians may now send their sons and wards to Lane Seminary with a perfect confidence, that the proper business of the theological school will occupy their minds; and that the discussion and decisions of abstract questions, will not turn them aside from the path of duty . . . there may be room enough in the wide world, for abolitionism and perfectionism and many other isms; but a school to prepare pious youth for preaching the Gospel, has no legitimate place for these.[3]

The rebels established themselves as a group at Cummensville, a short distance from Cincinnati, and began to publish their grievances.

Meanwhile, John J. Shipherd and Philo P. Stewart had founded a small school in northern Ohio called Oberlin Collegiate Institute. In February 1834, the charter for the new institution was granted. The school had actually opened its doors a few weeks earlier on December 3, 1833. The rebellious Lane students began to cast their eyes towards Oberlin.

The institute was located some thirty-three miles west of Cleveland on a lovely five-hundred-acre plot donated by some friends in New Haven, Connecticut. Situated in the township of Russia, Loraine County, it boasted a beautiful span of timber. The institution was named after John Frederick Oberlin, the distinguished French pastor of Alsace in the Vosges Mountains. His fame as a Christian philanthropist was just beginning to reach America's shores.

As Finney was about to inaugurate his lecture series on theology, Arthur Tappan put forward a startling proposal: he challenged Charles to go somewhere in Ohio, put down roots, and give his lectures to the young rebels from Lane. Tappan promised he would financially support the venture.

He felt strongly the need to evangelise the West, and these young men were the very ones to do it. And Finney was the man, under God, to prepare them.

Charles did not see how he could leave New York. He was sensitive to the needy situation in Ohio, but he had only been in the city a short time.

In January 1835, while Charles was debating the challenge, the Rev. John J. Shipherd and the Rev. Asa Mahan of Cincinnati came to New York. Finney knew these men well and deeply appreciated their friendship and their dedication to the cause of revivals. The two men had travelled east to ask Theodore Weld, at that time on a lecture and preaching tour for the abolition movement, to be Oberlin's professor of theology. It was said of the young man in those days: "He is as eloquent as an angel, and as powerful as thunder."[4] Weld declined the offer and told Shipherd and Mahan that Charles Finney was the only man for the post.

Mahan had been one of the trustees at Lane Seminary and had resisted the prohibition of free discussion on the abolition issue. Shipherd had obtained a charter broad enough to develop Oberlin into a full university, and was attempting to attract the Lane rebels to his new theological institution. They joined forces to challenge Finney to come to Oberlin. By this time, the new institute had attracted about one hundred pupils. The Lane rebels were also interested in coming to Oberlin, but *only* if Charles Finney could be persuaded to be their professor of theology.

Finally, after much prayer, it was decided that Charles could divide his time and efforts between the Broadway Tabernacle and Oberlin Institute. The plan was that he would stay in New York for six months in the winter and serve as pastor of the Broadway Tabernacle. Then in the spring he would move to Oberlin and teach the young ministers at the college during the six months spanning spring, summer and autumn. This would also release the students to teach school during the winter. Thus the decision was made.

When the Oberlin trustees heard the proposal, they met to vote. There was no problem for them; they felt that they had a great attraction in securing Charles G. Finney as their professor of theology. They unanimously accepted the proposal. Charles did make some stipulations. First, he refused to fill the professorial post unless the trustees agreed that they would never enter into the internal regulations of the institution. He did not want an Oberlin rebellion akin to the Lane revolt. Finney's conviction was that the faculty could make far more knowledgeable and meaningful decisions concerning student activities than the trustees. Further, Charles insisted that no one would be denied admission to Oberlin Collegiate Institute on the basis of race or sex. Black students were to be admitted on the same condition as white, women as well as men. This caused a problem for some of the trustees, but Finney, Shipherd, Mahan and others took a firm stand and the conditions were met.

The institute became the first co-educational college in the history of American higher education. It was one of the first institutions which accepted people regardless of race or colour, and, in fact, became perhaps the most avant-garde college of its day.

What about money? The mundane matter of funding had to be faced. The New York brethren were called together and in a matter of one or two hours the entire needs of the operational and developmental cost of the college were supplied – largely by the resources and influence of the Tappans, especially Arthur. Finney said, "Arthur Tappan's heart was as large as all New York, and I might say, as large as the world. When I laid the case thus before him, he said, 'Brother Finney, my own income averages about $100,000 a year. Now if you will go to Oberlin, take hold of that work, and go on, and see that the buildings are put up, and a library and everything provided, I will pledge you my entire income, except what I need to provide for my family, until you are beyond pecuniary want.' Having perfect confidence in Brother Tappan I said, 'That will do.'"

This arrangement was made in private with Finney. Tappan conditioned his promise on the agreement that funds would be sought from others as far as possible. Tappan also insisted that black students should be fully accepted, yet not to go overboard on abolition. He was trying to save Oberlin from the errors of Lane Seminary.

Finney prepared to move his family from New York City. He loved the people at the church and was loth to leave them even for the months when he would be away in Ohio. There were a number of factors in his reluctance to leave: New York was a great place to evangelise and it seemed he was perhaps giving up something of his evangelistic ministry for teaching. This caused apprehension, even though he was to teach future evangelists. Nevertheless, he was certain that God was in the matter, so in the early summer of 1835, he set his face west. Little did he realise this would be the last move of his ministry.

Charles spent his first academic period in Oberlin before the new Broadway Tabernacle building was fully completed. He went back to New York in the winter of 1835–6, accompanied by Asa Mahan who became his assistant pastor. The dual arrangement of professor and pastor proved quite successful for a time. But as the responsibilities grew, it became evident to Finney that he would have to give up either Oberlin or the Broadway Tabernacle. So in April 1837, he resigned as pastor of the New York church. The congregation wrote the following note of esteem:

> We gratefully acknowledge the goodness of God in so greatly blessing the labours of our pastor among us – while we bow with humble resignation with that Divine Providence which has brought us to the painful necessity of separation.[5]

Finney never really got the Broadway Tabernacle out of his heart. He said, "I felt great difficulty in giving up that admirable place for preaching the Gospel." It seemed as if he left a part of himself in New York. His impact on the sophisticated city had been profound. It demonstrated that the frontier preacher had matured to the point where he could reach the upper stratum of society. Yet he never lost any of his evangelistic zeal, as some friends feared he would. Though he changed his preaching style, he did not change his message.

The pastorate also made Charles alive to the need of doing something to establish the converts. It was while he was still in New York, that he gave his famous *Lectures to Professing Christians*, later published as a most influential book. The general lack of spiritual growth and maturity on the part of his new converts not only moved him to give those lectures, it also motivated him to develop his "perfectionism".

Now in theological education full-time, Finney was training men to do what he had so ably done: be an evangelist for God.

# PART III

# CHARLES GRANDISON FINNEY: AN EDUCATOR FOR CHRIST

# Finney's Lecturing for the Lord:
## The Evangelist's Early Oberlin Ministry

A banner fluttered in the brisk western breeze over a large three-thousand-seat tent in the college square in Oberlin, blazoning the words, HOLINESS TO THE LORD. Charles Finney's "Holy Band" had presented the evangelist-pastor, now theological educator, with a large, one-hundred-foot-diameter canvas shelter in which he could hold revival services. Bountiful blessings and countless conversions were granted by God's grace in that marquee. Soon the Oberlin Congregational Church was organised with Charles as pastor, a post he held until late in life.

When Finney first walked on Oberlin's campus in June 1835, few buildings had been erected. But Finney had his friends. Arthur Tappan had already pledged large sums of money. Others rose to help support the new educational venture. Construction could commence on the essential facilities.

Asa Mahan, trustee of Lane Seminary before the revolt, became Oberlin's first president, occupying that key role for fifteen years. Finney said Mahan had the best mind in western New York. He was an enthusiastic, optimistic man. An excellent preacher and a keen student of philosophy, he was dedicated to the Oberlin cause.

John Morgan, another renegade from Lane Seminary, was installed as professor of New Testament language and literature. He had served on the faculty at Lane and had sided with the students. He possessed a remarkable gift for languages and was an erudite scholar. In temperament he was the antithesis of Finney. Nevertheless, they were close friends, complementing one another beautifully. He constantly worked with Charles in Oberlin's revival services under the banner, HOLINESS TO THE LORD. Finney seemed almost lost if Morgan did not have some part in the services, not only during revival times but in the regular services of the Oberlin Congregational Church as well.

Another asset for the college was Henry Cowles, professor of Greek and Latin. His wife, Alice Welch Cowles, served as principal of the Oberlin Female Department, and was a significant figure in the moral reform movements of the day.

Academic disciplines other than religion enhanced Oberlin's curriculum. James Dascomb was professor of chemistry, botany and philosophy. A graduate of Dartmouth College Medical School, he taught scientific studies for forty-five years.

James H. Fairchild, an early graduate of Oberlin, became professor of languages and later of mathematics and natural philosophy. In 1858, he succeeded Finney in the chair of theology and in 1866 he followed his mentor as president of Oberlin.

Fervent abolitionist, James C. Birney, was elected professor of law and oratory, yet he never actually took up the post. Jonathan Blanchard, a committed Christian abolitionist, applied for a post at Oberlin. He was turned down. He moved to the presidency of Knox College and later became the prominent and loved president of Wheaton College. Blanchard grew into a significant figure in nineteenth-century evangelical circles.

The institution was structured on two academic levels: the liberal arts college and the theological seminary. Religion was the overriding theme in all areas of study. Symbolic of the spirit of Oberlin was what Finney said to the graduating class of 1851: "You are not only educated, but educated in God's college – a college reared under God, and for God, by the faith, the prayers, the toils and the sacrifices of God's people. You cannot but know that it has been the sole purpose of the founders and patrons of this college to educate you *men and women for God and for God's cause*."[1] Upon these foundations Oberlin began to grow and find its niche in American religious and educational life.

Advance was the theme for Oberlin, orchestrated by Finney and Mahan. In the first days, the facilities were quite meagre. The Finneys shared a house with the Mahans. The students all lived in a rugged one-storey, one-hundred-and-forty-four-foot long and twenty-foot wide dormitory. Its sides, partitions, ceilings and floors were of beech boards freshly cut from the nearby mill. One end of the hall was fitted out as a kitchen and dining-room. The remainder of the dormitory was divided into small rooms twelve feet square with a single window. A door opened out upon the forest. Two students were assigned to each room, but by the time the Rev. George W. Gale (on his way west to form Knox College) visited the new campus, he was much impressed. Tappan Hall had been completed, as were two brick homes, each two storeys high, one for Finney and one for President Mahan.

Manual labour was a part of Oberlin days. Many students had no financial resources for college training. Working on the school farm and buildings provided the funds they needed. Not only that, J. S. Shipherd said students should work so that they might "have health and muscle, with a disposition to 'endure hardness, as a good soldier of Jesus Christ'" (II Tim. 2:3). George Gale's Oneida Institute in western New York served as the model for this arrangement. The scheme actually kept the College afloat. Few students could have graduated without it. A severe monetary crisis overtook Oberlin in its early days. The building projects were barely under way when the Tappan fortune was literally devastated. Arthur Tappan saw all of his business properties reduced to ashes through a tragic fire. He was just recovering from that loss, when a financial crisis struck America's entire economic life. This wiped out Tappan and compelled him to declare bankruptcy. So serious was the crisis for Oberlin that Finney said, "To human view, it would seem that the college must be a failure." Had it not been for the student work programme, Finney's words would probably have been realised.

As the college struggled on, Charles may have had one or two second thoughts concerning his Oberlin move. For example, he had left a secure, successful pastorate. Moreover, when he and his family were on their way to

Oberlin from New York City, a tempting offer had come their way: the trustees of Western Reserve College at Hudson, Ohio, appointed him as professor of pastoral theology.

Charles had not turned down the offer, even though he was on his way to Oberlin. He was holding his final decision in reserve until he actually arrived in Ohio. The trustees at Western Reserve dispatched a committee to intercept the Finneys in Cleveland. Charles and his family were sailing into the Ohio city across Lake Erie. Out on the lake, a wind blew up and delayed the boat by several hours. The Western Reserve Committee finally grew tired of waiting and returned home. The negotiations thus fell to the ground.

The entire matter was surely in the hands of God, however. Charles discovered the trustees of Western Reserve were really attempting to secure his services only to silence him. They reasoned that there was enough "old school" thought at Western Reserve to overwhelm Finney and his "new school" ideas. Moreover, Western Reserve wanted Oberlin out of business. They must have felt that if Finney refused the Oberlin appointment, the institute would die and "new school" thought and "new measures" methods with it.

Finney found a letter waiting for him in Cleveland. His friend Arthur Tappan wrote apprising him of this unsavoury situation. It seemed almost inconceivable to Charles: he just could not believe the leaders at Western would resort to such tactics. Yet after he thoroughly investigated the affair, he was satisfied that Tappan was right. The whole affair spurred Finney to rise to the challenge at Oberlin with zeal.

While all this was going on, Finney's *Lectures on Revivals of Religion* had already arrived on British soil, and rich blessing had followed. Finney knew the British Christian public would be sympathetic to Oberlin's concern for abolition, co-educational college life and social reform. Therefore, John Keep and William Dawes were dispatched to Britain to raise funds. The college was thirty thousand dollars in debt and had no money to complete buildings or pay professors' stipends. The British Christian people responded warmly: Keep and Dawes raised six thousand pounds.

American Christians also responded. Funds came from sources as far away as the East Coast, although response in the immediate area around Oberlin was not good. Finney admitted that the large mass of Ohio folk were opposed to the Oberlin enterprise. The college's abolitionist views created hostility and feelings ran so high that there were even threats to tear down Oberlin's new buildings. Opposition grew to the point that the State Legislature of Ohio attempted to abrogate the college charter. But friends throughout the North-East, who were also friends of abolition and revival, generously came to the rescue together with the British. The college would survive, although there were many hard days and years ahead.

Charles' family personally felt the hardship, but Finney tells of God's wonderful provision in the midst of real want:

> At one time, I saw no means of providing for my family through the winter. Thanksgiving day came, and found us so poor that I had been obliged to sell my travelling trunk, which I had used in my evangelistic labours, to supply the place of a cow which I had lost. I rose on the morning of Thanksgiving, and spread our necessities before the Lord. I finally concluded by saying that, if help did not come, I should assume that it was best that it should not; and would be entirely satisfied with any course that the Lord would see it wise to take. I went and preached, and enjoyed my own preaching as well, I think, as I ever did. I had a blessed day in my own soul; and I could see that the people enjoyed it exceedingly.
>
> After the meeting, I was detained a little while in conversation with some brethren, and my wife returned home. When I reached the gate, she was standing in the open door, with a letter in her hand. As I approached she smilingly said, "The answer has come, my dear;" and handed me the letter containing a cheque from Mr. Josiah Chapin of Providence, for two hundred dollars. He had been here the previous summer, with his wife. I had said nothing about my wants at all, as I never was in the habit of mentioning them to anybody. But in the letter containing the cheque, he said he had learned that the endowment

fund had failed, and that I was in want of help. He intimated that I might expect more, from time to time. He continued to send six hundred dollars a year, for several years; and on this I managed to live.

With such privations, one might think that the Finneys would have had very little to share. Yet Charles was always generous, regardless of his own particular wants and needs. One day a kind-hearted woman told him about a certain Mr. Spencer, a missionary to the Ojibway Indians, who had no overcoat. Charles immediately sent him the best overcoat he had, one that had cost him about fifty dollars – a sizeable sum in the nineteenth century.

Finney had an unusual flair for catching the attention of the public. Without that ability, the new educational experiment in Ohio could well have failed. He was the spark that kept it alive and before the public. As one author expressed it, one could no more think of Oberlin without Finney than "of Harvard without Eliot, Williams without Mark Hopkins, or Yale without Dwight".[2]

In the early years of the Oberlin ministry, while Finney was still working in New York and Oberlin simultaneously, a new issue surfaced. Finney, together with Asa Mahan, worked out his concepts of perfectionism and sanctification. The series of "Lectures to Professing Christians" was reported in Leavitt's *New York Evangelist* and soon found itself in book form which was almost immediately read throughout America and most of Europe. A storm of protest arose: perfectionism was not a universally accepted idea in nineteenth-century Christianity.

The lectures were born because Finney was always on a constant search for truth: "I say again that true Christian consistency implies progress in knowledge and holiness, and such changes in theory and in practice as are demanded by increasing light."[3] When he discovered that what he felt was truth, he was adamant in his stand: "if upon further discussion and investigation I see no cause to change, I hold them [new ideas] fast."

Several things created Finney's concern and search for a higher Christian life. First, he found that after a revival series was over, a certain number of believers would slip into a state of spiritual stagnation. This was more true of older church members than the new converts.

Secondly, Finney himself confessed:

> I was also led into a state of great dissatisfaction with my own want of stability in faith and love. To be candid, and tell the truth, I must say, to the praise of God's grace, he did not suffer me to backslide, to anything like the same extent, to which manifestly many Christians did backslide. But I often felt myself weak in the presence of temptation; and needed frequently to hold days of fasting and prayer, and to spend much time in overhauling my own religious life, in order to retain that communion with God, and that hold upon the divine strength, that would enable me efficiently to labour.

Thirdly, viewing the Church generally, Finney asked if there were not something better and more enduring than most Christians were aware of – even those whose consecration and Christian maturity were evident. "Was there not", he inquired, "means provided in the Gospel, for the establishment of Christians in altogether a higher form of Christian life?"

Of course, Charles was not alone in his search. It is probably true that "Oberlin Perfectionism", as the fully-developed doctrine later became known, was the product of President Asa Mahan as much as Finney. However, because of Charles' popularity and his published lectures, Finney was seen as the prominent figure in the system. Finney's fame no doubt helps explain the depth of the controversy that followed.

Many gave testimony to being deeply impressed and helped by Finney's approach. Charles himself felt greatly blessed through the experience. He related in his *Memoirs:*

> The last winter that I spent in New York, the Lord was pleased to visit my soul with a great refreshing. After a season of great searching of heart, He brought me, as He has often done, into a large place, and gave me much of that divine sweetness in my soul, of which President Edwards speaks as he has attained in his own experience. That winter I had a thorough breaking up; so much so that

sometimes, for a considerable period, I could not refrain from loud weeping in view of my own sins, and of the love of God in Christ. Such seasons were frequent that winter, and resulted in the great renewal of my spiritual strength, and enlargement of my views in regard to the privileges of Christians, and the abundance of the grace of God.

Not long after the publishing of Finney's position, the cry of Antinomianism was heard. This traditional heresy grew from the idea that if a person were perfect, he could live in any way he pleased. As a consequence, morals and ethical living simply fell to the ground. Paul anticipated something of this reasoning when he said to the Romans: "What shall we say then? Are we to continue in sin that grace may abound? By no means!" (Rom. 6:1–2).

The cry of heresy was raised against Finney. Letters were written. Churches were warned. Ecclesiastical bodies went to war. A veritable army of ministerial influence took to the field to present Oberlin Perfectionism as Antinomianism and thus a great error. Much of the outcry came from the Western Reserve College at Hudson.

Finally, a convention was called at Cleveland to consider the matter. It looked like a repetition of the New Lebanon Convention but with a different agenda. The invitation implied the meeting would be an open affair, but it soon became clear that the entire proceeding was a closed shop: the Oberlin brethren were not allowed to be seated as delegates. They could attend as observers, but they were prevented from discussing any issue. The emotional heat of the meeting rose to the point that the Oberlinites were condemned as the severest of heretics. The whole convention seemed to be designed to hedge Oberlin in by creating negative public opinions and hence crush the influence of Finney and the college.

The leading light of the convention was none other than Lyman Beecher. Once again Finney and Beecher stood as adversaries. Although they previously had made peace over the "new measures" issues, this theological breach was never closed. Beecher seemed genuinely to reject Finney's views on the higher Christian life. Many well-meaning ministers had been drawn into the fray: the doctrine of Antinomian perfectionism was a serious issue at the time.

With all this going on while Oberlin College was trying to become established, it was extremely difficult for the young institution. Finney records an incident that occurred at this time. One day he was riding down the road in his buggy. He came upon a lady walking and stopped to offer her a ride, which she accepted. Finney tells the tale with these words:

> After riding for some distance, she said, "May I ask to whom I am indebted for this ride?" I told her who I was. She then inquired from whence I came. I told her I was from Oberlin. This announcement startled her. She made a motion as if she would sit as far from me as she could; and turning and looking earnestly at me she said, "From Oberlin! why," said she, "our minister said he would just as soon send a son to state prison as to Oberlin!" Of course I smiled and soothed the old lady's fears, if she had any; and made her understand she was in no danger from me. I relate this simply as an illustration of the spirit that prevailed very extensively when this college was first established. Misrepresentations and misapprehensions abounded on every side; and these misapprehensions extended into almost every corner of the United States.

Fletcher, the Oberlin historian, says that around 1840 the college was known to most Americans as "the home of racial amalgamation, unchristian heresy, inadequate scholarship, wholesale immorality, mob violence, and disgusting hypocrisy".

To Finney's credit, he never assumed a negative stance against his opponents. He had long since learned how to handle criticism. He just prayed and refused to go to public war with his detractors. Although Finney would always attempt to clarify his position against his critics, he did it with a positive spirit and purpose.

Because of the controversy, President Mahan and Professors Cowes, Morgan and Finney established the periodicals the *Oberlin Evangelist*, and later the *Oberlin Quarterly*. They became both an important media to reach people with Finney's ministry, and preserved much of Finney's personal writings and views.

Finney always felt that most people who were led into the opposition were really misled. He saw them for the better part as sincere, good people who had become caught up in the Antinomian cry and had not been properly informed.

Had it not been that during the heat of the battle there was a mighty revival spirit upon Oberlin, the days would have been difficult beyond description. As the battle grew in intensity, God seemingly poured out His Spirit in direct proportion. Finney said:

> During these years of smoke and dust, of misapprehension and opposition from without, the Lord was blessing us richly within. We not only prospered in our souls here, as a church, but we had a continuous revival, or were, in what might properly be regarded as a revival state. Our students were converted by scores; and the Lord overshadowed us continually with the cloud of his mercy. Gales of divine influence swept over us from year to year.

Some doubted that Charles would succeed at Oberlin as a professor of theology. John Keep wrote to a certain Garritt Smith that there were those who felt Finney would surely fail from "lack of science". But Finney's robust theological labours gained him considerable influence and reputation in educational circles. His influence also extended through his students, even to other educational institutions. Oberlin graduates and alumni were devoted to Finney's principles and propagated them wherever their preaching or teaching ministry led them.

Finney's educational philosophy was practical and workable. He believed in acquiring a good analytical grasp of Christian theology, but he was no obscure "ivory tower" theologian. Theology for Charles meant to address the Christian faith to real-life situations. He believed that young ministers needed to be trained to be evangelists and learn how to lead others to Christ and meet people's honest life needs where they found them. Not only that, he was committed to the fact that the spiritual life of students must be nurtured and developed as well as the mind. In Charles' view, personal consecration, prayer and Bible reading for soul nourishment are exercises as vital as purely academic ones. He saw a full head and an empty heart as a travesty for a Christian minister. Finney would always start his classes in prayer and at times pray throughout the entire hour. Elisha Sherwood, one of Finney's former students, recalled one of those days and wrote: "It was the richest hour of all my theological course. It was an hour that brought with it the enduring power of the Holy Spirit fitting us to be witnesses to the power of the Gospel. Oh, that every candidate for the ministry might enjoy such an hour."[4]

Lewis Tappan was a great encourager of Finney's educational pursuits. He would urge the professor-evangelist to block all efforts of other faculty members "who make Oberlin a literary institution at the sacrifice of its religious character".[5]

Charles was a pragmatic man and took Tappan's advice into all areas of learning. He would advise students on every practical matter. The young men were encouraged to be at ease in a mixed society since Oberlin was co-educational, but they were not to "trifle with the young ladies in conversation or in any way". A stronger piece of advice warned "beware how you write ladies; what is written is written". Finney cautioned the future ministers not to blow their noses with their fingers, not to use dirty handkerchiefs, nor to spit on the carpet. They were not to put their feet and muddy boots on the sofa or on the door-posts, and not to pull off their socks in front of families. Charles told his class about a young clergyman who "called on some ladies after walking some distance, took off his boots and hung his socks on the andirons the first thing". He related the story of another minister who "put his feet up in a window in a lady's parlour to enjoy the cool air!" The young parsons were further admonished to keep their nails clean and their hair and teeth clean. He said it was disgusting "in the anxious meeting to be obliged to smell the breath of a filthy mouth". It must be remembered that most of these students were reared in the rough, coarse, rugged frontier. Finney had that background himself. As the years unfolded, he acquired a high degree of culture and sophistication and he desired the best for his students as well.

Finney also wanted his students to gain a grasp of logic, languages and the sciences. Natural and revealed theology was the core of the course, but he also wanted what he termed "a sound mental philosophy".

Finney's teaching style would please most modern educators. His primary teaching technique was what we call in contemporary educational circles the "seminar" method. He would assign students a doctrine to study and then turn them loose to research for themselves. He expected them to engage in extensive reading and investigation. He would not tolerate intellectual laziness. After the research was thoroughly done, the students would then present their findings before the class and all would enter into the discussion. He identified with the students and regarded himself as a learner as well as an instructor. Finney confessed that by this method, "I have availed myself, to the uttermost of the learning and sagacity, and talent of every member of my classes in pushing my investigations. Thus I sustain the double relation of pupil and teacher."

Finney always displayed an inquiring, open mind. His "new measures", perfectionist ideas and logical theology would probably never have been conceived had this not been so. This attitude and approach no doubt deeply influenced his students.

In the midst of all these intellectual pursuits, if a revival broke out on Oberlin's campus, spiritual pursuits were always given prime position. For example, in October 1836, the students passed a resolution that a day be set aside for fasting and prayer so that revival might come to Oberlin. Classes were suspended. Finney and Mahan preached, and revival fires fell. This was quite typical of Oberlin in Finney's day. As Charles said, "I ploughed my own church up fresh every year."

The Oberlin revivals usually had their birth in the Congregational Church in Oberlin. Finney, as pastor, was an excellent model for the students. At the end of his sermons, Charles would often call for inquirers. It was not unusual at all for a large number of students to respond to the invitation. There were even times when Finney would preach all day. To find excerpts in the *Oberlin Evangelist* like, "Blessed with a special influence of the Holy Ghost" (Autumn 1838) was quite normal. Any young unbeliever who happened to be in Oberlin College in those days was either soon converted or soon left town.

The *Oberlin Evangelist* had its inception in 1838. Almost immediately it gained popularity and soon generated a circulation of over five thousand. For 1838 in the western part of America, that is an admirable figure. Finney, Morgan, Cowles and Cockran were the primary contributors. Even though the perfectionist controversy had brought the *Oberlin Evangelist* into being, its aim was to disseminate Christian truth on a broad basis. Issues such as education, slavery, moral reform, missions and a host of other subjects were discussed. A multitude of Finney's sermons are found in its many volumes. The paper was an especially influential voice for the abolitionist movement. It was eagerly read for twenty-four years before being discontinued.

Oberlin Collegiate Institute was doing what few if any other school of its day dared to do. In the December 1851 edition of the *Oberlin Evangelist*, the objectives of the college were published. They read as follows:

1. To afford the means of a liberal and thorough education at so low a price that it may be within the reach of the humblest and indigent class of students.
2. The union of physical and mental culture.
3. The thorough education of women.
4. To educate men for practical life.
5. The cultivation of the spirit of progress, the encouragement of every judicious and enlightened reform.
6. The inclusion of a liberal yet evangelical and practical Christianity.
7. The training of a band of self-denying, hardy, intelligent, efficient labourers, of both sexes, for the world's enlightment and regeneration.

All of Charles Grandison Finney's ministry could not have been confined to Oberlin and education, however. His resignation from the Broadway Tabernacle pastorate freed his winter months for evangelism: the world still needed his far-flung itinerant evangelistic ministry.

# Finney's Repeated Revivalism:
## The Evangelist's Travelling
## Ministry Resumed

As 1842 dawned, a new spirit of optimism and well-being rested on the campus of Oberlin College and Seminary. The Ohio community's attitude toward the college had grown far more positive. Several factors precipitated the change. First and foremost, a degree of the earlier anti-abolitionist sentiments had subsided. The reason for this centred on the fact that many of the escaping fugitive slaves from the South were relentlessly pursued by their owners, even as far north as Ohio. This raised the ire of all Northerners. Oberlin had become an important "station" point on the so-called "underground railroad" where escaped slaves from the South could find a place to rest in safety on their way to Canada. Although some historians say the "railroad" was not tremendously effective in liberating large numbers of slaves, the fact that Oberlin gave refuge to the harassed slaves secured much favour towards Finney's institution.

During the summer session of 1842, an urgent call came to Finney to spend the winter in Boston. Charles' close friend, Mr. Willard Sears, had purchased the old Marlborough Hotel in Boston and transformed it into a large chapel in which to hold services and reform meetings. Sears was a crusader for the same kind of reforms to which Finney was committed. He was encountering a tempest of resistance, not over divine worship services, but over the advocacy of social reforms.

At the same time, William Miller, the founder of the Adventist Movement, was riding a crest of popularity. He had "prophesied" the Lord's second coming would take place on April 23, 1843. The general unsettled religious convictions in the entire Boston area were causing all kinds of cross currents and Finney felt the burden of Boston and became convinced God was leading him there. So the winter of 1842 saw Charles leave his happy, peaceful Oberlin and move to Boston, prepared to confront and challenge the Bostonians at the new chapel Sears organised. Finney records that when he began his ministry "the Spirit of the Lord was immediately poured out". Inquirers started knocking on Charles' door from all parts of the city. Multitudes soon came to faith in Christ.

Farther south, Elder Jacob Knapp, a well-known Baptist revivalist, was labouring in Providence, Rhode Island. He was getting little results and much opposition. Josiah Chapin of Providence, a large contributor to Oberlin College, together with some other friends urged Charles to come to their city to hold meetings. He was reluctant to leave Boston while such a significant revival was in progress. Yet he felt he owed Chapin and his friends much, so he consented to leave Massachusetts and travel to the city where Baptists in America were born.

As Finney left Boston for Providence, Elder Knapp made the reverse trip in response to a timely invitation. In Boston, Knapp's ministry was met with warmth and success. Edward N. Kirk, an old friend of Finney's from the 1920s in Albany, New York, also laboured in Boston for a revival. The results were significant. Between the ministries of Finney, Knapp and Kirk, four thousand members were added to the Boston churches in the revival season of 1842. And these were the waning days of the movement of the Spirit that swept America between 1830 and 1842.

Down in Providence there were many striking and startling conversions. A former judge of the Supreme Court of Massachusetts was saved. His reputation as a sceptic had been widespread. After the work got under way, he started attending the services. The evangelist described him as "a very venerable looking gentleman". Although he was not accustomed to revival services, the judge nevertheless gave strict attention to Finney's messages. One night as Finney moved to the end of his sermon, the old judge rose and asked if he might address a few words to the people. Finney broke off his message and gave him the podium. Everyone knew the judge well – and his sceptical views. They strained to catch every word. With deep emotion he said,

> My friends and neighbours, you are probably surprised to see me attend these meetings. You have known my sceptical views, and that I have not been in the habit of attending religious meetings, for a long time. But hearing of the state of things in this congregation, I came in here; and I wish to have my friends and neighbours know that I believe that the preaching we are hearing, from night to night, is the Gospel. I have altered my mind. I believe this is the truth, and the true way of salvation. I say this that you may understand my real motive for coming here; that it is not to criticise and find fault, but to attend to the great question of salvation, and to encourage others to attend to it.[1]

He said this with much feeling and sat down. Conviction gripped the entire congregation.

The basement of the Providence Church where the services were held boasted a large Sunday School room. Its dimensions were nearly as large as the church building above. Because of the crush of the people, Finney began to call inquirers to assemble in the large basement room for counsel. That room soon filled with inquirers and rejoicing young converts. This continued night after night for two months as God graciously poured out His Spirit on old Providence.

In the spring, Finney started for home. Oberlin's academic term was about to begin and the exhausted evangelist must once again become the educator. College life would be a much-needed respite.

Striking out for Oberlin, Charles rested a day in Rochester visiting a friend. As soon as the word got around that he was in the city of his greatest revival, a leading judge of the state court of appeals called on him. He must stay and preach, the judge insisted. Several ministers also called and prevailed upon him. Rochester held pleasant memories, but his strength was absolutely threadbare and it was time to be back in Oberlin. All were so insistent, however, and Charles never learned to say no. "I decided to remain, and, though wearied, went on with the work."

Finney started preaching in George S. Boardman's Bethel Church. The Rev. James E. Shaw of the Second (or Brick) Church wanted to combine the services with Boardman's congregation, thus dividing the evangelist's time between the two congregations. Boardman refused, so Finney did his preaching at the Bethel Church. The work commenced in earnest.

At the outset of the meetings, the judge, together with several members of the Bar, presented Finney with a written request to preach a series of sermons to the lawyers of the city. Finney seized on the idea – that was his forte. Having been educated as a lawyer, he always felt a special concern for those of the legal profession. The evangelist had a thorough knowledge of the sceptical attitude of many of the barristers, yet he loved to preach to them because of their openness to argumentation. Good debate stimulated the best in Finney. Not only that, a good number of Rochester's lawyers had been converted in the great campaign of 1830–1. They would obviously be supporters and instrumental in helping others of their profession come to an understanding of the message of Christ. With all of these dynamics before him, Charles began with relish his ministry among the intellectuals of Rochester.

In the very first sermon to the lawyers, Finney raised the question: "Do we know anything?" He then proceeded to relate what we do know. The audience soon became quite select. The less thoughtful did not find this approach very appealing. Yet, the church was filled to capacity each evening. Moreover, the conviction of the Holy Spirit began to run deep among the attenders.

The judge who first issued the insistent invitation was, strangely enough, not a professing Christian. His wife was a fervent believer, however, and a close friend of Finney. She informed Charles that her husband was profoundly affected by the preaching. Not many days later the judge came to the evangelist and said, "Mr. Finney, you have cleared the ground to my satisfaction, thus far; but when you come to the question of the endless punishment of the wicked, you will slip up; you will fail to convince us on that question." Finney replied, "Wait and see, judge." Charles took the hint and when he came to that point in his series he discussed it with complete thoroughness. The next day the judge said to Charles, "Mr. Finney, I am convinced. Your dealing with that subject was a success; nothing can be said against it."

Up to that point in the revival series, Finney had not given any sort of Gospel appeal – no anxious seat, no inquirer's room, nothing to bring the lawyers to the point of decision. He realised that lawyers were accustomed to hearing the whole case before making a decision. So Charles persisted in his legal line of reasoning. Finney never gave an evangelistic appeal until he felt the Holy Spirit had done His work completely and that the reaping time had come. But now it seemed that the moment had arrived.

Finney was especially concerned for the judge, who had previously opposed the use of the anxious seat with some vehemence. The evangelist expected the same response, even though he was obviously deeply convicted by the Holy Spirit. As Finney began his invitation message, he could not spot the judge in the congregation. He had been in every service up to that point. Charles was disappointed; he had prepared his message with the judge in mind. Suddenly, he saw him up in the balcony.

As Finney preached on, the judge got up and left. Charles saw him and thought, "He will not get the message and the reason for inviting people to the anxious seat." He began to feel his sermon and appeal was about to fail for the very man for whom he was most personally concerned. But all of a sudden someone was pulling on his coat tail. It was the judge. He had left the building, walked through the basement, come up at the back of the pulpit and taken hold of Charles' coat. Finney stopped preaching. The judge said, "Mr. Finney, won't you pray for me by name? and I will take the anxious seat."

Finney shared with the people what the judge said. A tremendous wave of conviction came over the congregation. The evangelist had not so much as mentioned the anxious seat up to that point, but here was the judge ready to take it. Heads dropped. Weeping broke out among many of the lawyers. The men of the Bar crowded the aisle and filled all the empty seats at the front of the church building, many falling on their knees in prayer. The movement began without Finney even calling for a move. God's hour had struck.

Finney remained in Rochester for two months. The meetings grew in intensity and impact. Once again Rochester was stirred to its very soul by Finney's preaching. A certain Mrs. Elizabeth Spencer Eaton wrote to her husband concerning the awakening: "I am confident he [Finney] preaches the truth as no minister that I have ever yet heard, has preached it."[2] All denominations were helped and blessed as they became caught up in the moving of God's Spirit. Dr. Henry J. Whitehouse, rector of St. Luke's Episcopal Church, saw seventy converts confirmed in his church. One thousand conversions were recorded throughout the city. Many of the lawyers who were converted went into the Christian ministry. A large number of physicians found Christ.

Finney felt that the lawyers were much easier to reach for Christ than doctors. He said of lawyers: "I have always found, wherever I have laboured, that when the Gospel was properly presented, they were the most accessible class of men; and I believe it is true that, in proportion to their relative number, in any community, more have been converted, than of any other class." Finney found physicians rather sceptical. Their humanistic type of education was the culprit, Charles was convinced. Yet he said, "They are intelligent; if the gospel is thoroughly set before them, they are easily convinced."

Reflecting on the revival, Charles said, "I have learned, again and again, that a man needs only to be thoroughly convicted of sin by the Holy Ghost, to give up at once and forever, and gladly give up, Universalism and Unitarianism." The Holy Spirit alone can blast away the citadels of Gospel error.

In the midst of the moving of God, Finney realised the Oberlin call must be heeded. The college was remarkably understanding. When revival fires burned, they were considerate and let their evangelist-professor be used by God as the Holy Spirit directed. But now back to Oberlin Finney must go. Rochester was history again.

The beautiful Ohio summer soon passed and Finney enjoyed a delightful season with his eager students. As the autumn of 1843 began to paint the verdant Ohio forest with broad brush strokes of gold, brown and red, Finney returned to Boston and the Marlborough Chapel.

When Charles arrived, he learned the rather depressing news that his ministry of the previous year had not settled the controversial religious atmosphere of Boston. The evangelist himself said, "Their system is one of denials. Their theology is negative. They deny almost everything, and affirm almost nothing." Finney laid the blame for this depressing situation at the feet of the Unitarians, who caused the Orthodox to call into question every doctrine of the Christian faith.

To add to the trouble, all was not well at the Marlborough Chapel. The church had been launched with the primary goal of revivals of religion, but fostering the social issues of the day was also very important. Finney would never divorce the two. In the year that Finney had been away, however, the church failed to keep a proper balance and it filled with the more radical sort. Even though they were good people, as Finney granted, their dogmatic and inflexible views on various social issues destroyed that necessary visible unity so vital for spiritual fellowship.

On top of all of that, Millerism was causing great excitement: this was to be the year of the Lord's return. Miller wrote in the *Signs of the Times*, January 25, 1843: "I believe the time can be known by all who desire to understand and to be ready for His coming. And I am fully convinced that sometime between March 21, 1843 and March 21, 1844, according to the Jewish mode of computation of time, Christ will come."

During that winter of 1843, the evangelistic results were rather meagre. Yet it was a most refreshing time for Finney personally. Charles took a tremendous step forward in his own spiritual pilgrimage: "The Lord gave my own soul a very thorough overhauling." He acknowledged that Boston with its disturbing religious problems always precipitated a deep spirit of prayer in his own life. But this year he was more than ever "greatly drawn out in prayer, for a long time".

A personal crisis emerged; he was deeply exercised over his own dedication and holiness. In addition, the weakness and spiritual ineptness of so many church members – even his own converts – continually disturbed him. Finney gave himself to earnest prayer. After the evening services, he would immediately retire so he could arise at 4 a.m. for prayer. He was so immersed in intercession that he would often still be on his knees when called to breakfast at eight o'clock. After a quick meal, he would spend most of the day, as he was able, in the Scriptures. He read nothing all that time except the Bible. He said, "The whole Scripture seemed to me all ablaze with light."

Charles prayed and studied in this manner for weeks and months. Then the crisis came. He made an absolute surrender and commitment to God in a depth he had never known before. Strange that a man so significantly used of God could have had an even deeper experience of Christ. Surely he was yielded to the Holy Spirit as he understood it. But his understanding of what it meant to be totally yielded was profoundly deepened. Charles readily confessed it was "a great struggle to consecrate myself to God, in a higher sense than I had ever before seen to be my duty or conceived as possible". The issue that brought about this maturing step centred on his wife, Lydia.

Charles said he had often laid his family on the altar of surrender to God's will, but Lydia was back in Oberlin and very ill. It was evident she was going to live only a short time. Charles could not bring himself to give her up. He had a deep and abiding love for his wife, and to see her wrenched from his arms was almost unbearable. In his *Memoirs*, Charles says relatively little of his loved ones, but records his anguish over Lydia:

> I wrote to my wife, telling her what a struggle I had had, and the concern that I had felt at not being willing to commit her, without reserve, to the perfect will of God . . . But . . . I was able, after struggling for a few moments with this discouragement and bitterness, which I have since attributed to a fiery dart of satan, to fall back, in a deeper sense than I had ever done before upon the infinitely blessed and

perfect will of God. I then told the Lord that I had such
confidence in him, that I felt perfectly willing to give
myself, my wife and my family, all to be disposed of
according to his own wisdom.

After the struggle came *victory*. He gave up to the
perfect will of God not only his dear wife, but the interests
of the Church, the progress of revivals, conversion of
sinners, even the salvation or damnation of his own soul.
Immediately he sensed that he could rest in the will of God
with a deep assurance that nothing else really mattered
except God's perfect purpose. He was overwhelmed with
what he called "holy boldness". He said, "My mind settled
into a perfect stillness." Great joy flooded his soul. A deep
desire for God's will to be done on earth as it is in heaven
pervaded his whole being. The evangelist had not only
regained his first love, but in his own words, "a vast
accession to it".

He poured out his very soul, struggling to communicate
to the church all that the Holy Spirit was doing in his
life – and would do for them as well. Most of his message
made no impact. The people could not grasp it. He finally
concluded that it was not wise to share all that was in one's
own soul with those who had not yet arrived at that place of
heart hunger. Yet, there were a hungry few who did
understand, and were greatly blessed. That winter in Boston saw them grow in grace by leaps and bounds under
Charles' preaching.

The deep calm that came on the wings of Charles'
absolute committal to the will of God never left him. When
his beloved Lydia died at the age of forty-three in December 1847, he said he felt no murmuring or the least resistance to the will of God. He tells the beautiful story in these
words:

> The night after she died, I was lying in my room alone,
> and some Christian friends were sitting up in the parlour
> and watching out the night. I had been asleep for a little
> while and as I awoke, the thought of my bereavement
> flashed over my mind with such power! My wife was gone! I
> should never hear her speak again, nor see her face! Her
> children were motherless! What should I do? My brain

seemed to reel, as if my mind would swing from its pivot. I arose instantly from my bed, explaining, "I shall be deranged if I cannot rest in God!" The Lord soon calmed my mind, for that night; but still, at times, seasons of sorrow would come over me, that were almost overwhelming.

One day I was upon my knees, communing with God upon the subject, and all at once He seemed to say to me, "You loved your wife?" "Yes," I said. "Well, did you love her for her own sake, or for your sake? Did you love her, or yourself? If you loved her for her own sake, why do you sorrow that she is with Me? Should not her happiness with Me make you rejoice instead of mourn? If you loved her for her own sake, did you love her," He seemed to say to me, "for My sake? If you loved her for My sake, surely you would not grieve that she is with Me. Why do you think of your loss, and lay so much stress upon that, instead of thinking of her gain? Can you be sorrowful, when she is so joyful and happy? If you loved her for her own sake, would you not rejoice with her joy, and be happy in her happiness?"

I can never describe the feelings that came over me, when I seemed to be thus addressed. It produced an instantaneous change in the whole state of my mind. From that moment, sorrow, on account of my loss, was gone forever. I no longer thought of my wife as dead, but alive, in the midst of the glories of heaven.

Lydia was the wife of Charles' youth – always beloved. Later, in November 1848, when his grief abated, he married Mrs. Elizabeth Ford Atkinson of Rochester, New York. She was a widow.

Although Charles experienced a great personal revival in Boston and tried to communicate the spiritual lessons he had been learning, a general awakening did not occur that bleak winter. The orthodox churches were so caught up in their fight against the Unitarians that little thought was given to the maturing of their own lives or to reaching others for Christ. Theological controversy has always killed spiritual fervour. Finney was beginning to realise more and more that holy living and the unity of evangelical, orthodox people alone brings to the Kingdom of God the impact needed to reach a community for Christ, be that a Unitarian community or any other. Theological issues are important, but they cannot be a preoccupation. Moreover, holiness is the final argument that convinces the unbeliever. Thus Charles grew increasingly concerned for holiness of life among believers. A new milestone in the evangelist's journey was being passed.

Finney returned to Oberlin via the city of his old pastorate to hold some meetings. He began to preach, but as in Boston, the same general spirit of preoccupation existed in New York. Lewis Tappan wrote about the effort in these words:

> Brother Finney has done much good here, especially to professors of religion, but the city has been so excited all winter with the numerous lectures and debates on every sort of subject, that it has been more difficult than usual to get people together to hear plain sermons, especially from an Oberlin professor. The consequence is that thousands have lost a rich intellectual and moral treat. But there are those who have drunk in the truth, and who will be advantaged to all eternity by the labours of Brother Finney in this city. May the Lord reward him.

About this time, a general lack of interest in revivalism seemed to invade the entire East. There were probably several reasons for the decline. To begin with, there was obviously too much energy expended on various reform movements (as important as they were in themselves). Theological controversy took its toll, and the battles over slavery and Unitarianism had heated up dramatically. Then in the late 1840s, the Mexican War erupted. Priorities were very difficult to keep in balance.

Revival fires were burning other places, however. Ministers such as Edward Kirk, Horace Bushnell, Lyman Beecher and others found Europe quite open to revivals.

Thus with all these dynamics swirling about him, Finney returned to Oberlin for a new college term.

# Finney's Religious Reforms:
# The Evangelist's Social Consciousness

Back in Oberlin, spiritual priorities fared better than in many other areas. Revivalism flourished as each new spring season bloomed. So did social reform. The twin-pronged thrust of Oberlin moved forward with increasing momentum. A college critic wrote that Oberlin had become a "hot bed of revivalism and social reform". Little did he realise the compliment he was paying the college. The dichotomy between evangelism and social action so prevalent in the twentieth century was unknown in the nineteenth.

The America of the 1840s and 1850s abounded with reform movements. Literally thousands of local benevolent societies grew up. As the nation was expanding at an unbelievable rate, the expansion bred deep social problems. The positive influence of the revival spirit motivated multitudes to meet those needs. Societies grew in number and size together with the establishment of colleges, seminaries and Bible Schools. Religious journalism came into its own, as did the Sunday School movement. Other movements sprouted and budded in the fertile ground of revival: abolition, women's rights and temperance. American Christians felt the millennium would soon come to America. Thus they did all in their power to usher it in.

Not all reform movements were religious in origin, however. The Enlightenment coupled with the Industrial Revolution produced its humanitarians with their humanistic approach. They made their contribution, but the movements that had deep religious roots were by far the most long-lasting and influential. It took the revivals of the

1820s and 1830s to produce men like Theodore Weld and the Tappan brothers. That is where Finney made his contribution. In a sermon he said, "Many professed Christians hold that nothing is needful but simply faith and repentance, and thus faith may exist without real benevolence and good works . . . [no] mistake . . . [could] be greater than this. [The] grand requisition which God makes upon man [is that he become] . . . truly benevolent." In the spirit of the great seventeenth-eighteenth century thrust called the Puritan-Pietistic movement, he preached that genuine Christianity must have a practical expression in useful works of Christian love and benevolence. Evangelism and social action are brothers. Although Finney's relationship to the many benevolent societies was largely unstructured in his early years, after the great Rochester crusade he made a conscious effort to forge links between his revival work and the reform societies. For example, in 1831 Charles preached a sermon that netted seventy-eight dollars and three cents, a gold ring, and a pen knife to help educate poor children that a society had undertaken. He was heard and heeded by multitudes.

Finney's basic theology demanded such an approach. Finney held that God is benevolent; so His people should exemplify that spirit in all human relationships. God does good to His creation; so should God's people. Finney said, "The very profession of Christianity implies the profession and virtually an oath to do all that can be done for the universal reformation of the world."[1] Christian virtue is a "disinterested benevolence" that shows itself in works of compassion to others, "disinterested" in one's own selfish desires. Thus the motive for all Christian social action was rooted in the very nature of God. This fact, along with strong millennium views, was his basic position for social action. Moreover, Finney contended that motivation is the central issue. All action must be judged on the basis of its motives. *A benevolent attitude* matters most. Some historians go so far as to say that the evangelist's chief contribution centres not on the thousands he won to Christ, but on the motivating of his own converts to get involved in the reform movements of the day. He helped galvanise the millennial zeal of thousands. Thus Finney set Oberlin on the path of reform.

First, the college broke fresh ground in its attitude towards women. This was seen clearly in allowing women to be enrolled as full-time students. Charles' concern for women demonstrated itself first in his keen interest in the Female Reform Society of New York, an organisation founded by the young Presbyterian minister, John R. McDowell. The specific service of the society was to reform "depraved and abandoned females". Finney addressed the society while pastor at Chatham Street Chapel, New York City, in 1833. He told the Christian ladies that they should "visit these houses, and fill them with Bibles and tracts and make them places of religious conversation and prayer, and convert their wretched inmates on the spot".

Finney was disturbed that so many of the churches in the city were not willing to speak out more strongly on prostitution. He preached that people should be "engaged in a mighty conflict with the great sin of licentiousness . . . Where are these sworn reformers – these men and women who profess to waging an everlasting war against every form of evil? Where are the ministers? Do they lift up their voices like a trumpet? Do they cry aloud and spare not? Do they as John Adams says, 'thunder and lightning from their pulpit' every sabbath against these sins?"[2]

Mrs. Finney joined her husband, making her contribution to the Advocate of Moral Reform Society. It would not be correct to state that the Finneys were avid women's rights advocates in the contemporary political sense, but they were well ahead of many in their time.

Finney did not side-step political battles by reciting the cliché, "religion and politics do not mix". His political ideas grew out of Christian conviction. Christians are to be political, but they are to be *Christian* in those politics. Finney always reserved the right to advise his people – students or church members – on how to react to various political issues. He felt this was a duty incumbent on ministers. But to be a "party man" was anathema for Finney; pure party politics could not be Christian politics, for all parties will be un-Christian at times. Therefore,

Charles argued, one must never vote or stand for an issue simply because one's political party took a particular stance. He told his people, "Instead of voting for a man because he belongs to your party . . . you must find out whether he is honest and fit to be trusted."

Finney's political views emerged out of his understanding of "God's government". That phrase is the key that unlocks his entire theological treasure-store. In applying the principles to politics, he believed nations and human governments were obliged to live according to God's moral governmental laws. Finney preached that politicians and their politics must conform to God's government to be pleasing to Him and develop a viable society. Christians who understand the principles of God's government are thus obliged to throw themselves into politics and make their influence felt.

This leads to what Americans call "blue laws", that is, civil laws concerning activities on the Lord's day, the day of worship. Finney had decided views here, although he never joined an organised sabbatarian movement. He firmly believed that in the light of the secularisation of America, something must be done or the sanctity of the sabbath would soon shrivel away. He viewed the encroaching secularisation of society with alarm. He even feared that government offices would remain open on the Lord's day, let alone secular business. This, he contended, would corrupt the whole country. He exemplified the principle in his own life. Once while travelling by steamboat to Oberlin, he went ashore at Erie rather than steam on to Cleveland on the sabbath. He rested on Sunday and continued his journey by stage-coach the next day.

Finney had a deep conviction that people needed a day of rest from labour. Finney believed in work – manual work. He believed in what today we call the "Protestant work ethic". That attitude was exemplified in the very structure of Oberlin College. In the Ohio school, as already seen, every student was required to labour for four hours daily. The bulk of the work in the early days was the clearing of the forest and the erecting of buildings. After that phase was completed, the primary task for the men was to work on the college farm while the women did washing, ironing, mending and similar chores. In August 1836, one student turned in his report:

> two hours burning stumps
> three hours building a walk for Professor Finney
> three hours hanging gate, etc.
> four and a half hours preparing . . . service for Professor Finney

The students had callouses on their hands as well as on their knees.

Most nineteenth-century people held the Protestant work ethic in high esteem. This raises the question: what should a Christian do when hard work produces wealth? Did Charles see this as materialism to be condemned? He was quite harsh in his criticism of Christian merchants and others who transacted their business on the principle of mere commercial justice and amassing gain. God's people were to be benevolent. This does not mean Christians should not become wealthy. It does mean the wealth must be used for the good of others. This is Christian morality for Finney.

As a consequence, Finney created a "benevolent empire" of wealthy businessmen who did much to further reform and Christian movements. Men like Gerrit Smith, Lewis and Arthur Tappan, Anson G. Phelps and many others financially supported many of Oberlin's benevolent causes. The evangelist constantly challenged them. He preached, "If you make your business as God's business, transact it on right principles, and get your heart into a right state so that you do everything from religious motives, why, your business is then as much a part of religion, as praying and going to church is." Many matured to the point that they gained wealth only to distribute it to others less fortunate. The principle of Christian stewardship became their constant motivation. They were amazing men. They believed Finney when he said a person "cannot be pious without being philanthropic also".

Nonetheless, Finney always kept before the people – and himself – that the Gospel is for the "poor". In Boston in 1832, he was preaching in Lyman Beecher's church. In the course of one of his sermons, he reminded the people that Christ demanded all, including their wealth. Beecher's church was a very affluent congregation, and the pastor stood up after Finney's message to assure the people that they need not fear to give Christ all, because the Lord would surely give it all back to them anyway. Finney was immediately on his feet again, and refuted Beecher publicly. Charles said they must surrender all to Christ absolutely, without any thought of what God would permit them to keep for their own use. Everything one has belongs to God, Finney declared, and God must have full access to it. Charles could preach on such issues most forthrightly, because he exemplified the principle in his own life. He never amassed any wealth. He and his family were often quite seriously in need and always lived very frugally.

Another moral issue that Finney tackled was the drinking of alcohol. American evangelicals have always had something of a keen interest in this ethical question. Should a Christian drink? How often that query is raised even today in American congregations. Charles was a fully-committed temperance man. He held that a person was drunk "if you can smell his breath".[3] He clearly demonstrated his commitment by speaking at the founding meeting of the New York Men's Total Abstinence Society in December 1835. The formation meeting was actually held in his Chatham Street chapel.

Charles was convinced that ministers in particular had a responsibility to help people see the evils of alcohol. They were to excommunicate from their church anyone who traded in "ardent spirits", as he termed it. Finney said resistance to temperance ideals on the part of believers would grieve the Spirit and sidetrack revivals. A Christian stood guilty before God with "hands red with blood" if he stood aloof from the temperance movement. However, Charles did not believe in political action to curb the blight of alcohol. He manifested the same attitude towards land reform and women's rights. Although he took a strong stand, he did not believe in political intervention to bring about reform in those areas, although he believed in laws to curb other social evils.

The entire spectrum of bodily indulgence was an issue to

Charles Finney. Dietary reform, at one period, was a strong conviction at Oberlin College. Finney was concerned lest his students fail their spiritual goals by gratifying their natural appetites. He considered a good healthy diet a Christian duty. He said, "We are to eat no *more* and no *less*, than our health requires." Finney went so far as to state that an unhealthy diet was a pitfall making one susceptible to sin. Students at Oberlin were thus forbidden to use pepper or any other condiments at their meals in college. He said such spices were not only irritating to the lining of the stomach, they stimulated unholy passions. And he thoroughly enforced the rule. One one occasion, Professor John P. Cowles brought some of his own pepper to the table at a college meal. The trustees actually took action over the issue. He was later dismissed, and though the trustees said nothing about his use of pepper, Cowles felt that this was one of the issues in his dismissal.

Tea and coffee were never served. Meat was considered dangerous as well. Butter was even questioned. What did they eat? One student wrote home and said,

> Cold water, milk and wheat will make the sum almost entirely of our articles of food. Bread and butter or bread without butter, bread and milk, milk and toast, compose the variety of our breakfasts and suppers. We have not had what you call a meal of meat since we have been here . . . We frequently have what is called Graham pudding, made of wheat just cracked, and boiled a few minutes in water.[4]

Oberlin was an ardent advocate of the nineteenth-century Graham dietary plan. "Graham crackers" still linger as the American legacy of the fad. Moreover, Finney practised what he preached. He contracted typhoid during an epidemic in 1847. He refused all drugs as he had little confidence in any medicine, and ate only baked apples, gruel pudding and boiled rice. When their beloved professor recovered from his typhoid attack, all Oberlin hailed it as a victory for the health-food principle. To Finney's credit, however, he later abandoned strict "Grahamism". He came to believe that dietary questions had no real moral significance. Yet he continued to practise good eating and health habits. Charles felt that people should do the best by their bodies to serve Christ. It was said, "Brother Finney eats regular and sleeps good."[5]

Many other interests of moral concern occupied the mind and heart of the educator. He lent his influence to the education of retarded children. He was adamantly opposed to duelling, which was still occasionally practised in nineteenth-century America. At one time, he was even taken with phrenology and submitted himself to having his head examined and charted, thinking it might help him in understanding human nature. The Oberlin Peace Society, a pacifist group, commanded his attention also. He did not agree that *all* armed conflict was wrong, although he always saw war as a terrible tragedy and in many instances grossly immoral. Finney felt that as long as freedom, dignity and benevolence were involved, conflict was not immoral. Thus he felt justified in supporting the Revolutionary War.

The social reform that occupied the bulk of his time and interest was abolition. Finney tenaciously held that slavery must be totally and unequivocally eradicated. To this he gave himself with something of the same kind of conviction that he devoted to his evangelistic revivals, even though he was more moderate than some of the radicals. Abolition was, of course, the most important reform movement of pre-Civil War America. Although there was considerable secular abolition sentiment, the revivals gave the movement the fervour of religious emotions.

Finney's ardent dedication to the abolition of slavery started early in his ministry. In his New York pastorate, he often spoke about the issue:

> When I first went to New York, I had made up my mind on the question of slavery, and was exceedingly anxious to arouse public attention to the subject. I did not, however, turn aside to make it a hobby, or divert the attention of the people from the work of converting souls. Nevertheless, in my prayers and preaching, I so often alluded to slavery, and denounced it, that a considerable excitement came to exist among the people.

The Lane Seminary revolt caused him to take a slightly higher profile in abolitionist activities, but with due caution. It has been said that when the Lane rebels arrived at

Oberlin they were received by the new professor of theology with only "mild enthusiasm". Some of Finney's friends did not think he was outspoken enough. Lewis Tappan, for example, even threatened to withdraw his financial pledge to Oberlin if Finney failed to come out more clearly and strongly on the issue.

Still, Finney's lectures on revival in Chatham Street Chapel demonstrate how he stood unswervingly for abolition: "Christians can no more take neutral ground on this subject, since it has come up for discussion, than they can take neutral ground on the subject of the sanctification of the sabbath."[6] Finney saw man owning man as a blight to the country and America's great national sin. The Church simply could not be silent. When the Finney family moved to Oberlin in 1835, Charles quite naturally joined the Oberlin anti-slavery society. He refused communion to any slave holders wherever he was pastor.

Nevertheless, some of the more ardent abolitionists did not fully trust Finney's commitment. Several factors probably account for this disquiet. In the first place, Charles was afraid that a bloody civil war loomed on the not-too-distant horizon. Although he was not a thoroughgoing pacifist, he saw war and its carnage as a horrible alternative to the evils of slavery. In a letter to Theodore Weld, he said that unless Weld cooled his ardour, a holocaust was inevitable.

Secondly, Charles feared that abolition would "drink up the spirit" of a person so that other important concerns would be relegated to a minor role.

Finally, Finney feared absorption in the abolition movement would dampen concern and drain commitment from revivals. He had come to Oberlin primarily to train young ministers to save souls, not develop abolitionists. This is no doubt the prime reason he may have appeared at times as not completely dedicated to abolition, making it easy for the more ardent to criticise. One of the fervent abolitionist students wrote to Theodore Weld and said that Finney

. . . poured out his soul before us in agony in view of our continuing in the abolition field and said that his great inducement to come to Oberlin was to educate the young men from Lane Seminary "(our class)" that the revival part of the Church was looking anxiously for us to enter upon the work of Evangelists, and would be exceedingly grieved if we did not – that we would accomplish the abolition work much sooner by promoting revivals – that the present unholy excitement in the Church and state, which the *present system of measures* had raised, and was directly to *increase*, would soon end in civil war – that the only hope of the country, the Church, the oppressor and the slave was in widespread *revivals*.[7]

Charles Finney the revivalist wanted his students evangelising and converting sinners. For Finney the salvation of people mattered most. He wanted all his converts committed to anti-slavery, but he wanted his abolitionists converted. Furthermore, Finney was convinced that revivals did far more in the final analysis to foster reform than mere agitation over reform.

There was one rather serious deviation in the evangelist's views on abolition: he insisted on segregated seating in his churches in New York and in Oberlin. The Tappans took issue with him on this. In a letter to Arthur Tappan, Finney defended his views by saying, "You err in supposing that the principle of abolition and amalgamation are identical. Abolition is a question of flagrant and unblushing wrong. A direct and outrageous violation of fundamental right [sic]. The other is a question of prejudice that does not necessarily deprive any man of any positive right."[8]

Some historians have been critical on this point. But Finney was a pragmatist; a moral utilitarian. He firmly believed that integration, if coupled with abolition, would undercut the whole anti-slavery movement. He knew there were profound prejudices in the North as well as the South. Even though before the Civil War the North abhorred slavery, there were still deep-running emotions concerning the *complete* mixing of blacks and whites. Remember, the fire brigade of New York had refused to put out the blaze at the partially-constructed Broadway Tabernacle when they heard it was going to be an abolition centre. Finney's view was probably shared by most evangelicals in the North at that time.

As the days of America's Civil War drew near, Oberlin was more and more identified as an abolition centre, and at

Oberlin Finney took a different stance from his New York position on segregation. Some students suggested that black students be seated at separate tables during meals at Oberlin. Charles objected and carried the faculty with him. If white students refused to eat with blacks, they could sit by themselves, but no black student would be segregated at Oberlin. This practice also carried over into the public meetings and instruction periods. Soon all distinction between blacks and whites faded. If Finney's stance on racial equality was not revolutionary enough for the Tappans and a few others, it was far too revolutionary for the general population.

Finney's whole purpose was to maintain a balance between evangelism and social reform. American Christianity later failed on that very point in the theological battles between the so-called modernists and fundamentalists of the late nineteenth and early twentieth centuries. Social action somehow became identified with "liberal" theology and evangelism settled down with the "fundamentalist" image. The seeds of this tragic divorce were sown by men such as William Loyd Garrison who said that no slave-holding church could be of God. Garrison began his abolition crusade as a committed evangelical. Later, however, in the middle 1840s, he began doubting the authority of the Scriptures and became taken by Thomas Paine, the sceptic. This type of approach tended to secularise many social concerns and estranged the evangelistic-minded. Social action was thus torn from evangelism, and the rupture has not yet been healed in much American Christianity.

Finney saw the heart of the issue in the heart of man. The heart as well as the mind must be changed. Laws can create a certain coercion towards social justice, but the heart is the final issue. Only God can change the heart, and that change comes about by a conversion experience through faith in Jesus Christ. To see a revival was the way to see true reformation. This whole approach was basic to Finney. It even has eschatological dimensions. According to Finney, this is the way to usher in the millennium. To fail to grasp that foundational fact is to miss his rationale for uniting social concern and revivalism.

Perhaps this stance on revivalism is why some secular

historians have overlooked the profound influence and contribution the evangelist made on abolition and other social problems in the nineteenth century.

Finney indirectly made other significant contributions to great social advance movements. George Williams, the British founder of the Young Men's Christian Association, was profoundly affected by the life and ministry of Charles Finney. Hodder Williams, a man well acquainted with George Williams, says that Charles G. Finney was of tremendous religious influence in the life of George Williams who founded his movement in 1844. Charles' writings on revival and the spiritual life touched Britain some time before he actually arrived to minister personally, and it seems quite probable that George Williams knew of these writings while he was still in his early years of Christian services at Bridgwater. It is certain that he treasured Finney's writings later. When Charles went to London, Williams became personally acquainted with the evangelist.

William Creese, the only founding member of the Y.M.C.A. to outlive Williams, felt that the Association owed much in its early days to the young men who were brought to faith in Christ by reading Finney's *Lectures to Professing Christians* and *Lectures on Revivals and Religion*, published in London in 1840.

The genius of the Y.M.C.A. centred in small, praying groups. It was this intense and personal approach which fitted in so well with the traditions and atmosphere of the British evangelical scene. For this approach Williams was quite dependent upon Finney.

Moreover, Finney's emphasis on personal, religious experience greatly influenced Williams and other evangelicals. Finney had experienced a sudden conversion himself, and his preaching hammered home that principle to others. This greatly appealed to Williams and suggested that Christians should always be living on the cutting edge of revival fervour.

It is also important that Finney's effectiveness in revivalism left Williams and others with a lasting confidence in the efficacy and techniques of revivalism to win the lost and aid social justice. Although Lord Shaftsbury, one of Williams' friends, expressed doubt that revivals had a lasting impact, Williams was always committed to revivalistic evangelism. Williams, as did many evangelicals, constantly supported such campaigns.

Not only did the Y.M.C.A. feel Finney's impact, William Booth, the great founder of the Salvation Army, was helped by Charles' ministry. General William Booth said on one occasion that he could "remember rushing along the streets during my forty-minute dinner time, reading the Bible or Charles G. Finney's *Lectures on Revivals of Religion* as I went."

Finney was a man for all seasons. His profound social consciousness together with his ardent revivalism was touching circles undreamed of in the early days of the Evans Mills revival. The Spirit of God was fashioning a giant in the midst of the Victorian era.

## Finney's Evangelisation in England:
## The Evangelist's International Work

During the turbulent time of America's pre Civil War days, many in England kept asking Finney to visit them. The calm, stability and religious fervour of Britain appealed to the evangelist and his wife. Thus the decision was made. The autumn of 1849 saw the Finneys set sail for Southampton.

Greeting the Finneys on the channel coast on an early November day was the Rev. James Harcourt, pastor of a church in Houghton, a small town in the south midlands. Exciting reports of revivals in Wales, England and Scotland that occurred as a consequence of the *Lectures on Revivals of Religion* had spread across Britain. Finney, aware of these facts, expected a warm reception. He was not disappointed.

Mr. Potto Brown, a wealthy layman in Houghton, had been the catalyst of the Finney visit. He owned a milling business and was largely responsible for the financial base of the Houghton Church. The pastor who preceded the Rev. James Harcourt had substantially failed in his evangelistic ministry. He left under pressure, but under Harcourt, an open communion Baptist, God's Spirit began a good work in the town. Still, Finney felt the church did not really know how to consolidate and develop a significant revival.

Charles and his new wife of a year rested a few days in Potto Brown's home before taking up the work. Mr. Brown was a Quaker, but very ecumenical. His business partner had died and the six children of his deceased partner lived in his home. Not one of the six children, however, had met Jesus Christ in a personal conversion experience. While Finney laboured in Houghton, the Brown home was thrown open all day long so that invited friends could come, eat and converse on spiritual matters with Charles and his wife. They came in great numbers and filled the table day after day.

The six foster children of the Browns were soon brought to Christ, as were the friends that gathered in the Brown home for meals and fellowship. Joy spread throughout the community. In Ohio, the *Oberlin Evangelist* recorded the success of the mission in these words: "We learn that Prof. Finney's first labours in England have been chiefly in Houghton for a period of about three weeks, and signally successful. People have come in from a distance of forty miles to attend the meetings, and many are turned to the Lord. The state of things there is said to be very much as it was in this country twenty years ago."[1]

Mrs. Charles Finney was a significant figure in the revival. One of the first references concerning Elizabeth's work is in the *Oberlin Evangelist*. "Mrs. Finney is with her husband, abundant in labours, and jointly with him requests the prayers of Christian friends."[2]

The Finneys stayed some weeks in Houghton. In the middle of December, sensing the Spirit's lead, they moved to Birmingham. Mr. Roe, pastor of the Ebenezer Baptist Chapel, had invited Charles to come and labour among his people. The work began and a significant spiritual stirring immediately commenced. While in Birmingham, Charles also preached in Carr's Lane Church, served by the Rev. John Angell James. James had written the introduction to Finney's British edition of *Lectures on Revivals of Religion*.

In Birmingham, Charles discovered that James had received a number of critical letters accusing the evangelist of theological errors. It caused some questioning, so the pastor invited several ministers for breakfast and an open discussion. In the meantime, Finney gave James a copy of his *Lectures on Systematic Theology*. He also gave a copy to Dr. George Redford, a well-known British theologian. He wanted the influential ministers in Britain to know where he stood theologically; then, if he were guilty of any aberrations, to let the matter be fully aired.

Neither the pastor nor theologian Redford found any serious objection to Finney's doctrinal stand. After a thorough reading of Finney's *Theology* and an extensive conversation with Charles, Dr. Redford said, "I see no reason for regarding Mr. Finney, in any respect, as unsound. He has his own way of stating theological propositions; but I cannot see that he differs on any essential point, from us."[3] When Finney got into another theological controversy on his second British trip, Redford stood with him.

After this many ministers threw their influence and efforts into the work. The ministers urged Charles to move from church to church in the revival efforts. He declined, thinking it best to concentrate his labours primarily in Roe's Baptist church. Finney later regretted this decision. The British pastors had been right; Roe's church was too small to contain the crowd. Conversions multiplied nonetheless, and practically all of the one thousand five hundred unbelievers in James' church were saved.

The evangelistic methods used in Britain, Finney confessed, were "the same that I had done in [America]. Preaching, prayer, conversation and meetings of inquiry." Mr. Roe would stay in his vestry all day, receiving people who would drop in to converse about their relationship with Jesus Christ. Many found salvation through that means.

One of the citadels of British Unitarianism in those days was Dr. Priestley's church in Birmingham. Unitarianism in fact had a strong foothold in the Birmingham area. One of the Unitarian pastors of Birmingham attended a service and later wrote Finney:

> I found I must accept the Bible, or perish in darkness. You may imagine the agonies of spirit I had to endure . . . In this state of mind I heard your sermon . . . I felt the truth of your arguments. Your appeals came home irresistibly to my heart, and that night, on my way home, I vowed before God, come what would, I would at once consecrate myself afresh to that Saviour, whose blood I had so recently learned to value, and whose value I had done so much to dishonour.[4]

Finney received that letter while working in London.

The Rev. John Campbell of London, after reading it, said to Charles, "There, that is worth coming to England for!"

After three months in Birmingham, the next move under God was to Worcester, preaching in the church of Dr. George Redford. By this time, Redford was so satisfied with Finney's theology and methods that he wrote the preface to the British edition of the *Systematic Theology*.

While in Worcester, several wealthy men approached Finney with a proposition to build a portable tabernacle for use all over England. They wanted to construct a transportable building that would seat up to six thousand people. Charles declined, following the advice of local ministers who felt that the evangelist should keep to traditional church buildings. But no local church could contain the crowds he consistently drew.

Back in Oberlin, the hope was expressed that Finney would visit what Americans then called the "Queen of Cities", London. They were not to be disappointed. Dr. John Campbell, editor of the *British Banner* and a successor of George Whitefield in the London Tabernacle, wrote to Finney: "You are aware that it pleased God, now a century ago, through the instrumentality of an Englishman to bless America; and who can but tell it may please Him, by means of an American to bless England?"[5] Campbell was referring to the great George Whitefield. Could it be that Finney would actually become to England what George Whitefield had been to America? One of the greatest influences ever in American Christianity was that of George Whitefield during the days of the First Great Awakening. Now an American had the opportunity to return that blessing. The invitation from Campbell was too much to resist. In May 1850, Finney travelled with his wife to the "Queen of Cities" to preach in the Whitefield Tabernacle, Mooresfield. Dr. Campbell had published a small pamphlet giving Finney a sound recommendation, stating that Dr. Redford had heartily endorsed him. This gave Charles immediate rapport with London's Christian community.

Finney preached in the tabernacle for several weeks. Before long, Dr. Campbell told Finney he believed the evangelist was preaching to more people during the week nights than all the rest of London put together. When he felt the time had come to call for an inquiry meeting, Finney informed the pastor what he was about to do. Dr. Campbell thought it premature, but made no objection, suggesting that the infant schoolroom in the basement of the church be used. This room held about forty people. Finney graciously said this would never hold the group: "That is not half large enough. Do you have a larger room?" he inquired. Pastor Campbell said rather incredulously, "There is the British schoolroom. But that will hold between fifteen and sixteen hundred; of course you do not want that." "Yes," said Finney, "that is the very room." Campbell replied, "Mr. Finney, remember you are in England, and in London . . . You might get people to attend such a meeting under such a call as you propose to make in America; but you will not get people to attend here." Finney retorted, "Dr. Campbell . . . the Gospel is as well adapted to the English people as to the American people." The decision was made.

The evening service began in which Finney planned to extend the invitation for inquiries. At the conclusion of the meeting Finney made it quite clear that professing believers were definitely not to attend the meeting of inquiry. There was to be a communion service for them in the tabernacle after the service was dismissed. He laboured the point; only the unconverted were to make their way to the nearby schoolroom. He even insisted that what he called "careless sinners" should not attend. "I was determined not to have the mass of the people go into that room; and furthermore, that those who did go, should with the express understanding, that they were inquiring sinners." With that he dismissed the service of worship.

Dr. Campbell anxiously looked out of the window to see which way the departing people would go. Would they just filter out into the streets of London, or would they make their way to the British schoolroom? To his utter amazement, practically the entire mass of people crowded down Cowper Street leading to the British schoolroom. Finney joined them in a few minutes and found the building packed.

Campbell rushed through the communion service to join the host of inquirers. By his own estimation, some fifteen or sixteen hundred people had crammed themselves into the room. Finney addressed the inquirers for a short time on the immediate duty to repent and receive Christ as their Lord and Saviour. He carefully instructed the seekers, urging them to guard against emotional extremes. Finney knew Londoners of the nineteenth century and was concerned about theological extremes also. He said, "I tried therefore in my instructions, to guard them on the one hand against hyper-Calvinism, and on the other against that low Arminianism in which I supposed many of them had been educated." As he called on them to repent and pray, weeping and sobbing filled the house as many came to Christ.

Inquiry meetings became regular events during the London revival. Finney would also call on people who wished to receive Christ to stand while the service of worship was in progress. It was impossible to call people forward to any sort of an anxious seat; there was simply no room. On occasions as many as two thousand people would respond to Finney's invitation: "Indeed it would appear from the pulpit as if nearly the whole congregation arose." In the end, thousands were being turned away from the services due to lack of space in the tabernacle. People came from every part of the city, for miles around. The worshippers would sit spellbound. Finney normally preached for one and a half hours, but a report in the *British Banner* stated the people in the tabernacle would gladly have heard him throughout the night.

Finney would be stopped in the streets of London by people who knew him and had been blessed. Dr. Campbell was amazed at the results. He said to Finney, "I don't understand it. You did not say anything but what anybody else might have said just as well." Finney replied, "Yes, they might have said it, but would they have said it? Would they make as direct and pointed an appeal to the consciences of those people, as I did?" Finney reflected later: "That is the difficulty. Ministers talk about sinners; and do not make the impression that God commands them, now to repent; and thus they throw their ministry away."

The meetings at the tabernacle were due to end on August 14, 1850. But the interest had escalated to the point where it was clear they must go on. Finney confessed he was drawn out in prayer for the city in a way seldom experienced. The low spiritual ebb deeply burdened his heart. The Great Prayer Revival of 1858 had not yet come to Britain. But by the time Finney finally did leave, many churches were fully involved in promoting revivals.

Mrs. Finney took part in the women's meetings of the movement. These meetings were a completely new thing for London. She did not take a large leadership role at first, but Dr. Campbell asked her to help one day in what the Londoners called "tea meetings" for poor, uneducated women. She was expected to lead the service. She supposed that the men who were there would surely leave when the meeting began; women did not speak to mixed groups in those days. But the men did not leave. Mrs. Finney was much like her famous husband, so she rose to the occasion. When the men refused to leave, she addressed the group for forty-five minutes. The women seemed greatly moved, and the men expressed genuine appreciation. They said that they had held prejudices against women speaking in public, but could have no objection under these circumstances. They encouraged her to carry on with the work. Thus the women's movement spread and deepened. Walls were coming down in Victorian London. From this point on, Charles' wife began to take a more prominent part in the revivals.

As could be expected, opposition to the revival was not wanting. Some of the critics described Finney's preaching as "dull beyond measure". They accused him of being a promoter of "out-of-the-way opinions".[6] Finney certainly did promote some unusual measures. His advertising technique was to have people carry placards through the streets. The "new measures" controversies apparently stowed away and sailed with Finney across the Atlantic. Furthermore, critical articles were imported from America and circulated. But the opposition seemed to make no great impression, and the work went on unaltered with little serious hindrance.

As September days waned, the Finneys badly needed to

rest. Their friend, Potto Brown of Houghton, gave them fifty pounds to take a trip to the Continent for recuperation. They travelled across the turbulent channel to Paris. Brown said they should go to a country where English was not spoken so Charles could have some real rest. He probably knew if the evangelist were asked to preach, he surely would.

Charles wrote, "The influence of the change of climate upon my wife's health, was very marked. She recovered her full tone of strength very rapidly. I gradually got over my hoarseness." After about six weeks of restful travel, they returned to London and the Whitefield Tabernacle.

Back in Oberlin, although everyone understood Finney's involvement in Britain and had given him leave, things were getting tense. As London's winter settled in, letters kept coming asking if Finney ever intended to come back to his responsibilities at the college. It became obvious to Finney that he must make a decision about returning home. He had been gone an entire year. The college wrote, "fail not to relieve our minds at once, the anxiety is real and intense."[7]

Many of the students had gone to Oberlin because of Finney. The situation apparently developed that unless Finney returned soon, the students would probably leave. Professor John Morgan urged Finney to assure them he would return for the spring enrolment. Furthermore, Finney kept receiving innuendoes concerning the presidency of Oberlin College and Seminary. There was considerable dissatisfaction over Asa Mahan, and the faculty had decided to ask for his resignation. Mahan's critics accused him of being egotistical, overbearing and often rude to those who disagreed with him. Finney was a close friend of Mahan and the faculty wanted Charles to break the news to the president. Charles was spared the painful duty, however. When Finney's daughter, Helen, wrote to her father in August 1850, Mahan had already presented his resignation.

At that time, John Keep wrote to tell Finney that the trustees wanted him to become Oberlin's second president. Keep said they would have already appointed the evangelist if he had been there to confirm the election. He wrote,

"I regard it as essential that you return to this institution as soon as is practicable."[8] He was the natural leader of the college. In the light of all the circumstances, Finney wrote assuring his colleagues he would return in the spring. Finney was shortly thereafter elected as president of Oberlin College and Theological Seminary.

In the few months left in England, Finney stayed in the London area. A one-volume edition of his lectures on *Systematic Theology* was published by Messrs. Tegg Publishers. Another publisher produced thirty of his sermons in the *Penny Pulpit*.

Campbell felt that Finney was making a mistake to go back to Oberlin. He said Charles was "made for the millions – his place is in the pulpit, rather than the professor's chair." The good doctor also praised Mrs. Finney. He said, "Mrs. Finney is a woman of wholly kindred spirit with her husband; she sees everything in the same like, estimates all matters by the same standard, and by the same means seeks the same ends. Her heart is strongly set on advancing the kingdom of God, and to that end, like him, she perseveringly labours. She established the daily morning female prayer-meeting, which has been held in the tabernacle for the last nine months, and over which she has, while in London, uniformly presided."[9]

Dr. Henry Ward Beecher, Lyman's son, was visiting London during those days. He said of the Finney ministry in a letter to the *New York Independent*:

> At the close of the sabbath evening's service, more than a thousand persons presented themselves in an adjoining hall as inquirers. Nor have we ever witnessed in any place more solemnity, order, and unexceptionable propriety in the conduct of meetings, than has prevailed under Mr. Finney at the tabernacle. And now, if we were an English clergyman, and if we were inclined to doubt the reality of revivals, and, seeing the results of Mr. Finney's labours, should hear it testified from the land of revivals that they were spurious, that good as they might now seem, they would end in mischief, we should conclude, not against Mr. Finney, but against revivals. We should say, "If these are spurious all revivals are spurious."[10]

The Finneys left behind a host of friends in their now beloved Britain. A farewell party was held in April 1851 at the Royal British Institution, Cowper Street, London. Both Charles and his wife were given gifts to remind them of the visit. Charles received a copy of the Greek New Testament entitled, *English Hexapla*. The beautiful edition of the Greek text was in six translations. Mrs. Finney, also an avid reader, received a condensed version of the *Commentary of the Ingram Cobbin*. The London morning *Chronicle* ran the following article:

> Dr. Finney the celebrated American Revivalist, leaves England for his native country by the next Steamer. Though he came here for purposes of health and relaxation, he has not been idle. His fervid elegance has created a powerful and we hope a permanent effect wherever he preached. Perhaps no man since the days of George Whitefield, has succeeded in producing a more wonderful sensation.[11]

Charles left England with "great reluctance". The vast majority of those gathered on the pier waving a fond farewell were his new converts. Charles said, "Tearing away from such a multitude of loving hearts, completely overcame the strength of my wife. As soon as the ship was clear of the dock, she retired to our stateroom. I remained on the dock and watched the waving of handkerchiefs, until we were swept down the river out of sight." A sad day, but Britain would see them again.

The Finneys arrived back in Oberlin in May 1851, in time for the opening of the summer session. Now as president, Finney was ready for the new administrative duties that the position demanded.

The backwoods evangelist had come a long way. Although administration took some of Charles' time he was first and foremost a theologian at Oberlin. His theology demands an investigation. It is as exciting to delve into Finney's theological views as to investigate his revolutionary revival meetings. As he was a startling innovator in revivalism, he was a surprising innovator in theology.

## Finney's Theological Thought:
## The Evangelist as a Thinker

It has been said that a person behaves as he believes – or the reverse of that. Finney is perhaps a classic case of the latter. For Finney, theology had to "work". He was a pragmatic thinker; if a doctrine did not perform in actual ministry, he would seriously question it.

The Bible became Finney's primary basis for a systematic Christian theology but there were other influences. Jonathan Edwards, as an example, was a pervading influence. He was unquestionably the keenest theological thinker and philosopher America produced in the eighteenth century. As a pastor, educator, and prominent figure in the First Great Awakening, his impact was tremendous. Edwards' revival preaching was largely responsible for laying the foundation of the well-known "New England" or "new school" theology. Edwards came on the scene when hyper-Calvinism had just about run its course in precipitating dynamic Christian experience. The churches were at a low ebb. To bolster up church life, the "half-way covenant" was conceived and implemented. That arrangement allowed the children of believers to be baptised and become church members, but they could not participate in the Lord's Supper until they had themselves professed personal faith. This approach tended to fill the churches with people who had no real conversion experience.

In that spiritually cool atmosphere, Edwards started preaching the necessity of a true conversion to Christ. This implied people could be converted *if they would*. And the First Great Awakening burst on the early American scene. The preaching in the Great Awakening brought to the fore human responsibility, freedom to choose or reject Christ. That is most important, for it is the move which cleared the path for the development of "New England" theology that stressed human ability to exercise free will. Human responsibility thus began to be deeply ingrained in the minds of many early Americans.

As a consequence of the "new theology" and its spreading influence, New England Congregationalism divided. The "infection" became so widespread in Presbyterianism too that it caused a split in their ranks in 1837.

Regardless of the tragedy of church divisions that eventually came, Edwards' (and later Whitefield's) insistence on people coming to Christ made a most significant contribution to evangelism. The "New England" or "new theology" school had picked up some very illustrious names by Finney's time: Joseph Bellamy and Samuel Hopkins in particular.

Finney was first introduced to Edwards' writings in the home of Dr. Aiken in Utica, as we have seen earlier. He read Edwards' books: *On Revivals* and *On the Affections*. Aiken said Charles "often spoke with rapture" of these works. Finney constantly appealed to Edwards in his own writings and some say the Edwardian approach to declaring God's Word is what toned down Finney's earlier frontier harshness.

Nathaniel S. Beman was also a major influence in the development of Finney's theology. Charles' view of the atonement is almost identical to Beman's view.

Another contemporary whose impact must have been quite significant in the formulation of Finney's thought, was Nathaniel W. Taylor, a notable theologian. How much actual contact Finney had with Taylor is uncertain, although he did meet and talk with him. Finney developed his theology in much of the Taylor framework. Of course, "old school" Presbyterians completely rejected what they called "Taylorism". In "old school" circles, to label a man a follower of Taylor was to condemn him automatically. These charges were constantly raised against Finney.

There was another great influence on Finney's doctrinal stand: his law training. A most revealing passage is found in

Charles' conversation with Gale: "Your positions are not proved. They are unsusceptible of proof."

Finney's background in law made him acutely aware of the value of a convincing, rational argument. Law was probably the most significant foundation of his approach. Charles said, "I was bred a lawyer. I came right forth from a law office to the pulpit." He insisted, "Religion consists in the heart's obedience to the law of intelligence." As a result, he seemed uncomfortable with any theological tensions or any sort of a paradox. Even though Finney would have granted that there is mystery in the knowledge of God, he seemingly always resisted the tension mystery creates.

Above all, Finney firmly held to the absolute authority and total inspiration of the Scriptures. He said, "The question of the inspiration of the Bible is of the highest importance to the Church and the world, and that those who have called in question the plenary (total) inspiration of the Bible have, sooner or later, fritted away nearly all that is essential to the Christian religion."[1]

At the same time, Finney was an independent, free thinker. He had no tradition to keep. He would not be crammed into anyone's mould. As a man with a deep religious experience, he took the Bible for what he understood it to say, and with his analytical approach moved on from that foundational stance.

But now the question must be raised: what were the building blocks of Finney's theological position? The answer will be divided into two parts, one part implying the other, namely (1) Finney's systematic theology, and (2) Finney's perfectionist theology.

## Part 1: Finney's Systematic Theology

Finney's systematic theology was radical. One writer put it this way: "Welcome to the revolutionary theology of Charles G. Finney."[2] Although he wished to retain the Calvinistic concept of the absolute sovereignty of God, he was adamantly opposed to human passivity in conversion. After the First Great Awakening opened the door to human responsibility and the ability to decide for or against

Christ, Finney went one step further. He contended that the "old school" hyper-Calvinistic fatalism was unworthy of God himself. Finney was convinced of moral responsibility in every aspect of life.

Finney was sure the traditional doctrines of the "old school" would lead revivals into a cul-de-sac. His entire theological quest was something of a battle to wrest revivalism from its hyper-Calvinistic grasp. The preacher was not to be a mere proclaimer of the Gospel, he was also to be a persuader of the people. Finney stands significantly as the watershed between revivalists like Jonathan Edwards and mass evangelists like D. L. Moody, Billy Sunday and Billy Graham.

His belief concerning conversion can best be explained by looking at what theologians call the "order of salvation". Pure Calvinist thinkers hold the "order" to be regeneration and *then* repentance. They teach that God gives faith while people passively receive it and are thus regenerated. In that new regenerate state, the believer can exercise his reborn will in repentance. Only then can a person exercise true repentance. The later so-called hyper-Calvinists modified the scheme a little, but they all agreed that the responsibility for salvation primarily rests in the sovereign God, not the recipient.

Finney strongly reacted against this formulation. He was acutely conscious that this idea eradicated human responsibility and laid a serious charge on God, namely, if anyone was not converted, *it was God's fault*. He *totally* reversed the "order" by declaring that a person was fully responsible for exercising both repentance and faith, although he did see faith coming before repentance. People were to grow concerned, seek God, turn to Christ, repent, pray, believe, and thus permit Jesus Christ to come into their lives and save them. It is the sinner's role and responsibility to believe and repent. Charles declared, "Sinners, your salvation or damnation is as absolutely suspended upon your own choice, as if God neither knew nor designed anything about it." People are therefore as responsible to God for their conversion as God is to them. Finney argued that to wait on the Holy Spirit for regeneration, as "old school" men urged, is really to harden oneself against God. Thus he appealed to people to be converted *immediately*. He urged the unregenerate to turn to God and respond by repentance and faith then and there. To wait is rebellion, he preached. The only thing that stands in the way of salvation is a stubborn will. After all, he cried, that was his problem before he was saved.

In Finney's time these theological issues were of extreme importance. They even caused men of the "old school" like B. B. Warfield to accuse Finney of "Pelagianism". This heretical view, propounded by Pelagius in the fifth century, held that there was no such thing as original sin; people have perfect free will and therefore no absolute need of God's grace. The Pelagian system finally implied that humans are virtually the authors of their own salvation. This was a serious charge and unjustified against Finney. But he was obviously camped on the other side of the fence from the "old school". Along with Nathaniel W. Taylor, he took seriously the issue of human responsibility.

One of Finney's critics said: "It will be the less important for us to dwell further upon Finney's system because it may be dismissed in one word, 'Taylorism'."[3]

If the "old school" men from Princeton (the citadel of their theology) wanted to refute Finney or Taylor, they should have levelled their guns on Arminian theology. That is where the evangelist-theologian was coming from. Although Finney may have resisted being called Arminian, because he wanted to retain Calvinistic terminology and be known as a Calvinist, in many respects that is exactly what he was. Both Taylor and Finney worked out their system of salvation in the Arminian spirit of freedom of will.

What then was the theological basis for Finney's stress on human ability in deciding for Christ? It lies in what Finney called *God's Moral Government*. That phrase was not peculiar to Finney; Beecher and Taylor used it. They saw the world as operated by God on two levels: the physical and the moral. The physical has to do with natural laws like the law of gravity. The moral has to do with mind, motives, decision-making, conduct and the promoting of God's glory. These latter aspects relate to God's Moral Government. Finney would argue as follows:

If there is a moral government or order at the very heart of the universe with moral laws, there must of necessity be a moral governor. His name is God. Furthermore, there must also be moral agents subject to the moral government if there is any reality in the concept at all. These moral agents are human beings who are moral agents and morally obligated to obey God's government. But how could such people be real moral agents if they did not have the ability to exercise their minds, their wills, and make moral decisions. They obviously could not. Therefore, the choice must be a true choice; a genuinely volitional act wherein freedom is a reality. Freedom of moral choice must be absolutely genuine. How could one even be a moral agent subject to moral praise or blame if the choice was not real? The highest of all moral good is the pleasing of the moral governor. To have an authentic, free, accountable moral nature and to make decisions that are pleasing to the moral governor is one of God's most gracious "disinterested" benevolences he has bestowed upon his human creation. God is above all else, benevolent. That is, he seeks the highest good for his creation in all circumstances. God shows no partiality to any individual; his disinterested benevolence is given to all and the moral laws and the privilege of pleasing him applies to everyone.[4]

This concept is the very centre and core of his theological rationale. In the Preface to his *Lectures on Systematic Theology*, he says, "What I have said on the 'Foundations of Moral Obligation' is the key to the whole subject. Whoever masters and understands that can readily understand all the rest."[5] All that can be said of humanity and God is built upon the foundation of God as the Moral Governor supervising the Moral Government He has established.

Now if all Finney argues is true, the inexcusability of human sin must also be granted. If one can truly exercise free will in moral decision-making, one is genuinely guilty if the wrong choice is made. It follows, as over against the "old school", Finney would not condemn people because of the so-called "sin of Adam" inherited by nature. He considered the idea of an *inherited* sinful nature an "abomination" and "a relic of heathen philosophy". People are not culpable for what Adam did, though they have some share in the Fall. Finney rebuked people primarily for their *own* wilful, deliberate rebellion against God, not Adam's. Thus Finney would never say you *cannot*, but you *will not* receive Christ.

Finney's logic was incontrovertible, if one granted his basic premise. Even Hodge of the "old school" had to admit, "The author [Finney] begins with certain postulates, or what he calls first truths of reason, and these he traces out with singular clearness and strength to their legitimate conclusions. We do not see that there is a break or a defective link in the whole chain. If you grant his principles, you have already granted his conclusions."[6] What conclusions, therefore, did Finney draw from his "first truths of reason"?

On the issue of *original sin*, Finney did not depart completely from the Calvinistic concept of total moral depravity. He said the human mind is "in a diseased, lapsed, fallen, degenerate state, so that the healthy action of these powers (that is, of the mind) is not sustained."[7] Although that sounds very Calvinistic, Finney's emphasis was somewhat different. The fallen nature, which came about as an "original wrong choice", makes one *wish* to engage in self-gratification of the appetites rather than to do God's perfect will. But it does not *compel* one to do so, at least in the sense one becomes morally responsible for actions beyond one's control. The only moral bondage one is under because of the fallen nature is the *voluntary* bondage to one's own appetites and love of this world. Thus one could come to Christ and be released from sin's bondage if only he or she would. This is true even though a person will invariably choose moral evil; he can come to Christ if he will.

Some say Finney failed to distinguish between physical depravity and moral depravity. But Finney did make a distinction. He said physical depravity is the mind that is dependent on the body and in a diseased, lapsed, fallen and degenerate state. Thus the mind's healthy actions are not always sustained. Moral depravity is the depravity of the moral will in making bad choices out of one's own free will. Moral depravity, then, does not exist in infants; it is acquired by making wrong moral choices through life.

His critics constantly accused him of moving towards a works salvation. But faith was primary for Finney. Moreover, the Holy Spirit's work in salvation was central in the whole Finneyan scheme of redemption. Finney firmly believed the function of the Holy Spirit was to *persuade* people to come to Christ and make right choices. If that did not happen, no one could be saved. In a sermon the evangelist said:

> The preacher cries, "Turn ye, why will ye die?" The Spirit pours the expostulation home with such power, that the sinner turns. Now, in speaking of the change, it is perfectly proper to say, that the Spirit turned him, just as you would say of a man, who had persuaded another to change his mind on the subject of politics, that he had converted him, and brought him over. It is also proper to say that the truth converted him; as in the case when the political sentiments of a man were changed by a certain argument, we would say, that argument brought him over. So also with perfect propriety may we ascribe the change to the living preacher, or to him who has presented the motive; just as we would say of a lawyer who had prevailed in his argument with a jury; he has got his case, he has converted the jury . . . Now it is strictly true, and true in the most absolute and highest sense; the act is his own act, the turning is his own turning, while God by the truth has induced him to turn; still, it is strictly true that he has turned and done it himself. Thus you see the sense in which it is the work of God, and also the sense in which it is the sinner's own work. The Spirit of God, by the truth, influences the sinner to change, and in this sense is the efficient cause of the change. But the sinner actually changes, and is therefore, himself, in the most proper sense, the author of the change.[8]

Finney said, "Regeneration is always induced and effected by the personal agency of the Holy Spirit."[9]

In the light of Finney's premises, he would obviously reject the hyper-Calvinistic concept of a limited atonement, that is, Christ died only for the "elect". Finney argued that God's salvation is for all because all are able to receive it if they will. Secondly, the revivalist repudiated a legalistic approach to the atonement. The "old school" had a very wooden view of what Christ accomplished on the cross. They said every single, individual, specific sin was laid on Christ and he suffered the judgment for every single one in a legal, forensic sense. This frightened Finney because of the Universalist argument, so he developed what he called the "governmental theory of the atonement".

> The atonement did not consist in the literal payment of the debt of sinners, in the sense which the universalists maintain; that it simply rendered the salvation of all men possible, and did not of itself lay God under obligation to save anybody; that it was not true that Christ suffered just what those for whom he died deserved to suffer; that no such thing as that was taught in the Bible, and no such thing was true; that, on the contrary, Christ died simply to remove an insurmountable obstacle out of the way of God forgiving sinners, so as to render it possible for him to proclaim a universal amnesty, inviting all men to repent, to believe in Christ, and to accept salvation; that instead of having satisfied retributive justice, and borne just what sinners deserved, Christ had only satisfied public justice, by honouring the law, both in his obedience and death, thus rendering it safe for God to pardon sin, to pardon the sins of any man and of all men who would repent and believe in him. I maintained that Christ, in his atonement, merely did that which was necessary as a condition of the forgiveness of sins; and not that which cancelled sin, in the sense of literally paying the indebtedness of sinners.[10]

This theory of the atonement holds that Christ's passion was not to satisfy retributive justice as the "old school" Calvinists said, but to show to all the world the love and integrity of God and to satisfy *public justice*.

Finney's concept of public justice by no means precipitated a low view of the work of Jesus Christ, nor a low view of the person of the Lord Jesus Christ. Finney always saw Jesus as "truly God" and "truly man" in one divine-human Person. He was orthodox to the core on that issue. He embraced the so-called "Chalcedonian" view in its entirety.

In the area of foreknowledge and election, Finney's view of Moral Government once again comes to the fore. "The elect were chosen to eternal life because God foresaw that in the perfect exercise of their freedom they could be induced to repent and embrace the Gospel."[11] Finney probably would have said that election and predestination is simply God's way of getting the most people saved, and without it none would ever find salvation. Thus he desired to keep election as a viable concept, yet to defuse it of pointing to an arbitrary God.

Finney spent seventy-five pages in his *Systematic Theology* on the doctrine of the "perseverance of the saints", that is, one can never be lost after being saved. In the Bolton church in England, he wrote of many of the members being "reconverted" in the revival, which seems to imply a Christian could be lost. But in the end he said all true saints will in some sense persevere to the end. Genuine believers will keep their faith and thus be kept by the power of God. Finney did not say a Christian *cannot* fall from grace, he argued he *would* not. Thus he maintained an essential Calvinist view although he may have made something of a concession to the Arminians.

A word must also be said concerning Finney's "postmillennialism". Although he was not given to a great deal of doctrinal preaching on the second coming of Christ, in his eschatology he was a post-millennialist. Most nineteenth-century evangelicals were. This was the root of their zeal for social action. This view holds that Christ will return after the Church has established the Kingdom of God on earth. Finney believed that through evangelisation and social reform the world could see the establishment of the Kingdom of God in his own day.

This kind of utopianism was popular throughout the Victorian era. The ultra-optimistic Jeffersonian spirit of the day permeated much of America's sociological relationships. Finney was caught up in that spirit, arguing that if the atonement was for all, there was no reason why all could not be saved. As the world became increasingly Christian, it would become increasingly happy and prosperous. Naturally, the Church would be on the cutting edge of that glorious movement. Finney went so far as to assert in 1835: "if the Church will do all her duty, the millennium may come in this country in three years."[12]

A friend of the revivalist gave a good summary of the

Oberlin school of thought of which Finney was the supreme originator, motivator and mover. He outlined the system as follows:

1. The human will is self-determining in all its actions.
2. Obligation is limited by ability.
3. All virtuous choice terminates upon the good of beings, and in the ultimate analysis, on the good of being in general.
4. The will is never divided in its actions, but, with whatever momentum it has at each instant, it is either wholly virtuous or wholly sinful.
5. The total depravity of the human race is a biblical doctrine, and since the fall in Eden all the acts of man previous to regeneration are sinful.
6. Regeneration and conversion are synonymous terms, descriptive of an act in which the Holy Spirit and the human will co-operate. Truth, however, is in all cases the instrument through which conversion is secured by the Spirit.
7. The condition into which men are brought by regeneration is either that of continued holiness, increasing in volume, or of states altering from entire holiness to entire sinfulness, the former state predominating at last. The final perseverance of all who are once truly converted is a revealed truth which the reason cannot contradict.
8. The doctrine of election is our only assurance that the salvation of any will be secured. There is a divine plan of salvation whose means and ends were chosen from eternity, and which is now unfolding before us.
9. In this plan Christ is the central figure; a being who is both God and man, and whose humiliation and sufferings are a governmental substitute for the punishment of those who are sanctified through faith. The atonement satisfies the demands of general justice, and its provisions are freely offered to all men.[13]

Finney's systematic theology was generally accepted in many circles; it raised the ire of the "old school" men only; the "new school" advocates and all Arminians were quite happy. But when Finney's view of *perfectionism* became generally known, the cry of heresy began to rise from all circles.

## Part 2: Finney's Perfectionism

> Prone to wander, Lord, I feel it,
> Prone to leave the God I love.
> Here's my heart, O, take and seal it,
> Seal it for thy courts above.

All Christians empathise with the sentiment of the hymn-writer. Finney did especially – not only personally but for his converts. He found himself often in the spiritual "slough of despond". He confessed he knew all about Christ as a Saviour of sinners, but very little about Christ as the sanctifier of the saints. Christ forgives sin, but what about Christ delivering His people from its power? At that time, he saw sanctification purely as a process whereby God gained more and more control of the whole person. But he was seriously dissatisfied with the progress he and others were making.

In this womb of worry, Finney's quest for perfectionism was conceived. There were other influences, of course. When Finney became interested in sanctification, he read widely and avidly on the subject. Wesley's *Plain Account of Christian Perfection* was most important in this intellectual journey, and the Wesleyan concept of "perfect love" had particular appeal.

About 1832 a movement called "Antinomian Perfectionism" sprang up in the north-eastern part of America. A key figure in this movement was John Humphrey Noyes, a man influenced by Finney's revivalism. He founded the Oneida Community. The community was a typical utopian commune, very common in nineteenth-century America. Noyes was the self-styled leader of the group. He began publishing a paper called *The Perfectionist*. The periodical stayed in print for two years and was then replaced by *The Witness*. Noyes held three basic views:

1. Perfect holiness is attainable and when secured it is forever secured.
2. Perfect holiness is necessary to salvation.
3. The second coming of Christ occurred at the destruction of Jerusalem in A.D. 70.

Finney had some contact with Noyes, and read most of his work, but could not accept Noyes' basic tenets. Finney laboured to dissociate himself from his views being appalled at Noyes' Antinomian stance. Noyes' work deteriorated before long into a "free love" group. It was the Noyes Antinomian movement which some failed to distinguish from Finney's views that fuelled the fires of controversy in Charles' early Oberlin days.

Finney's early thoughts on perfectionism began with a question from an Oberlin student. The student asked President Mahan how much a Christian could expect in the area of sanctification. Mahan said he would give an answer later. Finney and Mahan went to New York and there began the study that eventually precipitated Oberlin perfectionist theology. At that particular stage, Charles made no claim to perfection himself. He said, "I do not myself now profess to have obtained perfect sanctification."[14] Even three years later, Finney said, "No individual could set up a claim to have attained this state without being a stumbling block to the Church."[15]

Later in life the crisis over the death of his first wife, Lydia, confirmed for him his essential views on sanctification. He said about his relationship to God in those days: "At this time it seemed as if my soul was wedded to Christ, in a sense in which I had never had any thought or conception of before . . . Indeed the Lord lifted me so much above anything that I had experienced before, and taught me so much of the meaning of the Bible, of Christ's relation, and power, and willingness, that I often found myself saying to him, "I had not known or conceived that any such thing was true.'"[16]

There were actually two distinct periods in the development of the doctrine at Oberlin. From 1836 to 1841, sanctification was stressed as an experience subsequent to regeneration, to be sought and received as a gift – "receiving the blessing". This followed quite closely the Wesleyan position. After 1841, most Oberlinites held one is "entirely sanctified" at conversion, but "permanent sanctification" occurs when the battle between holiness and sinfulness ceases. Growth in grace means more and more deliverance from the interruptions in entire consecration until permanent sanctification assumes command. This later view became traditional "Oberlin Perfectionism". The *Oberlin Evangelist* carried many articles on the subject. Henry Cowles, the editor, wrote a series of articles that were published in book form in 1840 under the title *Holiness of Christians in the Present Life*. He disagreed with the new development of 1841 as did Asa Mahon. John Morgan published a pamphlet entitled *The Holiness Acceptable to God*. Finney did some articles which were reprinted in book form, entitled *View on Sanctification*. By far the most influential book to come out of Oberlin, however, was President Mahan's work *Christian Perfection*, published in 1839. The new thrust entered Finney's preaching. Before developing the doctrine of sanctification, Charles preached the simple Gospel, directing his message primarily to the lost. Now he had a message to the saved. Consequently, he thereafter embraced both doctrines in his preaching ministry.

The question must now be asked: what did Finney actually believe about Christian perfection? At the outset, it is very important to realise that the term "perfectionism" was used quite differently in Finney's approach than is commonly understood today. For Finney and many of his contemporaries the term was used in the same sense as we now speak of sanctification, Christian maturity, victory over sin, or complete surrender to God's will. Perfection and sanctification in fact became all but interchangeable terms for Finney. Charles said, "Call it what you please, Christian perfection, heavenly-mindedness, the full assurance of faith or hope, or a state of entire consecration; by all these I understand the same thing."[17] For Finney, perfection did not mean a spiritual state where one can never sin again, as it tends to connote in contemporary thought. It certainly did not mean perfection in the sense that God Himself is perfect.

Secondly, Finney never claimed in any dogmatic fashion to have "arrived" to a state of perfection himself although at Boston his description of his experience sounds somewhat like it. He tended to hold it up as a goal, a goal that is attainable.

What Finney was trying to communicate was that sanctification rested in being willing to be taught by the Holy Spirit and obeying God in everything. *Obedience* to God's understood will was the crux of the matter. Finney's perfectionism rested upon his doctrine of God's Moral Government. If one could obey God at all, why could not one obey God's will perfectly? There was no reason, at least in principle, to the contrary. He defined the concept in these words: "By permanent sanctification understand, then, a state not only entire but of perpetual unending consecration to God. Simple obedience to the law of God is what I understand to be present, and its continuance to be permanent sanctification."[18] In his *Systematic Theology* he outlined the idea:

1. We argued the possibility of attaining this state from the fact that God expressly commands it.
2. From the fact that man by virtue of his moral agency was naturally able fully to obey God.
3. From the fact that provisions are made in the Gospel for the entire sanctification of believers in this life.
4. From the fact that we are commanded to pray in faith for the entire sanctification of believers in this life.
5. From the fact that Christ and the Apostles prayed for this.
6. From the fact that the entire sanctification of believers in this life is expressly promised in Scripture.[19]

Therefore, one can be "perfect" by exercising one's free moral choice in the power of the Holy Spirit. Could perfectionism last? Finney replied, "You shall be perfect as long as you continue to be perfect." Or, to put it another way, you are perfect as long as you are perfectly obedient to God's will as it is understood at the moment. This can be done by resting in the power of Jesus Christ. Only the grace of the Sovereign God can make it possible. Approached from this perspective, Finney's thinking is rather difficult to refute. As one writer expressed it, "If you accept his definition, you can accept his conclusions."[20]

Finney's quest was the development in believers of an attitude of complete surrender to the will of God. That basic attitude was expressed first in the act of repentance that introduced the Christian experience and procured salvation. Commitment to the Sovereignty and Lordship of Jesus Christ should be carried on through life as one grows and matures in spiritual apprehension. The principle that brought salvation should bring entire sanctification. Finney never saw perfection from a humanistic attainment perspective any more than he would have viewed salvation from that vantage point. As faith in Christ and His power is central for salvation, faith in Christ and His power is basic in the exercise of the human will in choosing God's will and thus bringing about sanctification.

Finney would probably argue that if there is victory by faith over sin through the Lord Jesus Christ, why cannot one have victory over *every* known sin? Finney's definition of sin always seemed to be a *knowledgeable* act. He would probably argue one could hardly be guilty before God for that which he did not understand as rebellion. He did not deal in detail with what is commonly called "unconscious sin".

Did the scheme work? Many objected. Yet, President Fairchild (Finney's successor as leader of Oberlin) while not too happy with the theology of Oberlin perfectionism, had to admit that in those early days there were remarkable transformations of character.

Lyman Beecher denounced the view as did several synods of the Presbyterians. Some of the synods felt so strongly that they would not even ordain Oberlin graduates. Even Samuel Aiken, Finney's old friend and host in the great Utica revival of 1826, signed a statement condemning Oberlin perfectionism. This deeply grieved Finney. Some of the Congregational groups joined the protesters also.

As the controversy spread, some of Charles' friends suggested he use another term rather than "perfection". William Wisner said it would be best to use a phrase like "assurance of faith". Such terms would have a wider acceptance. But Finney continued to use the term, and paid the price for it. His "new measures" controversy died down; even his "new school" theology was tolerated; but perfectionism continued a volatile issue for years.

There was a definite positive side to the controversy nonetheless. The Methodists, for example, with their background in Wesleyan perfectionism, were happy with Oberlin. Perhaps the most positive contribution of Oberlin perfectionism was in relation to the Keswick movement in England. The Higher Life Movement which blanketed Europe from about 1870 onwards had some of its roots in Oberlin. And the Higher Life Movement gave birth to the now famous, worldwide Keswick movement. The basic theology of early Keswick was in essential agreement with Finney's perfectionism, even if some details, and especially terminology, were somewhat different. For example, Finney used the term "baptism" of the Holy Spirit where Keswick used "filling" and Keswick would prefer "sanctification" to "perfection". Asa Mahan, co-author with Finney of the perfectionist idea, later lived in England and participated with Pearsall Smith in the famous Oxford Convention of 1874. Mahan collaborated with Smith in planning the first Keswick Convention, although Smith himself returned to America before the convention met.

As the years moved on, Oberlin became more balanced on the subject. Fletcher, the historian of Oberlin College, said, "Oberlin Christians became so busy as missionaries, preachers, teachers, and advocates of Christian reform, that they found less and less time to court the 'baptism of the Holy Spirit'."[21]

Oberlin perfectionism left its mark on many a movement. Indeed, the quest of godly, holy living should always be central in Christianity.

Thus Finney made his contributions to Christian thought. He threw open wide the portals of salvation so all could go in, and those who did enter were to experience a genuinely changed life.

## Finney's Reviving of the Revival Route: The Evangelist's Travels Continued

Finney's first year as president of Oberlin College and Theological Seminary went very well. All that Oberlin was, Finney personified. But now that the initial term was completed, the revival ministry called again, and Finney could never resist.

Charles had been invited to return to the Broadway Tabernacle in New York City for the winter. Dr. Thompson was pastor at the time. Finney looked forward to the winter with anticipation. As he travelled east, he hoped to see a real revival take place in his old pastorate. His anticipation soon cooled. The Broadway Tabernacle people had been renting out their building for public lectures. This became a serious hindrance because of the image it created around the tabernacle. Charles despaired of seeing a revival. Nevertheless, the *Oberlin Evangelist* recorded that Finney was still preaching to large audiences each evening. But Charles felt the situation would not allow maximum results, so he made plans to leave.

Finney had received an invitation from the Rev. William Patton of Hartford, Connecticut to hold a series of meetings in New England, and he accepted. Patton was a pastor of an influential Congregational church in the city and a good worker. Horace Bushnell and Joel Hawes were also pastors in Hartford at the time. Finney preached in both their churches as well as to Patton's congregation.

People generally felt that Hawes and Bushnell should settle quite a serious division between them. The burden seemed to rest on Hawes; he had been very vocal in his criticism of Bushnell. Finney, acting as a peacemaker, talked to them both and urged them to establish fellowship, and publicly. The Spirit of God spoke to the men, and they followed Finney's advice. Hawes acted graciously in the matter and took the initiative. Their differences were thus resolved, the people of the city were informed, and as Charles expressed it, "A great obstacle [was] removed".

The revival now went on and great grace was on the work. By the middle of February 1852, people were turned away due to overcrowding at the Central Church where Finney was doing the major part of his preaching. Many converts were added, but Charles himself said, "I was never in the habit of ascertaining the number of hopeful converts". The *Oberlin Evangelist* recorded, "It is known to Brother Finney's friends that he is seldom wont to say much of revivals in which he is labouring while they are in progress; we are therefore obliged for the most part to depend on other informants for news respecting such revivals."[1]

The people of Hartford were frightened of any evangelistic methods except prayer meetings. This attitude restricted Charles from calling on sinners to come forward. Dr. Hawes was especially fearful of any revolutionary "new measures". Finney always tried to fit into the pastor's plan if possible, so he decided to have no more than an inquiry meeting in Hawes' vestry. But even that was a shock to the timid pastor. Prayer, therefore, became the main motif of the meeting. However, God used the prayer meetings marvellously. Young people gathered in groups for prayer and intercession. The new converts especially drew themselves together in prayer. They would invite inquirers to join them in their prayer sessions so as to help them to Christ. This measure seemed to satisfy everyone and many were reached by the method.

The limiting of revival measures did not in this instance impede the revival. Perhaps there were times when Charles actually did put too much stress on "measures".

An interesting experience occurred in a boys' school during the revival. The local pastors had agreed some time earlier that no evangelistic work would be done in the schools of the city. Yet the presence of God was so real in all of Hartford that one morning many of the lads in one of the schools were so disturbed about their relationship to Jesus Christ that they could not study. They asked their teacher to pray for them. The teacher was not a professing believer, so he sent for a local pastor to come and pray for them. The pastor refused because of the agreement. The teacher sent for another and another with the same results. All the pastors told him he should pray for them himself. Finally, in desperation he rose to the occasion and prayed for the students – and gave himself to Christ along with a large number of his students.

Mrs. Finney, with the valuable experience she had gained in Britain, started prayer meetings for the ladies of Hartford. The meetings were well attended as the women became deeply involved. The women's prayer meetings became a significant source of strength in the revival.

The Hartford revival resulted in some six hundred new members being added to the churches. On April 1st, the Finneys left Hartford to return to Oberlin. On the way home they stopped by New York City and Charles preached in the Plymouth Church of which Henry Ward Beecher, Lyman's son, was pastor. The next autumn the Finneys left Ohio once again for the East.

Finney had received an insistent invitation from the pastor of the Congregational Church in Syracuse, New York, while he was still in Hartford. Finney agreed to come, although there were many other places he had not yet visited. The Syracuse church was small and very discouraged, but on the first Sunday Finney preached, God moved in a marvellous manner on the congregation. So Finney stayed for another week, then another, and a revival was soon under way. As the evangelist said, "Soon I began to perceive a movement of the dry bones." Thus, he settled in for an extended ministry.

The fact that Finney would go to a small, discouraged church, especially in the light of his fame and the thousands that would come to hang on his words, gives an insight into his genuinely humble character. He would always go where he felt God was leading, regardless of the size or condition of the church. Finney was not a "mass evangelist" in the sense of conducting city-wide crusades as was true of D. L. Moody later. He was a "local church revivalist". Yet, his organised, planned and structured meetings helped pave the way and set the style for the later ministry.

The larger Presbyterian churches threw open their doors to the developing awakening in Syracuse. That was a significant move; fellowship between the Presbyterians and the Congregationalists had been lacking.

Finney met an unusual woman in Syracuse. Charles came to call her "Mother Austin". She was very poor, entirely dependent on the charity of others, but had great faith. She told the evangelist, "Brother Finney, it is impossible for me to suffer for any of the necessities of life because God has said to me, 'Trust in the Lord and do good so shalt thou dwell in the land and verily thou shalt be fed.'"

On one occasion, the dear saint was visited by an unbeliever. He offered her five dollars as he left. She felt she could not take it in case the man thought it an act of self-righteousness. She had just enough fuel and food in the home to last over the weekend and no means of getting any more. The five dollars would have come in quite handy. On Sunday, a snow storm began, and by Monday morning the snow was several feet deep. All the streets were blocked. When she arose that morning, the woman's small son asked, "What are we to have for breakfast?" "I do not know, my son; but the Lord will provide," she replied. But the streets were impassable. The little lad began to weep, fearing they would starve or freeze to death.

The mother went about making provisions for breakfast as best she could with no food. At that moment, she heard loud talking in the snowbound streets. She went to the window to see a man in a single sleigh with some other men shovelling a path before them so the horse could get through. Up to her door they dug themselves, burst in with ample food and fuel for several days. God had kept His promise. The dear lady told Finney many such stories. It must have deeply impressed the evangelist. He devoted three pages in his *Memoirs* to her life of faith.

The winter of 1853–4 saw Finney stay in the West. During November and December, he preached in the Plymouth Congregational Church of Cleveland. In January, he went to the Tabernacle Presbyterian Church in Cincinnati.

The next winter, at Christmas time, the Finneys travelled east again to their much loved Western in Oneida County. This was a happy return to an area of earlier triumphs. Charles started preaching with his old zeal and enthusiasm. The church was without a pastor, but many conversions took place. For example, a young man, though reared in a godly home, became bitter, speaking almost blasphemous things about the revival. His parents were grieved almost to despair. But God's Word kept challenging the young man until he could stand the inner pressure no longer. He sought out Finney and said, "I have committed the unpardonable sin!" "What makes you think so?" asked Finney. He told the evangelist that some years earlier he had read a book on piracy. It so enchanted him he decided to become history's most notorious pirate and bandit. But his godly home and teachings stood as a bulwark in his way. Therefore, he set himself to blaspheme the Holy Spirit. That should take care of the bulwark – or so he thought. After that he decided it was time to commit a crime, so he set a nearby schoolhouse on fire. But now that God was speaking to him, what was he to do?

Finney told the young man that the school trustees must be informed. Charles went to the officials with the miserable youth, and the head of the trustees freely forgave him and put the matter right. Still, the young man was not at rest. He felt he must make a public confession. Several young men in the community had been suspected, and he felt all must know who had actually perpetuated the crime. One night in the service, he made a clean breast of it all. It so moved the congregation that weeping broke out all over the building. This gave the young man real peace, and he had a firm faith in Christ until his death in the Civil War.

Throughout Finney's ministry, confessions of all sorts were abundant. Charles said it would take hours just to recount the crimes that he had heard confessed. When such a situation presented itself, the evangelist always insisted upon restitution as Jesus said in Matthew 5:23–4, "So if you are offering your gift at the altar, and there remember that your brother has something against you, leave your gift there before the altar and go; first he reconciled to your brother, and then come and offer your gift."

Several people from Rome came to Western while Finney was there, and urged the evangelist to come to them. So after several weeks in Western, Finney travelled to Rome to evangelise once again in that city. The meeting in Rome was a disappointment. The church had originally been Congregational. Some time before Finney arrived for his second revival effort, the congregation had called a Presbyterian minister. He had led the people to become a Presbyterian church. This had caused dissatisfaction among several church members. The unrest that resulted, Finney argued, hindered the meeting, thus putting the blame on the pastor.

A prominent Presbyterian historian had another story, however. He said the Rome revival of 1855 was not as successful as the 1826 meeting because Finney's style of preaching and revivalism was *passé*. He felt Finney should not have blamed the pastor. The historian even charged that Finney was so out of touch with the current situation that even friends in Utica who had wanted to invite him back there decided against it. Yet other accounts of the revival claimed that the Rome Presbyterian Church was filled to capacity each night. Finney actually devotes little space in his autobiography to Rome – it cannot have been too exciting, even though he said God blessed in many respects and "conversions were occurring very frequently".

In the autumn of 1855, Finney again visited his old domain where he reigned as the evangelism king: Rochester, New York. At first he had no mind to go there again. But the requests were most urgent – even from unbelievers. So after much prayer, he complied with their wishes and made his way to Rochester. The invitation was no doubt of God. Charles began preaching and tremendous blessings were immediately forthcoming.

The First Presbyterian Church of Rochester, committed to "old school" theology, closed its doors to Finney. He divided his preaching between the Brick Church and the Washington Street congregation. Before long, the Baptists, Methodists, and Congregationalists all got caught up in the spirit of the breaking revival. In the church services, Finney preached to professing Christians concerning holy living as well as declaring the Gospel to the lost.

The remarkable thing about the three Rochester revivals, according to Finney, rested in the fact that the highest echelons of society were reached in unusual numbers. Many that had not been converted in the first two revivals were touched in this significant third meeting. Finney stayed the entire winter as the work progressed.

Elizabeth Finney was well acquainted with the city, having lived there some years before their marriage. She had witnessed the two previous revivals, and in this one she "laboured, as usual, with great zeal and success", as her husband Charles expressed it.

Many men connected with the railroads were converted. So profound was the touch of God upon these, that Sunday railroad operations were practically stopped. Merchants arranged their business to allow their employees to attend the day-time services. The influence of the awakening soon spread to nearby villages, as had been the case in the previous revivals.

Finney confessed in his *Memoirs* that he "never preached anywhere with more pleasure than in Rochester".

In the winters of 1856, 1857 and 1858, Boston was again the scene of Finney's work. He generally found New England a difficult place in which to labour for a revival, but he seemed continually drawn to that area. Finney did much of his Boston work in the Park Street Church. His style of ministry in Boston commenced with searching sermons to the believers before preaching to the unconverted. By this approach, he attempted to stir up the church and reveal the self-deceived. It was most effective. In the winter of 1856, the pastor of the Park Street Church told Finney he needed the message himself as much as anyone else, and was soundly converted. This produced a very deep impression on the church, and God used it to help many others to Christ. The Finneys promised to return the next winter.

In the meantime, the Congregationalists raised considerable opposition to Finney's return to Boston in the winter of 1857–8. The problem of Oberlin perfectionism surfaced again. Only two Congregational churches joined in the return invitation. Charles went on to Boston regardless.

During 1857–8, the Great Prayer Revival burst on the American scene and swept through much of the land. It covered the country with such an awareness of God that for two years there was an average of ten thousand new converts added to the churches every month. Finney told of a man who travelled from Omaha, Nebraska, to Boston. On the journey east, he said he found a continuous prayer meeting two thousand miles long.

The Great Prayer Revival had its birth at the old North Dutch Church, Fulton Street, New York. The church had experienced hard times for several years. In order to reverse the tide and to reach the lost, Mr. Jeremiah Lamphier was employed as a lay missionary. It occurred to him that a prayer meeting for the businessmen of the city might help the apathetic situation. A noon prayer meeting was arranged for Wednesday, September 23, 1857, in a room on the third floor of the consistory building of the church. Only six persons attended. The following week; twenty were present and at the third meeting this number doubled. They decided to hold the noon prayer meeting daily. The influence of the work of the Holy Spirit extended throughout New York and Brooklyn, until by spring there were more than twenty places where daily prayer meetings were conducted.

From New York the work extended to other cities across the North until there was scarcely a city or hamlet throughout the Northern States that was not affected by the revival. The daily papers of the great cities devoted considerable space to the reports of this remarkable religious awakening. Within a year's time it was estimated that more than five hundred thousand people found Christ. While there were for a time daily preaching services at Burton's Theatre in New York, for the most part the revival was carried on by the daily union prayer meetings normally conducted by laymen.

Despite the blessing flowing all around, in Boston Finney had to struggle. Divisive influences were constantly trying to thwart the work. Theodore Parker, for example, hurled ridicule on it. He had a quite deviant theology and was a man of influence. Finney tried to heal the situation. He said, "I called twice myself to see him, hoping to have an opportunity to converse with him; but in both instances he declined to see me as was told me on account of his health." However, Parker's opposition precipitated much prayer. Finney described the prayer for Parker in these words: "The Spirit of prayer for him seemed to increase and took this type; that the Lord would convert him if He wisely could; but that if He could not do this, his evil influence might in some way be set aside." Parker heard of this and criticised it severely. Soon after however, he became ill and unable to preach. He went to Europe and there he died. Finney seemed to think this was an answer to the prayer.

Prayer soon became the theme of Boston. Businessmen set up special prayer meetings. Mrs Finney led the ladies in prayer services. All over the city, the spirit of prayer was poured out to the extent that people could not get into the buildings to pray. Every prayer meeting was crowded with intercessors. The Prayer Revival was beginning to touch old Boston. Objectors were soon overrun by the magnitude of the movement.

Finney felt that the South was not touched by the Great Prayer Revival, and blamed the South's adherence to slavery. But in this he was not historically correct. It can be well documented that the Prayer Revival of 1858 significantly stirred the South as well as the North.

Thus, Finney had his share in the Prayer Revival – not a large share, for no one prophet came to the fore as was often the case in other awakenings.

Still, all of America was caught up in the promotion of the prayer awakening. Finney said, "The Church and ministry in this country had become so very extensively engaged in promoting the revival, and such was the blessing of God attending the exertions of laymen as well as of ministers, then I made up my mind to return and spend another season in England, and see if the same influence would not pervade that country." So England was to be visited once more. Could Charles bring something of the Great Prayer Revival to that land? What would his second reception in the British Isles be like?

## Finney's British Blessings:
## The Evangelist's Second British Ministry

Believers had been begging Charles and his wife to come back to Britain for some time. Under God, Finney longed to plant some of the seeds of blessing of the Great Prayer Revival in British soil. So in December 1858, the Rev. and Mrs. Charles G. Finney sailed for Liverpool on the steamer *Persia*. On the dock to greet them was their old friend Potto Brown. When the news of Finney's arrival spread around, invitations immediately poured in. It seemed as if the whole country were before them.

Finney first preached in Houghton and St. Ives. Houghton had benefited under Charles' first visit, and again the people saw what the evangelist called a "precious revival".

For many years, St. Ives had never seen a real revival of religion. There was only one free church in St. Ives. The pastor had been there for some time, but his ministry had minimal evangelistic effect. He was not at all in favour of a revival effort. Moreover, he had personal problems that Finney thought an impediment to his usefulness. Nonetheless, a powerful movement began even in the face of the pastor's opposition. The minister stood adamantly against Finney until the tide of feeling in favour of the effort was so strong that he actually left town. Many were converted and a new church emerged.

The Rev. James Harcutt, former minister of Houghton, had taken up a new pastoral charge in London, the Borough Road Chapel. As soon as he heard of Finney's arrival, he urgently pressed the evangelist to come to London and minister in his chapel. At that time, Harcutt's church was in a serious state of spiritual stagnation because of internal problems. In Finney's own words, it had been "torn to pieces". The issues were so volatile that the previous pastor had left broken-hearted and the deacons forced to resign. Discouragement, disorganisation and depression reigned. Harcutt said that unless the church itself were converted, there could never be any spiritual success in the ministry at Borough Road.

After a farewell to the Christians in St. Ives, Finney arrived in London and started preaching. After assessing the situation, even Charles doubted that the congregation could be resurrected. But once again God met the need, poured out the Holy Spirit and sent conviction to the entire church. The grace of God so took hold of the community that hardly a family was left unaffected.

Soon after Finney began his work in London, Dr. S. P. Tregelles, a renowned scholar and formulator of many modern concepts on biblical textual problems, challenged Finney's theology, stating the evangelist was not orthodox concerning the conditions of salvation. Finney made it clear what he believed in his *Systematic Theology*. The problem seemed to be that Tregelles had not read the *Systematic Theology*, but was going on mere hearsay. He wrote several articles opposing Finney. A letter was dispatched to Dr. Campbell, who sided with Tregelles though he had previously agreed with Finney's theology. A friend wrote to Finney in the heat of the battle encouraging him: "I have read with intense pain the criticisms which have appeared in the *British Standard*, on your views of Theology, and I regard them as very unnecessary and unfair – unnecessary because your views have been before the public for years – and unfair because they misrepresent your views."[1]

To make matters worse, the *Oberlin Evangelist* reported the issue. That annoyed Charles. In a letter to his daughter in America, Finney wrote:

> If you are at Oberlin when this reaches you will you call on one of the editors of T. O. E. [the *Oberlin Evangelist*] and ask who committed the blunder of representing the piece they published from the *British Standard* as Editorial and Dr. Campbell as so great a theologian . . . Dr. C. [Camp-

bell] is anything but a great theologian. When I was with him he professed agreement with my views. He now claims to differ from me and is out upon me in his paper and claims to be real Old School.[2]

After the smoke cleared, Campbell seemingly saw the situation more clearly and subscribed to Finney's orthodoxy. Redford never deserted Finney at all.

Finney's health was deteriorating once again, when a Christian physician invited him to visit his Huntingdon home for rest and treatment.

The rest was restoring. After two or three weeks, Finney began to regain his strength and was soon preaching. There had never been a significant revival of religion in Huntingdon – they did not even know what one was like. Finney preached in what he called a "temperance hall". It was the only large building in the town. It soon filled as God's Spirit moved on the services.

The physician with whom the Finneys stayed had eight children. Not one of them was saved when Charles and Elizabeth arrived in town. In a very short time, however, every one of the children accepted Jesus Christ as Saviour. The first to come to faith was the eldest son, a physician himself. Many families in Huntingdon tasted the goodness of God.

After the Huntingdon revival, the Finneys went back to London and worked in the north-east part of the capital. Charles preached through the summer in one of the old Huguenot chapels in Spitalfields.

At about that time, an invitation came to visit Edinburgh. That was in August 1859. It was delivered through John Kirk of the Evangelical Union Church of Scotland. The Evangelical Union was formed after the revival that had spread over Scotland which to some extent was a consequence of Finney's *Lectures on Revivals of Religion*.

Dr. Kirk was a great lover of revivals. Finney preached in his church and remained in Scotland for three months. The pastor's hands were so full counselling inquirers, that he scarcely had time to do his normal pastoral duties. The church building was large and multitudes came to hear the Gospel.

Kirk was not only pastor of a large congregation, he was a professor in a theological college of Edinburgh as well as being editor of the *Glasgow Christian News*. This gave Finney wide exposure and a golden opportunity to disseminate the revival, as well as defend his views in the face of opposing hyper-Calvinists.

Mrs. Kirk, a great Christian lady herself, joined hands with Elizabeth Finney and together they did very fine work among the women of Edinburgh. They established ladies' prayer meetings which continued for decades after the Finneys left. Mrs. Kirk published a volume some years later on the impact of the prayer meetings. Answers to the intercession of the dedicated women of Edinburgh were marvellous. Prayer requests came in from all over Scotland. From those meetings, similar groups sprang up covering the country.

The Finneys evangelised in Edinburgh for three months and then journeyed north to Aberdeen. November had come when they accepted the invitation of the Rev. Fergus Ferguson, Jr., pastor of the Evangelical Union Church in Aberdeen. As the work began, the old opposition flared up. James Morrison, a pastor in Glasgow, was at the root of it. He was regarded as the theological authority and organisational founder of the Evangelical Union churches. Morrison said, "An eminent Revivalist, by holding meetings in a church already formed, threw the pastor into the shade and made the people discontented with his less exciting ministrations, at the close of a season of protracted effort."[3] This sort of unfounded, unkind criticism grieved Finney. The pastor encouraged the evangelist, saying he should not be distracted by this opposition. The paradox was that Finney's *Lectures on Revivals on Religion* had contributed so much to the birth of the Evangelical Union churches; but the children often despise the father.

Still, Finney could not get a hearing in Aberdeen except in Ferguson's church. He admitted, "I became a good deal discouraged." Such statements are seldom seen in Charles' *Memoirs*. And that was in the light of the fact that a general revival spirit pervaded Scotland at the time. He must have been very depressed over the situation.

At that stage, Finney received a letter to come and work

in Bolton, Lancashire. He accepted. Strangely, as he was about to leave, the Congregational church opened its doors to Finney. Mr. Brown, pastor of the Presbyterian congregation, also invited him to hold services in his church. Invitations multiplied. But he had agreed to go to Bolton. He stayed in Aberdeen as long as he possibly could, filling the invitations, and then turned to Bolton. He left Scotland a little before Christmas in 1859.

Charles and Elizabeth had received many letters inviting them to work in the Evangelical Union churches of Glasgow. Yet because of the general confusion concerning his ministry among the Union churches, he declined. He decided not to work any longer in the Evangelical Union congregations. Thus he dissociated himself from the group. He loved the brethren, but felt that his decision was best for his own usefulness in revivals.

Christmas 1859 saw the Finneys arrive by rail in Bolton, a town of about thirty thousand people. Situated only a few miles from Manchester in the heart of the great industrial Midlands, it was a strategic spot for a revival effort. Even in the middle of the nineteenth century, three million people lived within a sixty-mile radius of Manchester.

A Methodist layman and his wife entertained the Finneys. The lady of the host home had a Quaker background, but she had never truly submitted herself to Jesus Christ in repentance and faith. Charles led the family in prayer, and as he lifted his voice towards heaven, heaven came down upon them. The hostess fell under immediate conviction and Charles soon led her to Christ. The husband and his newly-converted wife rejoiced together. Just at that very moment, the son of the family burst in, announcing that one of the servants was deeply moved. In a very short time, salvation came to that servant. Then Charles learned another servant was weeping in the kitchen. He went to her straightaway and led her to Christ. Thus the work began.

The first service of worship was held in the chapel of the Rev. Mr. Davison. The building filled the very first night. The minister of the Methodist church in Bolton opened the service with prayer. He prayed so fervently, Finney discerned they were to experience a powerful movement. Charles then rose to speak upon the subject of prayer.

Finney said that whenever and wherever he spoke on prayer, God always poured out His Spirit to challenge the people to a life of intercession. The first week saw the spread of a spirit of prayer throughout the area. The meetings in the chapel increased in power. After the third or fourth service, Finney moved to a larger church and called for inquirers. The vestry was packed with people seeking the Saviour. After a week, a large temperance hall was secured that could adequately accommodate the multitudes wanting to attend.

Finney adopted another "new measure" in Bolton. He challenged the people to go out two by two and canvass the entire town. They were asked to visit every home, and if possible, pray in that home, and urge people to come to Christ and to the revival services. The Christian workers responded courageously. They secured a large number of religious tracts, handbills and posters, and went to work with enthusiasm.

The Methodist movement in Bolton was very strong, and had been since Wesley's day. The Methodists far outnumbered all other Christian groups. They were spiritual folk and zealously thrust themselves into the revival. As they joined hands with the Congregationalists, all sectarianism was banished. Finney said, "It was very common to see a Methodist and a Congregationalist, hand in hand, and heart in heart, going from house to house, with tracts, and praying wherever they were permitted, in every house, and warning men to flee from the wrath to come, and urging them to come to Christ."

The impact of the awakening spread until people began to travel there from Manchester. They were so impressed by the movement that they urged Finney to visit the great industrial city to conduct meetings. But Charles could not tear himself away from Bolton. The work became so powerful that he remained there three months. Crimes were confessed, including questionable business dealings. One businessman restored fifteen hundred pounds simply because he felt that he had not acted in Christian love. Bolton was canvassed and covered by the visiting laypeople until one minister said that every home had been touched in some way by the revival. Charles himself stated that if they had a building large enough, ten thousand people would have attended – and that in the town of only thirty thousand.

Regardless of their need for rest, Finney and his wife left Bolton and started ministering in the metropolis of the industrial Midlands. Before they left the lovely little town of Bolton, a beautiful testimonial was given to them. It read:

> To the Rev. Charles G. Finney, principal of Oberlin College, Ohio, United States, America.
>
> Rev. and Dear Sir: It is with deep regret, but also with cordial feeling and devout gratitude to the Father of mercies and God of all grace, that we assemble and bid you "Farewell" at the close of your arduous labours in our midst. We own the Providence which directed your steps to our town, and we feel that we can never cease to be your debtors for the earnest and self-sacrificing efforts which you have made, while with us, to deepen the spiritual life in our own hearts, to increase our devotion and enjoyment of the gospel, to secure the salvation of our friends, and to extend the Redeemer's kingdom in this important and densely populated district . . . Wherever you go, we will follow you with our earnest prayers and deepest sympathies. May you be long spared to labour, and after you have finished your course with joy, may you receive the crown of life that fadeth not away, and shines as the brightness of the firmament in the kingdom of our Father forever and ever.[4]

With these gracious and loving words ringing in their hearts, the Finneys left Bolton and gave themselves to Manchester.

The work began in Manchester in a large hall, independent of any denominational label. The prospects looked bright, but there appeared to be a general spirit of distrust among certain brethren in the city. With little community spirit, there was dissatisfaction with some of the leaders who were in the forefront of the work. This state of affairs, Finney stated, grieved the Holy Spirit and crippled the work. Tragically, the revival effort never became as widespread as in Bolton.

By this time, Charles and Elizabeth were simply worn

out. Even though many in Manchester wanted them to linger, they decided it was God's will to suspend the work and sail home. They had brought at least something of the Prayer Revival blessings with them, even if a general awakening did not follow them everywhere. On August 2, 1860, they travelled to Liverpool and boarded the *Persia* bound for New York City. As they left the brethren behind, with their faces set towards Oberlin, they must have well remembered the words of their dear friend Campbell who wrote: "You will leave behind you in both nations, multitudes to whom your name will be long dear."

## Finney's Oberlin Objectives: The Evangelist's
## Role as Professor, President and Pastor

Oberlin was no longer a small wilderness school. They needed their president. The college had grown tremendously. The student body increased from one hundred and one in 1835 to four hundred and eighty-four in 1840. When Charles came to the presidency in 1851, enrolment jumped from five hundred and seventy-one to one thousand and twenty in just one year.

When Finney arrived in Ohio, the religious state of the college had seriously declined. The leaders knew that if there were to be a rise in the general level of Christian commitment on the part of the students, they must have a revival. And whom could God use more than their president? Finney put his tired hand to the old revival plough and started to turn the "fallow ground".

The revival began with the traditional prayer meetings, fully attended from the outset. Spiritual hunger invaded the campus. The evangelist-president preached twice on Sunday and several nights during the week. Every Lord's day he would hold an inquiry meeting. Conviction spread and conversions increased. Finney's free hours were filled with people seeking private conversation on the means of salvation. The work grew week after week until a general awakening was sweeping the entire area. Before it was all over, the movement produced, as Finney expressed it, "a clean sweep of the unconverted in the place". The demanding work went on for four months.

One evening, after a service, Charles came home and suffered a severe chill. He was put to bed and confined there by sickness for almost three months. Finney's prolonged illness, with a different man in the pulpit, dampened the revival spirit. Attendance dwindled. But as soon as the old Trojan was on his feet again and able to preach, the conversion flow began once more.

This kind of ministry was typical of Finney in the years he served Oberlin College and the Church. If he were not out of the Oberlin community evangelising and winning the multitudes elsewhere, he was constantly giving himself to the students in lecturing, leading, preaching and meeting their various spiritual needs. Finney's rapport with the student body was warm and personal. He had a great sense of humour that appealed to the young people. On one occasion, his class met in his home for a lecture. A student who had chosen a comfortable chair fell asleep in the midst of the professor's dissertation. Charles closed the hour with prayer, asking God to keep the class sufficiently interested at least to keep them awake. The next day, the group returned to his home for another lecture, and they found the room with nothing but wooden, straight-backed chairs from the kitchen. "You see, young gentlemen," said Finney with a twinkle in his eye, "I have found a way to answer my own prayer."

There was a touch of humour in the Oberlin chapel services too. One day the choir rendered a very heavy anthem. Charles got up and prayed, "Oh Lord, we trust that thou hast understood the song which they have tried to sing, but thou knowest that we did not understand any of it."[1] Whether it were mere humour or his old frontier brashness resurrected again, it certainly caused some laughter. Finney said to himself, "I'll probably hear about this from my wife." No doubt, he did!

His students loved him dearly and respected him profoundly. He was a spiritual father-figure to many. In the late 1880s, an evangelist was preaching in the Santa Clara Valley of California when a revival broke out. A stranger came up to him and said, "You're a Finney man, aren't you?" Tears filled the eyes of the preacher and he replied, "Yes, thank God! I'm one of the thousand other lights."[2]

Finney continued to be equally interested in the temporal, earthly problems of his people. For example, the summer of 1853 was a difficult time for the farmers of northern Ohio. The whole area was suffering from a severe drought. The pastures were dried up, and the prospects for a crop were very slender. The Oberlin church gathered one Sunday for worship. The burden of Finney's prayer was a plea for rain: "Lord, we want rain. We do not presume to dictate unto thee, but our pastures are dry, and the earth is gaping open for rain. The cattle are wandering about and lowing in search of water. Even the little squirrels in the woods are suffering from thirst. Unless thou givest us rain, our cattle will die and our harvests will come to naught. O Lord, send us rain, and send it now! Although to us there is no sign of it, it is an easy thing for thee to do. Send it now, for Christ's sake. Amen." Before the service was over, the rain descended in such torrents that Finney could scarcely be heard. He paused and said: "Let us praise God for this rain", and gave out the hymn:

> When all thy mercies, O my God,
> My rising soul surveys,
> Transported with the view, I'm lost
> In wonder, love and praise.

The congregation was so moved that many could not sing for weeping. But then, that is real Christianity – God Himself being vitally interested in our temporal, earthly problems.

Oberlin began to evolve as an institution. College societies and exhibitions multiplied. The evangelist-pastor found it increasingly difficult to promote a revival during the academic term. Sentiment was growing that the best time to promote a revival was during the winter break, not the summer academic session. This was difficult for Charles. To be hemmed in some place where he could not hold a revival was completely foreign to his nature. He often felt an urge to leave Oberlin and give himself totally to itinerant evangelism. Yet, as he said, "I have come to Oberlin and resided here, for the sake of the students, to secure their conversion and sanctification; and it was only because there was so great a number of them here, which gave me so good an opportunity to work upon so many young minds in the process of education, that I had remained here from year to year." In this general period Finney travelled as far as Detroit, Michigan and elsewhere.

The spiritual awakening that came to Oberlin during term-time after the second British ministry, proved the college could be mightily revived, even though academic demands and institutional concerns were mounting. Finney could also live out his evangelistic ministry many times over through the lives of the hundreds of young ministers he moulded through his faithful teaching.

In the winter of 1866–7, there was another powerful moving of God's Spirit on Oberlin's campus. There were revivals in much of America: it was the continuing legacy of the Great Prayer Revival of 1858. But in the midst of the Oberlin effort, Charles again broke down in health and others had to carry on. He was now seventy-five years old.

Charles' second wife, Elizabeth Atkinson Finney, had passed away three years after their return from the second British ministry. They had been together for fifteen years. She was in Syracuse, New York, at the time and on November 27, 1863, she went home to be with the Lord she loved and served. After the awakening in the college subsequent to their British trip, she wrote to some friends in Britain:

> It is such a season as we have not seen in Oberlin as long as I have lived here and as much as I have seen in days gone past of the working of our Lord in this community. On Sunday evening I go to the ladies' hall where I meet a large number of young ladies; on Monday I meet about two hundred more; Tuesday, Wednesday and Thursday I hold a general meeting for all females and besides that I have two other meetings a day to attend.[3]

Elizabeth's contribution to the work was great. When God saw fit to take her home Charles felt a tremendous loss. But he had learned how to face sorrow.

Finney married again in 1864. He took as his last wife Miss Rebecca A. Rayl. He was seventy-two years old at the time. She had been assistant principal of the ladies' department of Oberlin. The third Mrs. Finney died in Kentland, Indiana on September 12, 1907, surviving her husband by thirty-two years.

Calls to hold meetings continually poured in, but after the mid-1860s, Charles had to refuse most of them. He wrote in the *Memoirs*, "Since 1860, although continually pressed by churches, East and West, to come and labour as an evangelist, I have not dared to comply with their request. I have been able, by the blessing of God, to perform a good deal of labour here; but I have felt inadequate to the exposure and labour of attempting to secure revivals abroad."[4] Such refusals pained him. "No" was hardly in Charles' vocabulary, but his health would not permit the itinerant style he had loved and practised so long. He still preached, but with more caution as to the toll it took on his strength.

In August 1865, Charles resigned as president of Oberlin College and Seminary. He had reached his seventy-third birthday. The trustees reluctantly accepted the resignation, but hoped he would continue on as professor of theology, his health permitting. They paid him the following glowing tribute:

> Permit us to say that we esteem your connection with the Institution as the main earthly source of its popular power and spiritual influence. You came to it in the day of small things. You have stood by it in the days of trial and adversity. You have lived to see it prosper, honoured, and useful. You have always been, and always will be while you live, its recognised head.[5]

Several friends wanted Finney to travel again, others urged that he stay in Oberlin. Realising his strength was failing, he stayed. As a tribute to the wisdom of that decision, a significant revival broke out at Oberlin once again. The passion to win souls to Christ never left Charles. In a letter to his daughter Julia as late as 1868, he spoke of his regret that some students had not yet been converted.

During these latter years, pressure was on Finney to write his life story. There was so much to tell. He went to work writing an account of the revivals; in the process he produced a classic. The results of his efforts are the famous

*Memoirs*. They will always stand as the superlative narrative on the power of God in revival ministry.

Finney lost none of his fire with age. He was always the crusader. So he took on Freemasonry. After 1865, most of his correspondence was an attack on that movement. He wrote several articles on the subject and finally produced a book entitled *The Character, Claims and Practical Workings of Free Masonry*. Some may have said he was just a misguided old man, but his mental alertness was retained to the end. The situation was simple; anything he saw as an impediment to revivals, he challenged. There was, in fact, a lot of strong feeling on the subject of Freemasonry in those days. In 1828, for example, an anti-masonic party was formed in western New York. So Finney's writings were not out of character for the time, even though much of the anti-masonic sentiment had died down by about 1865.

Although Finney had laid aside the presidency in 1865, the trustees' hopes concerning his teaching were realised; he continued to lecture in the college and serve as pastor of Oberlin's First Congregational Church. Not only that, he could still preach with great power. Charles achieved a singular triumph at the organisational meeting of the National Congregational Council at Oberlin in November 1871. He was asked to speak on the subject: "The Gift of the Holy Spirit". The weight of years was upon him, but he preached with such power that tears flowed down the faces of that great audience as he dwelt upon a subject which had been so central to his life-long ministry. Dr. Buddington, the moderator of the council, said concerning the message and its messenger, "I rejoice to stand this day upon the grave of buried prejudice. It is true that Oberlin has been a battle-cry in our ranks for a generation. It is so no longer, but a name of peace, of inspiration, and hope."[6]

At the age of almost eighty, Finney tendered his resignation to the church. That was in May 1872. He had rendered the entire denomination a great service, and had been used of God to reconcile a score of factions among the Congregationalists. Above all, revival had come to many people. If ever a man gave himself to God and to the people, it was Charles G. Finney.

## Finney's Final Fight of Faith:
## The Evangelist's Last Days

Finney will always be remembered as probably the most spiritually powerful preacher America has ever produced. Despite his early crude mannerisms – a crudeness he largely lost after leaving western New York – the sheer power of God upon the man is virtually without parallel in American evangelism. He was first and foremost a man of God, filled with spiritual might and reality.

Finney's preaching set a whole new trend. His call for immediate repentance was a pattern for many. A contemporary said:

> Mr Finney is one of the most remarkable preachers in America. His strong logical powers, and educated as a lawyer, he deals much in convincing argument . . . he preaches more the love of God, and wins as well as alarms to repentance. His strength of mind is equalled by that of few . . . for a certain scope of preaching he is unequalled – that of impressive argument, and such presenting of the relations of religious truth as in its completeness and clearness works irresistible conviction, and brings sceptic, infidel, and atheist alike into broken hearted submission to the power of God.[1]

Finney was also a gifted and influential reformer. As seen, abolition, women's rights, racism and temperance were all of great importance to him. His concept of "disinterested benevolence" enabled him to embrace all movements for the betterment of oppressed people.

As a writer, he made vast contributions. His *Lectures On Revivals of Religion* sparked revivals in many parts of the world. The *Memoirs*, his *Systematic Theology* and *Lectures to Professing Christians* stimulate the mind and continue to deepen the seeking spirit. The multitude of articles, written sermons and letters that appeared in various periodicals are still read today with appreciation.

One of Charles' longest-lasting ministries was his work with his students. Young men and women came from far and near to sit under him, and then filled with zeal went out to evangelise their world.

Charles' fame not only attracted students, it brought in funds as well. Yet he never acquired any wealth himself. It was for Oberlin he built his "benevolent empire". The new college in the western wilderness probably would not have survived five years had not Finney been the man around whom the institution revolved. It remains alive and viable to the present moment because of his contribution to its birth and early days.

Above all, Charles G. Finney will be remembered as the great revivalistic evangelist. The use and popularising of prayer meetings for revivals, the call to public response to receive Christ, the personalising of the message of salvation, the counselling of inquirers, the protracted, structured and organised meeting, using any kind of building or hall in which to preach the Gospel, and many other revolutionary methodologies – these are his greatest contributions. Of course, the "new measures" are no longer "new" today: they are accepted as standard procedures. They became part of the programmes of evangelists like D. L. Moody, Billy Sunday, Billy Graham and a host of others. All these owe so much to this man.

Finney's revivalism proved to be a ministry of maturity and substance. History attests to this. He cannot be charged and found guilty of creating a "burned-over district". Even conservative England and Scotland received him well. Finney was personally a man of depth and his ministry reflected that profundity.

Thus Finney will always stand as a key figure in world evangelisation. Even one of his critics, B. B. Warfield of Princeton, said Finney "conducted the most spectacular evangelism activities the country has ever witnessed".[2] Others claim he was instrumental in winning more people to Christ than anyone since Whitefield's day. He wanted true conversions, and God gave him a multitude.

David Livingstone was among the Christian leaders worldwide who were impressed by his ministry. While waiting to explore Africa in 1839, he forwarded his first salary to a younger brother in Scotland, urging him to use the money to study under Finney at Oberlin. Livingstone's brother responded and graduated from Oberlin in 1845.

But the twilight had to come. There was a crown waiting. In July 1875, he presented his last series of lectures at the college. He was eighty-two, yet the burden of the years seem to rest light upon him. He still stood erect and had the demeanour of a young man.

In the last month of his life, he preached one Sunday to his beloved First Congregational Church of Oberlin. The fire glowed in his piercing eyes as the congregation felt deep appreciation for his spiritual power and keen insight into the Christian experience.

His last full day on earth was a quiet Sunday, August 15, 1875. It had been a lovely day. He sat in the cool of the evening with his beloved wife at his side. They probably reminisced on all the goodness God had showered upon them. At sunset, he walked with his wife over the college campus to stand near his old church to hear the singing. The congregation was lifting up their voices in the grand hymn "Jesu Lover of My Soul". How the words blessed them! That truth had transformed him on that significant October 10, 1821 and had sustained him through the many years of his glorious ministry. Charles and his wife quietly joined in the singing from the outside. They then leisurely strolled home, thanking God for His matchless grace and love. He retired. It had been a beautiful restful Lord's day; the kind of a sabbath he deserved, but because of his work he had seemed to have so few.

Later, about 2 a.m. on August 16th, Charles was seized with severe chest pains. His wife was up and friends gathered. He asked for water, but his thirst could seemingly not be satisfied. He said in his pain as he looked into the loving, anxious eyes of those gathered about his bedside, "Perhaps this is the thirst of death." A moment later he softly added, "I am dying." Those were his last words as he gently closed his eyes. He suffered on a few more hours. Just as a beautiful new morning was dawning on the Finney home on Oberlin's lovely wooded campus, a glorious new dawning arose in Charles' heart as he quietly went to be with the Lord he loved so deeply and served so faithfully. He was home at last, with the thousands he had won to his wonderful Lord waiting to greet him on heaven's shores.

His legacy of evangelism will always remain. As a tribute to the memory of this giant of revival and profound man of the Spirit, in the vestibule of Oberlin College Chapel, built by his son, Frederick Norton Finney, these words are inscribed:

THAT THE YOUTH
OF THIS FOUNDATION OF LEARNING
MAY DAILY MEET TO WORSHIP GOD
AND THAT A SON MAY HONOUR
THE MEMORY OF HIS FATHER
THIS CHAPEL IS BUILT
AS A MONUMENT
TO
CHARLES GRANDISON FINNEY
BY
HIS YOUNGEST SON
FREDERICK NORTON FINNEY
IN THE YEAR OF OUR LORD
1908

# Events in the Life of
# Charles Grandison Finney


1792 – August 29. Born, Warren, Connecticut.

1794 – Parents moved west via the Ox-Cart Trail to Hanover, New York. Attended elementary school two years: the Indian school and the Hamilton Oneida Academy at Clinton.

1808 – Parents travelled west again, settling in the wilderness of Lake Ontario, at Henderson Bay, in the village of Henderson, New York.

1809–12 – Taught in a rural school.

1813–15 – Attended Academy at Warren, Connecticut.

1815–17 – Taught school in New Jersey.

1818–21 – Studied law as a junior partner in the office of Judge Benjamin Wright, at Adams, New York.

1821 – October 10. Converted to Christ.

1822–3 – Studied theology under the Rev. George W. Gale, First Presbyterian Church, Adams. Licensed to preach, December 30.

1824 – First ministry and revival at Evans Mills and Antwerp, New York.

Married Miss Lydia Andrews.

The great revival ministry began. Ordained at Evans Mills, July 1, Presbyterian Church.

1824–32 – Nine years of itinerant revival ministry.

1832 – April 29. Began New York City pastorate in Chatham Street Theatre.

1833–5 – Broadway Tabernacle ministry.

1834–5 – Revival Lectures delivered, autumn and winter.

1835 – Left Presbyterian Church for Congregational Denomination.

1835 – Summer, moved and began ministry in Oberlin College and Theological Seminary.

1835–7 – Three years of summers in Oberlin and winters in Broadway Church, New York.

1837 – Discontinued New York pastorate.

1837–72 – Assumed pastorate First Congregational Church, Oberlin.

1847 – Death of Lydia A. Finney.

1848 – Married Mrs. Elizabeth Atkinson.

1863 – Death of Elizabeth Atkinson Finney.

1864 – Married Miss Rebecca A. Rayl.

1851–66 – Presidency of Oberlin.

1837–72 – Thirty-five years of ministry in college, church and world evangelism.

1872–75 – Retired from Oberlin but had three years of student involvement.

1875 – August 16. Within thirteen days of his eighty-third birthday, he passed on to glory.

# ENDNOTES

Some quotations in this biography are not bibliographically cited. Only those passages felt necessary for historical verification are noted. Most of the statements of Finney not cited are from his *Memoirs*.

## PART I

### Chapter 1

1. J. H. Fairchild, "Introduction" to Charles G. Finney's *Systematic Theology* (abridged), (Minneapolis: Bethany Fellowship, Inc., 1976).
2. Ibid.
3. Ibid.
4. Ibid.
5. Ibid., quoting Leon McBeth, *Women in Baptist Life* (Nashville: Broadman Press).
6. Ibid.
7. J. Edwin Orr, *The Role of Prayer in Spiritual Awakening* (Los Angeles: Oxford Association for Research in Revival), p. 1.
8. Lewis A. Drummond, *The Awakening That Must Come* (Nashville: Broadman Press, 1979), pp. 15–16.
9. Ibid., p. 16.
10. Ibid., pp. 16–17.
11. Ibid., pp. 17–18.

### Chapter 2

1. Thomas D. Clark, *Frontier America: The Story of the Westward Movement* (New York: Charles Scribner's Sons, 1959), p. 566.

2. I. W. Barber, *Incidents in American History* (New York: George F. Cooledge and Brother, 1847), p. 264.

## Chapter 3

1. *The Oxford Companion To English Literature*, Compiled and edited by Sir Paul Harvey, 3rd edition (Oxford: The Clarendon Press, 1946), pp. 726–7.
2. Frank Grenville Beardsley, *A Mighty Winner of Souls* (New York: American Tract Society, 1937), p. 11.
3. Ibid., p. 11.
4. William Cochran, *Charles G. Finney: Memorial Address*, (Philadelphia: I. B. Leppincott and Company, 1908), p. 20.
5. Beardsley, *A Mighty Winner of Souls*, p. 14.
6. Charles G. Finney, *Memoirs of Rev. Charles G. Finney* (New York: Fleming H. Revell Company, 1876), p. 12.

## Chapter 4

1. Frank Hugh Foster, *A Genetic History of the New England Theology* (Chicago: The University of Chigaco Press, 1907), pp. 26–7.
2. Samuel Eliot Morrison, *The Oxford History of the American People* (New York: (Oxford University Press, 1965), p. 526.
3. Finney, *Memoirs*, pp. 12–18 (with additions from original manuscripts).
4. Ibid., pp. 18–23.
5. Beardsley, *A Mighty Winner of Souls*, p. 34.

## PART II

### Chapter 1

1. George F. Wright, *Charles Grandison Finney* (Boston: Houghton Mifflen and Company, 1891), pp. 18–19.
2. Finney, *Memoirs*, p. 78.

### Chapter 3

1. P. H. Fowler, *Historical Sketch of Presbyterians, Within The*

*Bounds of the Synod of Central New York* (Utica: Curtiss and Childs, 1877), pp. 260–1.
2. Finney, *Memoirs*, p. 165.
3. Ibid., p. 177.
4. Ibid., pp. 193–4.

## Chapter 4

1. Beardsley, *A Mighty Winner of Souls*, p. 67.
2. *Oberlin Evangelist*, April 23, 1845.
3. Barnes and Diamond, *Weld-Grimke Letters*, II, p. 432.
4. Finney, *Memoirs*, p. 201.
5. Nettleton to Aiken, January 13, 1827, cited in *Letters of Beecher and Nettleton on "New Measures"*, pp. 18–19.
6. Beardsley, *A Mighty Winner of Souls*, p. 78.
7. Bennet Taylor, *Memoirs of the Life and Character of Rev. Asahel Nettleton D.D.*, 2nd edition (Hartford: Robins and Smith, 1845), pp. 213–14.
8. *Autobiography, Correspondence, Etc. of Lyman Beecher, D.D.*, Vol. II, edited by Charles Beecher (New York: Harper and Brothers, 1883), p. 99.
9 Richard Ellsworth Day, *Man of Like Passions* (Grand Rapids: Zondervan Publishing House, 1942), p. 139.
10. Beardsley, *A Mighty Winner of Souls*, p. 81.
11. Finney, *Memoirs*, p. 215.
12. Beecher, *Autobiography*, *II*, p. 101.
13. Finney, *Memoirs*, p. 219.
14. Wright, *Charles Grandison Finney*, p. 94.
15. Samuel I. Baird, *A History of the New School* (Philadelphia: Claxton, Ramsen and Hoffelfinger, 1868), p. 216.
16. G. Frederick Wright, *Charles G. Finney*, pp. 94–5.

## Chapter 5

1. Frost to Finney, May 2, 1826, Finney Papers.
2. Beman to Finney, October 23, 1829, Finney Papers.
3. Poughkeepsie Session, A. Welton, Moderator to Finney, March 29, 1830, Finney Papers.

## Chapter 6

1. *Rochester Observer*, October 15, 1830.

2. *New York Evangelist*, November 20, 1830.
3. *Publications of the Rochester Historical Society*, Edward R. Foreman, ed. (The Rochester Historical Society, 1925), iv, pp. 288–9.
4. Day, *Man of Like Passions*, p. 54.
5. Beardsley, *A Mighty Winner of Souls*, p. 37.
6. Charles P. Bush, "Mr. Finney in Rochester and Western New York", *Reminiscences of Rev. Charles G. Finney* (Oberlin: E. J. Goodrich, 1876), p. 12.
7. Beardsley, *A Mighty Winner of Souls*, p. 42.
8. *New York Evangelist*, February 26, 1831.
9. Henry Mitchell MacCracken, *Lives of the Leaders of Our Church Universal, From the Days of the Apostles to the Present Time* (New York: Phillips and Hunt, 1879), p. 735.
10. *Rochester Democrat and Chronicle*, December 26, 1926.
11. Finney, *Memoirs*, pp. 300–1.

## Chapter 7

1. Charles Howley, *The History of the Presbyterian Church, Auburn, New York* (Auburn: Daily Advertiser and Weekly Journal Stoan Book Print, 1876), pp. 49–51.
2. O. Smith to Finney, April 4, 1831, Finney Papers.
3. Charles C. Cole, Jr. "The Free Church Movement in New York City", *New York History* XXXIV July, 1953, p. 287.

## Chapter 8

1. E. M. Clarke to Finney, May 23, 1832, Finney Papers.
2. Beecher, *Autobiography*, II, p. 224.
3. Robert Samuel Fletcher, *A History of Oberlin from Its Foundation Through the Civil War* (Chicago: The University of Chicago Press, 1907), pp. 159–61.
4. Day, *Man of Like Passions*, p. 74.
5. J. H. Colton to Finney, April 6, 1837, Finney Papers.

## PART III

## Chapter 1

1. *Oberlin Evangelist*, September 10, 1851.
2. Fletcher, *History of Oberlin*, p. 191.

3. Charles G. Finney, *Lectures on Systematic Theology* (Oberlin: E. J. Goodrich, 1847), Preface.
4. Elisha B. Sherwood, *Fifty Years On The Skirmish Line* (New York: Fleming H. Revell Company, 1893), pp. 37–8.
5. Lewis Tappan to Finney, March 31, 1846, Lewis Tappan Letter Books, Tappan Papers in Library of Congress, U.S.A.


*Chapter 2*


1. Finney, *Memoirs*, p. 355.
2. Ibid., pp. 353–8.


*Chapter 3*


1. *Oberlin Evangelist*, January 2, 1846.
2. *Oberlin Evangelist*, January 21, 1846.
3. Charles G. Finney, *Lectures on Revivals of Religion* (New York: Fleming H. Revell Company, 1868), p. 145.
4. Robert S. Fletcher, "Bread and Doctrine at Oberlin", *Ohio State Archaeological and Historical Quarterly*, XLIX (March 1940), p. 40.
5. Day, *Man of Like Passions*, p. 56.
6. Finney, *Lectures on Revivals*, p. 275.
7. James A. Thome to Weld, August 9, 1836.
8. Finney to Arthur Tappan, April 30, Finney Papers.


*Chapter 4*


1. *Oberlin Evangelist*, January 16, 1850.
2. Ibid.
3. Finney, *Memoirs*, p. 394.
4. Ibid., p. 398.
5. John Campbell to Finney, March 28, 1850, Finney Papers.
6. John Ross Dix, *Pen Pictures of Popular English Preachers; With Linnings of Listeners in Church and Chapel* (London: Partridge and Oaky, 1852), pp. 195–9.
7. John Keep to Finney, June 3, 1850, Finney Papers.
8. John Keep to Finney, August 30, 1850, Ibid.
9. *British Banner*, April 2, 1851, Ibid.
10. Beardsley, *A Mighty Winner of Souls*, p. 150.
11. Payne Kenyon Kilbourne, *A Biographical History of the*

*County of Litchfield, Connecticut* (New York: Clark, Austine and Company, 1951), p. 343.

## Chapter 5

1. Wright, *Charles G. Finney*, p. 188.
2. Fairchild, "Introduction" to Finney's *Systematic Theology*.
3. Frank Hugh Foster, *A Genetic History of New England Theology* (Chicago: The University of Chicago Press, 1907), p. 467.
4. "Finney would argue as follows." This is a condensed form of Finney's views. See Finney's *Systematic Theology* for the full presentation.
5. Charles G. Finney, *Lectures on Systematic Theology* Preface (E. J. Goodrich, 1878).
6. *Biblical Repertory and Princeton Review* XIX, 1847, p. 237.
7. Wright, *Charles G. Finney*, p. 228.
8. Charles G. Finney, *Sermons on Important Subjects* (New York: John S. Taylor, 1836), pp. 21–2.
9. Wright, *Charles G. Finney*, p. 231.
10. Finney, *Memoirs*, p. 50–1.
11. Finney, *Sermons on Important Subjects*, pp. 229–53.
12. Finney, *Lectures on Revivals of Religion*, p. 306.
13. Wright, *Charles G. Finney*, pp. 198–9.
14. Charles G. Finney, *Lectures to Professing Christians* (Oberlin: E. J. Goodrich, 1837), p. 266.
15. Charles G. Finney, *Views of Sanctification* (Oberlin: James Steele, 1840), p. 9.
16. Finney, *Memoirs*, p. 378.
17. Finney, *Lectures on Systematic Theology*, p. 595, 616.
18. Beardsley, *A Mighty Winner of Souls*, p. 134.
19. Finney, *Lectures on Systematic Theology*, III, p. 204.
20. James E. Johnson, "The Life of Charles Grandison Finney", unpublished Ph.D. Dissertation for University of Syracuse, 1959, p. 325.
21. Fletcher, *History of Oberlin*, pp. 228–9.

## Chapter 6

1. *Oberlin Evangelist*, March 3, 1852.

## Chapter 7

1. Thomas Lawson to Finney, April 20, 1859, Finney Papers.
2. Finney to Daughter Julia, May 5, 1859, Ibid.
3. Fergus Ferguson, Jr., to Finney, November 14, 1859, Ibid.
4. Beardsley, *A Mighty Winner of Souls*, pp. 156–7.


## Chapter 8

1. Beardsley, *A Mighty Winner of Souls*, p. 178.
2. Day, *Man of Like Passions*, p. 175.
3. Fletcher, *History of Oberlin*, I, pp. 212–13.
4. Finney, *Memoirs*, p. 475.
5. The Board of Trustees of Oberlin College to Finney, August 21, 1865, Finney Papers.
6. Beardsley, *A Mighty Winner of Souls*, p. 190.


## Chapter 9

1. Henry Fowler, *The American Pulpit* (New York: J. M. Fairchild and Co., 1856), p. 37.
2. B. B. Warfield, *Perfectionism*, II, 20; Oneida Circular, XII (August 30, 1875), p. 278.

## ANNOTATED BIBLIOGRAPHY OF
## IMPORTANT WORKS ON FINNEY

Charles G. Finney, *Memoirs* (New York, Fleming H. Revell Company, 1876). This autobiography has long been the basic work on the ministry of Finney. Some have criticised the *Memoirs*, implying Finney could not have remembered all the details he recounts; he had produced the work in his seventies. However, George W. Gale states Finney used many of the incidents in his ministry as sermon illustrations, thus keeping them fresh in his mind. Gale declares Finney's memory was accurate on the scores of anecdotes and stories he tells and several of Finney's friends also edited the work for accuracy. The book probably suffers from no more subjectivism than most autobiographies. A most helpful new edition of the *Memoirs* by Dr. Garth Rossell and Dr. Richard A. G. Dupuis was published in 1983. The old edition (1876) was edited by James Harris Fairchild, president of Oberlin and successor to Finney. Fairchild's edition was rather extensively edited, leaving out much valuable material. Rossell's and Dupuis' new and un-abridged edition of Finney's autobiography has been invaluable and will continue to prove a rich source on the Finney ministry. The *Memoirs* remain a classic in revivalism.

James E. Johnson, *The Life of Charles Grandison Finney*, an unpublished Ph.D. Dissertation from the University of Syracuse, New York, June 1959. This Ph.D. thesis was the most valuable secondary resource in preparing this biography. It is a scholarly and well-balanced work. Particularly helpful was the original research the author produced. It was also most helpful in the material on Finney's friends, theology, perfectionism, social action, educational philosophy and the New Lebanon Convention. This was a most worthy and valuable work.

G. Frederick Wright, *Charles Grandison Finney* (Boston, Houghton, Mifflin and Company, 1891). This biography is un-questionably the best biography ever published on the life and ministry of Finney. Unfortunately, it is old and has been out of print for years.

Frank Grenville Beardsley, *A Mighty Winner of Souls* (New York, American Tract Society, 1937). This is a good biography. Yet it lacks the depth of some works. Nonetheless, it is insightful and a valuable resource on Finney.

Several other popular biographies have merit:

*Man of Like Passion* by Richard Ellsworth Day.

*Charles G. Finney* by Basil Miller.

*Finney Lives On* by V. Raymond Edmon.

All these works are now out of print.

A vast source of Finney's original works still remains in print, e.g. *Revival Lectures*, *Systematic Theology*, *Memoirs*, *The Promise of the Spirit*, *Reflections on Revivals*, etc.